An American Family in World War II

Cover design by
Minker Design
Bethesda, Maryland

Printed in the United States of America.

ISBN 10: 1-59571-081-7 • ISBN 13: 978-1-59571-081-9
Library of Congress Control Number: 2005929705

Word Association Publishers
205 Fifth Avenue,
Tarentum, Pennsylvania 15084
www.wordassociation.com

Dec. 30, 2016

For Julia,

These letters tell the story of courage and sacrifice that is the price of our freedom.

Sandra O'Connell
Mrs. Ralph Lee Minker

An American Family in World War II

Edited by
Ralph "Lee" Minker
Sandra O'Connell
Harry Butowsky

For the men of the 447th Bomb Group
Rattlesden, England 1943 -1945

And the families who loved them.

Table of Contents

Preface

World War II was the greatest man-made cataclysm in history. When the battle sounds finally ceased, nearly 60 million people were dead. Innocent civilians were caught up in a conflict of which they knew little and understood less; nearly 30 million of the civilian population across Europe, Russia, and Asia were lost among the ruins and rubble. How can we possibly understand an event of such magnitude? The history of the generals, the soldiers, and the battles has been studied and written about these past sixty years. The experience of the families who lived through that extraordinary time—when the outcome of the war was uncertain—has not been told.

The Minker family of Wilmington, Delaware, were among the millions of Americans caught up in the vortex of World War II. In 1941 Reverend Ralph L. Minker Sr. and his wife Edna were living quietly in Wilmington, Delaware with their three teenage children: Ralph Jr., Shirley and Bernice. Their life centered on work, school and church, and the business of growing up in the post-depression years.

This was all to change on the morning of December 7, 1941 with the news that the Japanese had bombed Pearl Harbor. The portent of this event would be felt by all and especially 17 year-old Ralph "Lee" Minker Jr., a freshman at Dickinson College in Carlisle, Pennsylvania. In a little over one year after Pearl Harbor, Ralph would find himself in the army training to be a pilot to fly the famous B-17 bomber of World War II. For the Minkers and families across America, the world was forever changed by events over which they had no control but were to witness and play a part.

Millions of young men and women signed up for military service, Lee Minker among them. A few weeks after he left for Army Air Corps training in early 1943, he asked his mother to save his letters, as a diary of his military experience. In turn, he saved all of the letters his parents and two sisters wrote to him.

The collection of over 800 letters, written between February 1943 and August 1945, and other wartime memorabilia were donated to the Historical Society of Delaware in 1998.

Through these letters we are able to tell the story of one family in World War II – largely in their own words. We are part of the intimate family discussions of the war, Lee's training to be a combat pilot, and the concerns on the home front; bond drives, rationing, and occasional black outs. The writing is intensely personal and yet universal as each member of this family shares not only events of daily life, but their fears for a world at war and their hopes for peace. The letters exchanged by Lee and his family bring a vibrant reality to the war and the people who lived it. Through *An American Family in World War II* we see the titanic battles in both Europe and in the Far East. We meet the famous and not so famous: Joe DiMaggio, Hedy Lamar, General "Hap" Arnold, the young Princess Elizabeth, Colonel Jimmy Stuart, and Ralph's crew who would fly the *Blue Hen Chick* in action over Germany during 1944 and 1945. Though these compelling letters we share the hopes and fears of the Minker family for the safety of their son and other young Americans who fought and lived through the war.

An American Family in World War II is the product of the efforts of many individuals who contributed their time and talent over a period of five years. We want to thank each of them for sharing their knowledge, giving honest feedback, willingness to seek out long forgotten photos and memories, and most of all, their enthusiastic belief in this project.

First, our appreciation to two marvelous women, Bernice Minker Pettit and Shirley Minker Hunsberger, who through their girlhood letters to their brother allow us to experience what it was like to grow up in those years when classmates marched off to war. We were saddened by the loss of Shirley in June 2004; her gay spirit and generous nature will continue to shine through in her letters and her family. Our special thanks to the talented Janet R. Minker who designed the cover and gave us an attractive package for the book; a gift of love for her father, as well as Aunt Shirley, Aunt Bunny, and her grandparents, Ralph Sr. and Edna Minker.

Our greatest challenge was selecting some 200 letters from the 800 letters that the family wrote. We were interested in letters that told the story of both the Home Front and the War Front, while at the same time revealing the dynamics of the family. In selecting and editing the letters, every effort was made to maintain the quality of the original conversations among the family members. Of necessity, a few of the letters have been edited to remove private references or simply to eliminate redundant material. Many of the early letters in the collection, from March – April of 1943, were undated. Where we could infer the sequence, dates have been added in brackets. The immediacy of conversation comes through every page, punctuation in the letters was minimally edited for clarity, and spelling was mostly left as written and unique to the writer, a known spelling error is acknowledged by the [sic] notation. Where the editors provided explanation or definition within a letter, the material is [bracketed], material in (parenethes) is original to the letter.

The reunions of the 447th Bomb Group, that grand annual gathering of the gallant young men who went off to England, now white haired and slow of movement, were a source of information and inspiration. The size of the group is diminishing with the years, but not their spirit. And what stories they can tell! Our gratitude to Denis Grant, sent to the English countryside as a child to escape the bombing of London, for his memories of war time Rattlesden. Mr. Grant and Ernst Osborne of Suffolk, England, entertained us with stories of two nine year-old boys living in a small village, suddenly surrounded by 2200 "Yanks" and their magnificent airplanes. Denis and Ernst are unparalled in their dedication to the men of the 447th Bomb Group. Our research and writing brought us new friends who enrich our lives.

Whenever a question arose about the 447th Bomb Group, we turned first to two rich sources: *History of the 447th Bomb Group* by Doyle Shields (710th Squadron), which describes each mission including a listing of the first pilots, and to www.447bg.com, created and maintained by David Warren, the son of ball turret gunner Arthur Wayrynen (708th Squadron). The web site gives instant access to photos, crew names, aircraft names, and serves as a model of an electronic museum. When we needed to check our facts about the 447th , the missions, and the planes, David Warren, Stub Warfle, Rob Kirkwood, and Iver Iverson quickly brought their expertise to our rescue. Yet, we wanted to know more about each of Captain Minker's missions, which led us to the National Archives in Maryland. The papers of the 447th Bomb Group are stored in box after box; a treasure trove of crumbling brown paper of mission orders, weather reports, intelligence, navigation maps, and pilot debriefing reports. We are so grateful that the army found it necessary to document and preserve everything! Hours patiently looking through the files, one by one, yielded Ralph "Lee" Minker's mission reports.

For the narrative of the story which surrounds the letters and connects the events of both war and home, we used a multitude of resources. Patrick "Skip" Stevenson, Dickinson College, provided the first written analysis of the wartime letters in his history honors project, "The Good Soldier for the Good War." We are indebted to Skip and the direction provided by history Professor Lisa Lieberman for their work on this project which also resulted in the website, www.dickinson.edu/-history/rlm/. Skip conducted a three hour video taped interview with Ralph in January, 2000. That oral history is now a time capsule of Ralph Minker's experience and memories. Ralph gained a new friend, separated by nearly 60 years in age, but not at all in their dedication to service to their country. At the time of this writing, Captain Patrick "Skip" Stevenson is serving as Battalion Logistics Officer (S4) for the 260th Quartermaster Battalion, Hunter Army Airfield, Savannah, GA. Is it mere coincidence that Hunter Army Airfield was the point of departure for Lieutenant Minker over sixty years ago? Our thanks for oral history also go to Dr. Robin Sellars from the *Institute on World War II and the*

Human Experience at Florida State University who interviewed Ralph Minker in March 1999. With the fading of memory, the oral history transcripts from Dickinson and Florida State have proven to be an invaluable resource in completing the book. Daniel Martinez, National Park Service historian from the *USS Arizona Memorial*, offered valuable suggestions and the insight that the Minker story was as much about the Home Front as it was about the War Front.

Colonel Elwyn J. (Stub) Warfle (USAAF ret.), author of *One Lucky Bastard*, helped us understand what it was like to fly in combat with runaway propellers, assemble in bad weather, hit the target through clouds and other technicalities of flying a B-17 in combat. Colonel Warfle and his wonderful wife, Jo, read many sections of the manuscript, providing comment and corrections where needed. John Kirkwood, navigator of the second crew for the *Blue Hen Chick*, and his son, Rob Kirkwood, read the chapters on the 447th Bomb Group, providing information on the Mustaleski crew and their missions in the *Blue Hen Chick*. The current 709th Airlift Squadron of the U.S. Air Force Reserves stationed at Dover Air Force Base, is keeping alive the traditions of the 709th squadron begun at Rattlesden. We will always remember the day we dedicated the C-5 Galaxy now named the *Spirit of the Blue Hen*. Our thanks to Colonel David Wuest and the men and women of the 709th Air Squadron for their service and for seeing to it that the *Blue Hen* flies once again.

Librarians were responsive, eager to help, and a fount of information. Connie Cooper, Director of Library and Archives, Historical Society of Delaware, is now the guardian of the Minker Collection of papers. She cheerfully pulled out the archive boxes for us on multiple occasions and answered an endless stream of questions about Wilmington, Delaware during the war. James Gerstener, Archive Librarian at Dickinson College helped with the history of the Minker family at Dickinson, especially the freshmen class of 1941-42. Mary Ellen Ducey from the Archives and Special Collections of University of Nebraska-Lincoln Libraries supplied photos and information to clarify the months Ralph Minker spent in Lincoln in 1943. Other librarians who willingly took the time to search for old photos and provide digital files were Julie Dougherty from Lycoming College, Pennsylvania and Lynne Tesch of the Tower Hill High School library, Wilmington, Delaware, and Sandra Farmer from the University of Delaware archives library.

We read some of the letters to an audience at the Rust Branch of the Loudoun county library on Memorial Day, 2003. Their heartfelt response encouraged us to keep working. Linda Holtslander, from the Loudoun County, Virginia Library system, believed in the project from the beginning and provided the use of space in the library when needed. Thanks to Nancy and Cynthia Schmit, who volunteered to proofread several chapters, giving us valuable suggestions that made the manuscript more interesting and useful for the reader. They, too reenforced our belief that "this story has to be told." Classes at the Writer's Center in Bethesda, Maryland provided Sandra with a consistent deadline for writing along with useful feedback from classmates and the writers who teach in this unique program. Even with all of this help, research, and internet access, any and all errors of fact or syntax are the responsibility of the editors.

Many friends contributed to the final product by encouraging us, even as the scope of work grew and grew. Lois Butowsky read portions of the manuscript offering valuable suggestions and uncomplainingly saw her husband spend endless hours and Saturdays on this work over a period of five years. Her faith in the project never flagged. Sandra's great-niece, Sarah Stone, deserves credit for going to college and working, while living for a year in a house where a book was in the making. With the grace befitting a Princess, Sarah tolerated frozen dinners, made lunch during long work sessions, and endured Sandra's occupation of the computer, and preoccupation with an earlier decade in history. Sarah also bugged me to get on with "the book" as she did her homework and made the honor roll.

More than thanks to Roxane Kerr, Sandra's friend extraordinaire, who read a very early draft, telling us the letters needed context and cheering me on throughout the book's development. Her direct feedback combined with loving support are the best definition of friendship. How can we thank Chris Nicoll, for his feedback on rough drafts, and for meticulously building not one, but two models of the *Blue Hen Chick*? (One of the models resides at the Historical Society of Delaware.) He has been the most steadfast of friends to Ralph, may your Friday morning coffee together continue for many years. Maurice Rudiselle, Ken Bonner, Buzz Bury and others in Ralph's caring support network helped out on many days. Their steadiness and love contributed to the book in a most special way. Lydia Macdonald Colwell, in her genial fashion, introduced Ralph and Sandra to historian Harry Butowsky, but did not know we would form a new partnership and lasting friendship.

Finally, we would like to thank the crew and the families of the *Blue Hen Chick* for their courage during the war that contributed to the success of this one B-17 and to eventual victory in World War II.

Ralph L. Minker
Sandra E. O'Connell (Mrs. Ralph L. Minker)
Harry Butowsky
Reston, Virginia, April 2005

PROLOGUE TO WAR

On Christmas night 1944, Edna Minker wrote a poignant letter to her son, Lee Minker, a B-17 pilot in England, that expressed the love and longing felt by every family engulfed by World War II.

Dearest Lee, *Christmas Night 1944*

And now, dear, another Christmas is almost over. I wish I could think the day had been for you just a little bit like ours, - with friends and loved ones, warmth and a nice dinner; but always there has been in the back of our minds the thought that you had to go out on a mission regardless of the fact that it was Christmas.

I hope the Christmases we have spent together have been pleasant memories which have helped you through the day. Today grandmother Minker said she hoped that some Christmas just once more she could have all of her children and grandchildren with her for dinner. That may not be possible – at least not at her house – but maybe we can all celebrate together sooner than we think.

It will perhaps be a new year when this reaches you. May it be a year we shall always remember as the one when hostilities ceased and men worked as hard to make a lasting peace as they had to wage a terrible war!

Love,
Mother

Edna's Christmas night letter reveals the longing for peace felt by millions of families on the home front. Mothers and fathers, brothers and sisters, wives and sweethearts read the frightening headlines every day, wrote letters, watched for the mailman, and prayed they would not get a telegram announcing their loved one was wounded, missing or killed in action. Although many books and studies have been published about nearly every battle of World War II (WWII), the experience of the families who waited anxiously for an end to the dark days of war has been largely unreported.

This book is the intensely personal and moving account of the life of one such family – told in their own words. Our story is extracted from the 800 letters, written between February 1943 and August 1945, by the five members of the Minker family of Wilmington, Delaware: Lee Minker, his parents Edna and Ralph Minker Sr., and sisters Shirley and Bernice. Lee's letters chronicle the transformation of a young college student into a seasoned bomber pilot; the family's letters are a portrait of the home front during the most crucial time of the twentieth century. We introduce the family briefly here, their individual relationships will emerge on the coming pages.

The Minker Family of Wilmington, Delaware

Ralph "Lee" Minker Jr.

A high school senior in 1940 when the rumblings of aggression came from both Europe and Japan, Lee entered Dickinson College in Carlisle, Pennsylvania in the fall of 1941. The news that the Japanese had bombed Pearl Harbor changed everything for young people in nation. Along with millions of young men, Lee registered for the draft but the army lacked the bases, officers and equipment to train them. In the summer of 1942 he returned to Dickinson as colleges across the country went to year-round sessions. In February 1943 he received orders to report to Miami Beach, Florida for basic training. Lee Minker was four months shy of his 19th birthday when he left Wilmington, Delaware to begin the journey that would make him a combat pilot in the Eighth Air Force assigned to the 447th Bomb Group, Rattlesden, England.

Edna Minker (mother)

Ruth Edna Jones attended Dickinson College in Carlisle, Pennsylvania for two years, from 1920–22, an unusual accomplishment for a young woman in the early 1920s. She married Ralph Leland Minker on March 31, 1923 and began her life as a wife and mother. Their first child, Ralph Leland "Lee" Minker Jr., was born June 16, 1924, and Shirley was born December 7, 1926. The family was completed with the birth of Bernice on November 22, 1928. Shortly before her 20th wedding anniversary in 1943, Edna Minker saw her 18 year-old son off to war. Her letters paint a collage of a full family life, replete with a son in the service, two teenage daughters, a job as secretary at the Ferris School, and an active social and civic life in Wilmington, Delaware. She was the mainstay of the family, providing her son with encouragement and practical advice. She bought Christmas and Valentine gifts for Lee's girlfriend, did his income taxes, mailed packages of cookies, and found scarce items such as camera film. Edna's letters gave her son a strong link to the family and the Wilmington community. She wrote to him several times a week for two and a half years, during 18 months of training and 11 months of overseas duty in England.

Ralph Leland Minker Sr. (father)
Ralph L. Minker graduated from Dickinson College in 1920 and then attended Boston University Theological School. After serving several pastorates in New England, Rev. Ralph Minker Sr. became the Superintendent of the Ferris Industrial School for Boys in Wilmington, Delaware from 1936 until 1945, where the family lived on the school grounds. He also served as part-time pastor at Grace Methodist Church, as Civilian Defense Warden for New Castle County, a fundraiser for government bonds, and was an avid fan of the Wilmington Blue Rocks baseball team. Rev. Minker's letters to his son were filled with pride and advice on each step of his progress from private to pilot. From the activities of the Ferris School to bond fund drives and commentary on the war, Ralph Sr.'s letters portray Wilmington civic life during the war years.

Shirley Minker (sister)
Lee's oldest sister, Shirley Minker, was beginning her last semester in high school when he left for the service in early 1943. She graduated from Alexis I. duPont High School in a class bereft of boys and went on to attend Dickinson Junior College in Williamsport, Pennsylvania. She wrote encouraging letters to her brother and worried along with him about his progress with flight training. Shirley's war-time letters are full of sisterly teasing of her big brother. In her lighthearted manner Shirley shared her experience of college life, singing

lessons and performances, and new friends. In the summers she sang with the Brandywiners, a unique organization that presented a large-scale musical production every summer at Longwood Gardens in Kennett Square, Pennsylvania, and contributed the proceeds to cultural, educational and civic causes throughout the Delaware Valley. Taken together, her letters are a charming portrait of a young woman during the uncertain years of 1943 – 45. Shirley's letters are also a record of the pervasive effects of the war on young people as she reported on friends in the service: the boys killed, wounded, or taken prisoner of war.

Bernice Minker (sister)

A teenager of 15 when her brother left for training, Bernice supplied the knock-knock jokes, humorous escapades, and a lively sense of fun. In her letters she shared her high school years, the transfer to Tower Hill High School, singing with the Brandywiners, and trips to see her sister Shirley at college. She was always eager to cheer her brother up and looked for items to send in packages to him. When the war was finally over, her vivid descriptions of V-E Day and V-J Day let us experience the celebrations through the eyes of a teenager. Bernice's teenage years culminated in the summer of 1945 with high school graduation, acceptance to college, and the end of the war.

Our story begins in the summer of 1940.

"This is Trafalgar Square. The noise that you hear is the sound of the air raid siren."

The rich baritone voice of CBS correspondent Edward R. Murrow crackled over the radio on an August night in 1940. Sixteen year-old Lee Minker lay in bed in his third floor room, listening to every word of the rooftop report from London. The news of the Battle of Britain was a disturbing reminder of the world outside of Wilmington, Delaware and the war in Europe that had already begun. He thought about the possibility of Americans going to Europe to fight Adolf Hitler, wondering "Would we be involved in it?" (Stevenson 2000)

Lee Minker began his senior year at Alexis I. duPont High School in the fall of 1940 as Europe was overrun with a flood of violence. That summer and fall the British Royal Air Force (RAF) battled against the German *Luftwaffe* (German Air Force) for control of the skies of Britain, a prelude to Hitler's plan to invade Great Britain. The Germans had already overrun Belgium, the Netherlands, and northern France. In late September 1940, Germany, Italy and Japan formed the Axis powers with the stated purpose, " to establish and maintain a new order of things." The Axis pact was a warning to the United States to stay out of the war in Europe and the Pacific.

Lee became president of his high school senior class in an isolationist America that was just beginning to feel the effects of the conflict in Europe and Japan. President Franklin Delano Roosevelt (FDR) placed an embargo on oil and other supplies to Japan in the fall of 1940 in response to their aggression in China. As a further reaction to world hostilities, he signed the Selective Service Act in mid-September, enacting the first peace time draft. Sixteen million men registered for the draft in October of 1940. Throughout the fall and winter of 1940, Murrow reported from London on the nightly air raids, the bravery of the RAF fliers, and the loss of life for the English people. The aerial attacks on

London and other British cities abated in May 1941 when the *Luftwaffe* bombers were moved to the eastern border of Germany to prepare for the invasion of Russia. The months of *Luftwaffe* bombing had wrecked havoc in England. In London alone 41,000 people died and 46,000 dwellings were destroyed during the Blitz. When the devastating raids finally ceased, Winston Churchill paid eloquent tribute to the airmen who fought in the skies defending their homeland. "The gratitude of every home in our island, in our Empire, and indeed, throughout the world, except in the abodes of the guilty, goes out to the British airmen, who, undaunted by the odds, unwearied in their constant challenge and mortal danger, are turning the tide of world war by their prowess and by their devotion. Never in the field of human conflict was so much owed by so many to so few!"

In the spring of 1941 as Lee's high school graduation approached, President Roosevelt signed the Lend-Lease Act which provided for food, fuel, and war supplies to an embattled Britain. The Nazi conquest continued its march across Europe with the invasion of Greece and Yugoslavia in April. Against this backdrop of ever building aggression and violence, the class of 1941 graduated from Alexis I. duPont High School.

Lee Minker entered Dickinson College at age 17 in September 1941, following in his parents' footsteps. Lee joined the Theta Chi fraternity and the debate club, pursued his studies, and a social life – he was a typical college freshman. He also had a girlfriend from Wilmington, Julia Taylor, who would go to Oberlin College in Ohio the next year. Lee was well aware of the debate over U.S. entry into the war. The sentiment on campus and throughout the country, was changing from isolationist to recognition of the inevitability of war. A 1939 survey conducted on the Dickinson campus showed 501 students opposed to joining the Allies, and only 17 in favor. Attitudes shifted quickly after the attack on Pearl Harbor. The events in Europe and the Pacific developed into a tornado that was gathering strength, growing larger and more destructive every day.

Lee Minker (left) with buddies from the freshman class.
Echo, 1941 Courtesy Dickinson College Archives

On Saturday December 6, 1941, Julia Taylor came from Wilmington to attend Lee's fraternity pledge dance. The next day, Lee and a friend helped to clean up the Theta Chi house after the party. As they walked back across the campus, economics professor Cornelius Fink came out of his white frame house on West High Street shouting the news: *"THE JAPANESE HAVE BOMBED PEARL HARBOR!"*

In that moment the idyllic peace-time life of college students across the country changed – totally and completely. Lee knew that the allies in Europe needed help and now there would be a war in the Pacific. The United States declared war on Japan on December 8, 1941; Germany declared war on the United States on December 11, 1941. Millions of young men volunteered immediately, Lee had to wait until he turned 18 in June to register. He then volunteered for the Army Air Corps (A.A.C.), and received his acceptance in October 1942. (In 1947, the Army Air Corps became a separate service, the United States Air Force.)

REGISTRATION CERTIFICATE

This is to certify that in accordance with the Selective Service Proclamation of the President of the United States

RALPH LELAND MINKER Jr.
(First name) (Middle name) (Last name)

FERRIS SCHOOL WILMINGTON DELAWARE
(Place of residence)
(This will be identical with line 2 of the Registration Card)

has been duly registered this 30 day of JUNE, 1942

(Signature of registrar)

Registrar for Local Board 2 CARLISLE Pa.
(Number) (City or county) (State)

THE LAW REQUIRES YOU TO HAVE THIS CARD IN YOUR PERSONAL POSSESSION AT ALL TIMES

D. S. S. Form 2
(Revised 6/9/41) 16—21631

Ralph Leland Minker, Jr.
(Registrant must sign here)

Lee Minker's registration card.
Historical Society of Delaware

Lee's choice of the Army Air Corps was influenced by his slight size; he thought he would have more control in a plane than "charging across a field with a bayonet." Another factor was his childhood memory of seeing Charles Lindbergh land a plane on a field in New England. (Stevenson 2000)

The peace-time Army was not prepared to train the millions of new recruits all at once. Colleges across the country went to a year-round schedule so that "students could receive as much college level learning as possible before adequate military training was made available." (Sellars 1999) The summer of 1941 Lee returned to Dickinson, the accelerated college schedule allowed him to finish his sophomore year in January 1943. He received orders from the Aviation Cadet Examining Board to report to Army Basic Training Center # 9 in Miami, Florida on February 25, 1943. Ralph Sr. drove to Carlisle to pick Lee up from college for a few last days at home. It had been 14 months since the fateful attack on Pearl Harbor. Now the hostilities had come home – the Minker family, along with millions of other American families, were about to be swept up in the tumult of world war.

Chapter One

Don't Worry About Me

February 25, 1943 – April 3, 1943

Dates: February 25, 1943 – April 3, 1943	Location: Miami Beach, Florida

January 1943	Lee completed his sophomore year at Dickinson College.
February 17, 1943	He received orders to report to Miami, Florida Training Center.
February 25, 1943	Lee left Wilmington on the train, arriving the next day in Miami.
March 1943	Lee completed basic training.
April 3, 1943	Lee left Miami headed for Lincoln, Nebraska.

On Thursday, February 25, 1943 Ralph and Edna Minker took their 18 year-old son, Lee, to the Wilmington train station; along with other parents they said good-bye to their Delaware boys who were leaving for basic training in Miami Beach, Florida. The United States had been at war for just over a year, the end of hostilities was not on the horizon. Reverend and Mrs. Minker did not know if he would pass the rigorous requirements for pilot selection and training, or when they would see their only son again.

On board the *Silver Meteor*, the sleek, stainless steel, long distance train that operated between New York and Miami, Lee traveled with several boys he knew from Dickinson College. From the modern 60 seat coach they watched the countryside speed by, with the signs of mobilization for war prominent on the landscape. Lee wrote his dad almost immediately after his first day of army life.

Sunday noon
[February 28, 1943]

Dear Dad,

Gradually a semblance of order is coming out of the chaos of the last several days.

My first impressions: There were hundreds of planes lined up at the Glenn L. Martin plant outside of Baltimore. It was really an impressive sight to see all the new planes, the huge plant and airfield and the numerous mushrooming villages nearby.

I saw Stowell and Springer [classmates from Dickinson] in Union Station while waiting for the Silver Meteor which came at 9:30 (at last). We had a fairly comfortable journey down in this really classy streamliner. We arrived in Miami at 10:30 Friday night after a monotonous journey through the poverty stricken south.

Finally a truck came for us and we were taken to the Cadillac Hotel at 12:15 a.m. They weren't expecting us so we were temporarily assigned to the Hotel Good and given our mess equipment – two steel plates, knife, fork and spoon. We were followed by eight more (including Stowell and Springer) at 12:30 and twelve more at 2:30. We got two hours sleep before being called for breakfast at 4:45. (We have fifteen minutes to dress, wash and line up outside.)

Meals have been very good although not like mother's and we have to stand in line from thirty to sixty minutes beforehand.

We just stood around and waited most of Saturday. We were taken from Flight 635 [a flight was the term for a group of recruits] and assigned to Flight 629 in the Coral Reef Hotel. Michels of Dickinson, Phi Psi, was one and I am at present one of six with him in one room although I will probably have another room shortly as they are shipping quite a few out.

We just came in from getting our outfit except for gas masks, ties, handkerchiefs and certain sizes of certain things. Hyde, Stowell and Springer are still in my group and I have seen the other Dickinson boys for they are in [flight] 635 mostly.

My address is *AAC Pvt. Ralph Minker*
TSS 1129 Flight 629
BTC 9
Miami Beach Florida

I'll write more later but probably will be rushed for the next few days. Don't send any packages yet.

Tell everybody hello for me.

Yours,
Lee

Each day Edna and Ralph Sr. waited eagerly for news of Lee's safe arrival, driving to the downtown post office hoping for a letter from their son. All over the country, the delivery of mail took on a new significance for families. The postman was welcome as he went about his rounds, block by block and house by house. A letter meant that their serviceman was safe and well, at least for the time being.

Tuesday evening, March 2, 1943

Dear Lee: --

We thought for sure we would receive a letter from you today, especially after Mr. Hyde called daddy and said he had received one from Bill. I'll start one to you, in the hopes that tomorrow morning's mail will bring something.

You left here just in time to miss some cold weather, for on Friday it snowed all afternoon and today has been quite cold. I am glad you are in a warmer climate during the month of March. Just be careful that you don't get too much Florida sunshine at one time and come down with a bad case of sunburn.

I was interested in reading an article in the Star on Sunday about some residents at Miami making objection to the early morning singing of the soldiers. According to the newspaper the following reply was sent to them by Col. Ralph M. Parker, commander of the base. "The singing will continue. Moreover, please arise at the first sound of military activity each morning and get down on your knees with all the members of your household who are disturbed thereby, and offer thanks to God Almighty, with me and all the rest of us, that those are Americans singing American songs and not Germans or Japs singing victory songs in American Streets." You must have a pretty decent commander.

Wednesday morning

Daddy and I drove in town about 10 o'clock last night and were delighted to find the letter which you had written Sunday afternoon. What does the world look like at 4:45 in the morning? I'm glad that you are with some boys from Dickinson and know you will have some great experiences. Are you and Bill Hyde still together?

It is colder here this morning and snowing, so take in plenty of sunshine for all of us up here shivering. I want to get this letter off air-mail this morning. I suppose that will reach you a little bit more quickly than ordinary mail, won't it? Let me know, for I think I remember reading somewhere that it was not advisable to send mail to camps that way.

We are all thinking of you and wondering about what you are doing. That was a nice letter. Keep up the good work.

Love from everyone one of us, including your grandmothers.

Mother

Tuesday evening [March 2]

Dear Shirley,

Oh what a day we've had –eight hours of review in a boiling hot sun which I later found out to be practice for a four hour review for General Weaver tomorrow. I only hope I don't get sun poisoning. We stood at attention for one full hour, alternately saluting about every officer there could be in all Miami Beach. The total twenty thousand men of Basic Training Center # 9 took part and there was the biggest band I have ever seen, two hundred pieces plus a fifty piece bugle and drum corps and an immense drum Major. Several fainted out of the ranks.

We have also been interviewed and given our G. I. Haircuts – not as bad as I anticipated.

Tell mother to airmail all letters and packages as you can [guess] the long time it takes otherwise. Rush me stamps, towels, underwear and socks also please in my laundry case.

By the way, the General inspects our hotel tomorrow so we'll really have to clean it up. There are seven boys in our room and two (including me) have to sleep on cots and keep all our clothing and equipment in a duffel bag. It's very inconvenient but the whole program down here is the same way and shows not much real preparation.

Love,
Lee

First G. I. hair cut, Miami, March 1943
Historical Society of Delaware

Lee began the adjustment to military life with a G.I. haircut and K.P. duty. The barracks were one of many ocean front hotels that now housed soldiers rather than tourists. He lived with six roommates crammed into one room. Although an eager air cadet, he was discouraged by army inefficiency as each week they packed up and moved from hotel to hotel along the beach front and reported for inspection in the sweltering Florida sun.

Wednesday evening the 3rd of March, 1943

Dear Lee: -

Your letter was a tonic. Mother and I rode into the Post Office last night as I had done Sunday and Monday nights, and the letter was there. We didn't wait to get home to read it. We put the inside light of the Packard on, and, in front of the Post Office we read it. You sense from this that letters from you mean a lot to us.

I realize something of the rush and hurry of these early

hours in the new situation, and I know it meant a lot to find the few minutes it took to write those paragraphs to us.

Wilmington's new siren is in place and we have a test blackout tomorrow night along with Maryland and Pennsylvania. We test our new signals. From the way Hitler is talking we may need to use our Civilian Defense Organization. It may be just the bravado sputterings of a dying or trapped bandit.

Well, kid, the best to you. Keep yourself in the old tip top shape, and first be yourself. They don't come any finer than you, and you don't have to apologize to any of them when it comes to real manhood. I'm pulling for you every minute.

As always,
Dad –

RALPH L. MINKER
Superintendent

Ferris Industrial School of Delaware
BOX 230
Wilmington, Delaware

Wednesday evening
the 3rd of March,
1943.

Dear Lee:-

Your letter was a tonic. Mother and I rode in to the Post Office last night as I had done Sunday and Monday nights, and the letter was there. We didn't wait to get home to read it. We put the inside light of the Packard on, and, in front of the Post Office we read it. You sense from this that letters from you mean a lot to us.

Opening of Ralph Minker Sr.'s first letter to his son.
Courtesy Historical Society of Delaware

Shirley, starting her last semester in high school, wrote weekly to keep Lee up to date on their high school friends. Her teasing relationship with him does not mask the love and concern she felt for her brother.

Saturday night
March 6, 1943

Dear Lee –

Well, I imagine that by now your face looks like a big red beet. It sounds like it might be a little warm down there. This afternoon Mother sent you some cookies but I imagine you have eaten them all up by the time that you get this.

This first week of school has just flown by and I haven't been to bed before midnight yet. They certainly piled the work on the seniors. Several of the boys are talking about leaving before school is over if they can get their diplomas. I guess we won't have such an awfully large graduating class.

When the Senior Issue of the Echo [their high school newspaper] comes out, would you like one? I think all of the alumnae in the service are getting one free, but if not I'll send you one. It should be quite good and will probably be rather thick as the pictures of the class members and of service men will be in it along with other senior things.

I wish you would please note the big stationery and the longer-than-usual letter and if you say that I wrote bigger or left more space, I'll crown you so help me. I'll write again next week and Grandmother sends you her love.

Lots of love –
Shirley

P.S. Have you heard any good jokes? They're all stale up here.

Saturday evening
[March 6]

Dear Mother,

I'm writing this right after P.T. [physical training] in the ocean and right before my K.P. duty [kitchen police] which will extend from 6:30 P.M. to 4:30 A. M. and will consist in the main of cleaning up the mess hall and preparing for tomorrow's meals. I'll write you in detail about it later.

Tomorrow night twelve fellows from rooms at the end of the hall have to G.I. the hotel lobby because we didn't get the call to fall out yesterday.

This morning we were reviewed in parade by Secretary of War Stimson, the head of the Chilean army and Air Corps Chief Lieutenant General "Hap" Arnold. It was very impressive.

I've run out of writing paper and so I use this unearthly green which is furnished by the Miami Women's Club.

Got to run so so long.

Love,
Lee

Lee found U.S. Basic Training Center # 9 massive, sprawling, and disorganized. Hampered by the lack of training facilities at the beginning of the war, the Army had taken over 300 hotels and apartment buildings in south Miami Beach, nicknamed the Gold Coast, for housing and training headquarters. Rather than build large training bases, hotels such as the Coral Reef, the Atlantic, and the Boca Raton became barracks, the beaches and golf courses became training fields.

The war had already come to the Florida coast where German U-boats prowled in 1942, attacking merchant ships. The vessel *Pan Massachusetts* was sunk 20 miles south of Cape Canaveral, the *Republic* was sunk off West Palm Beach, and on May 19, 1942, the *Portero del Llano* was torpedoed, then burned and sank in sight of Miami Beach. Debris began washing up on Florida's gold coast beaches, effectively ending the tourist trade for the duration of the war.

Wednesday night [March 10, 1943]

Dear Dad,

I'm rather blue tonight and so are most of the other fellows.

It was announced that we would have to stay here in basic training for at least eight weeks, instead of the original four. It's going to be a rather trying time for all of us because we are packed in this place, hotel and beach, worse than sardines. There are seven in our room and I am one of the two latecomers who has to keep everything in one duffel bag.

Would you see about getting a doctor's prescription to wear sun glasses. Doctor Pierson told me to a few years ago and I want to keep my eyes in the best possible shape.

After our two months here we'll spend five months in college according to the newly instituted program.

Lee

Shirley reported with dismay that some of her classmates were going to work before high school graduation, they were needed to alleviate the local manpower shortage. A national problem, by the end of 1943 nearly 13 million men and women had been called up or enlisted in the military. The war economy simultaneously created millions of new jobs and drained the economy of able workers for military service. To close the enormous gap between available labor and needed workers, war plants increased the work week from forty to forty-eight-hours, and new groups (women, blacks, Hispanics and teenagers) were brought into the labor pool.

March 11 – '43

Hi! Peeler!

How is the little beet face? I bet you are a beauty. Of course, you always were. Boy, you must have a swell place to live. Do you have pull with the General or something?

Beginning next week all senior commercial students and some general [students] are going out to work until May 20 – senior exams. I guess this is to relieve the manpower shortage, but some of them don't want to go. There won't be half our class at school.

We got our schedule for senior exams, baccalaureate, and commencement the other day. It makes one feel funny. Well, I'll write again and send you some gab.

Lots of love,
Shirley

"Little beet face" Sun burned Private Minker, March 1943
Courtsesy Historical Society of Delaware.

In a time when few people traveled far from home, Lee met a diverse group of Americans while in training. He enjoyed meeting boys from different parts of the country as they marched and sang and did K.P. [kitchen police] together. In the forced camaraderie of military life, millions of Americans found themselves thrown together with people they never would have met in times of peace. Lee was swept into a tide of cultural change brought about by the war.

Friday evening [March 12]

Dear Bernice,

We had eight more hours of drill today – my face is so

sore it hurts to wash it. But they sure are beginning to toughen us after the first couple of days of breaking us up. My leg muscles are gradually coming in to shape. I certainly would never have believed that that injury of several years ago had made so much difference in my two legs though.

One distinctive thing about our life down here is that we march everywhere we go and as we march we sing as loud as possible. Everybody's voice has changed a notch or two because of the sudden strain. Mine has become deeper. We sing quite a collection of songs as you can imagine we would with all parts of the country, different colleges, and the armed forces represented here. There are Yankee flights, Virginian, Rebel, Pennsylvanian, Michigan, etc. and there is much razzing of the different groups.

Lee

Sunday night [March 14, 1943]

Dear Mother,

At last luck has hit me and us – this morning flight 629 was moved from the Coral Reef Hotel at 36th and Collins Avenue to the Atlantis at 26th and Collins. This marks the fourth hotel I've been in so far by the way but this one will probably be my home for the duration of my stay here as they moved all of the aviation cadet candidates up to this part of BTC#9 [Basic Training Center].

This hotel is a beauty – it has all the rugs and furnishings left and we have only five in a much larger room than before. I again have a sea front room which formerly rented for $ 40 a day. It is real luxury. And here *we have a canteen downstairs which is run by a Miami Women's Club which boasts of a fine reading and recreation room and which promotes dances, contests, war classes and cultural classes.*

Last night we had our first "open post" which is free time until 11:00 P.M. It was a real tonic to us all. I met several of the Dickinson boys from other flights, bought a dress uniform, had my picture taken (4 for $ 3.25, I am feeling so I don't know what they will look like but I'll send you one as soon as I can pick them up) and enjoyed a snack – a chocolate shake sure tasted swell.

I'm sending home my army insurance receipt. Keep it on file for in a year I can make it a 20 year or life policy at very special rates and without examination.

More later for the guard just yelled, "Lights Out."

Love to you all,
Lee

Throughout March 1943, ominous headlines of the German advance in Russia dominated the *Wilmington Morning News* along with the news of the Eighth Air Force in England: "FLYING FORTS HIT ROTTERDAM IN DAYLIGHT RAIDS" The B-17, known as the flying fortress, was the dominant American bomber in the European Theater of War, carrying out missions over France, Holland, and Germany. For Edna and Ralph Sr., the news had to be disturbing, knowing that their son was in the Army Air Corps and could be assigned to a flying fortress. Any parental anxiety did not come through in their letters which continued to encourage Lee through the early, confused days of training.

[March 16, 1943] Tuesday morning

Dear Lee:

Your airmail letter addressed to daddy came yesterday afternoon – fast work – and the letter you wrote me Saturday evening came this morning.

We have not received any pictures yet nor your laundry bag.

How often do you have to do K.P.?

With the reorganization I suppose your Sunday was pretty well taken care of. Are there any church services there for the boys, and if so how do you work it, -- each group in their own hotel? Who is the chaplain? It might be someone daddy knows.

Have you put on any weight yet?

I know all this reorganization must be upsetting, but try not to let it get you down. Are you still in the same room and with the same roommates?

I hope mail from some of those to whom you have written is beginning to "roll" now.

Lots and lots of love,

Mother

March 19, 1943

Dear Lee:-

The reports you send of the shifting around and re-arranging you are subjected to lead me to believe that even this seeming confusion is part of basic training. There is a certain haphazardness you have to harden yourself toward. Even in life as we carry it on normally you have to face some of this. Mr. Hering [family friend] remarked rather suggestively the other evening when he and I were discussing you before his fireplace that "you were getting a taste of the endurance test army life for the most part is." I know you can take it, and here's to you. And take it smiling.

Enclosed are a few hundred clippings. All of us are alert for paper articles you might be interested in, and on my desk that ordinarily carries enough stuff is piled high with material my various sub-editors, Mother, Shirley and Bernice, have collected. Hope you enjoy these items.

I hope those cookies have arrived by this time.

Every good wish.
As ever,
Dad

Sunday noon [March 21, 1943]

Dear Dad,

It's happened again! We have been reorganized. We were all called out at 8:00 A. M. this morning to reorganize after having had only three hours sleep. It's really disgusting – the inefficiency which is prevalent throughout this center! I'm lucky however in that I am still in the Atlantis – which is the cleanest and most efficient hotel on the beach. Captain Young is tops and so on down.

K.P. was very monotonous. Results – 41 bushels of potatoes sliced, 1/3 fried, pancake batter mixed, the whole mess hall G.I.'d, millions of grapefruit halved and tables set for breakfast. Our mess hall, by the way has to feed 3,000 men in two hours time three times a day so you can gauge the immensity of it all.

The last few days a great wave of homesickness has swept over everybody here due probably to a great extent to the futility brought on by inefficiency.

It's time for dinner so I've got to quit. Let everybody you can reach know about my address change.

As always,
Lee

Sunday 7 p.m. [March 21, 1943]

Dear Lee:-

This is the first day of spring, according to the calendar, and we are having another snowstorm. The tulips, daffodils and crocus are up and I hope this cold does not kill them.

We were delighted with the snapshots which came in Bernice's letter yesterday, and then this morning before I left for church your four pictures arrived. We think they are fine, even tho your peeling nose is quite prominent. Let me know how you wish me to dispose of them. Do you want Julia [Julia Taylor was Lee's girlfriend] to have one or not? The girls will take one to school tomorrow for Mr. Yingst [high school science teacher] to use in the duPont Echo. When your sisters saw the two pictures of you as "Baldy" they let out a scream which could be heard as far away as the airport.

Of course you will let us know as soon as there is any change in your address, won't you? Should you be sent back to this part of the country do you suppose you will have any time off to run home, or must you keep moving?

Lots of love from all of us. Your pictures look as though you are well and happy.

Mother

Lee came down with an unspecified illness towards the end of basic training. He spent five days in sickbay while the doctors tried to decide if he had spinal meningitis, rocky mountain spotted fever, or the measles. Frustrating for Lee and worrisome for the family; the illness delayed his departure from Miami. The symptoms cleared up in a few days, he was able to leave with the very next flight of cadets. In an effort to reassure his parents, he wrote "don't worry," a phrase that he would repeat many times, from many Army Air Corps bases.

Monday Morning [March 22, 1943]

Dear Dad,

Right now I'm feeling both blue and happy but am perfectly well.

Friday I developed a cough and high temperature and [was] given some aspirin to take. Saturday I awoke with dime size purple blotches all over me. From that moment until this I have been in the station hospital with all the army doctors here trying to find out what I had for it has disappeared entirely now. The Captain says he thinks I can rejoin squadron 10 in a couple of days and I'm hoping against hope that I can ship out with them. The doctors said that the spots were internal hemorrhages and that they might mean either Rocky Mountain Spotted Fever or Spinal Meningitis [sic] but I feel fine after the run down feeling of Friday and Saturday. They haven't even given me any medicine.

I'll let you know more when I get time. Don't worry mother with this.

Lee

P.S. I could be kept here for 28 days if my blood culture is bad and thus loose [sic] my flight [a unit of trainees].

After only a few weeks in the service, the eighteen year old private realized that he would want a record of his life in the military. He asked the family to save his letters so he would have a diary. Lee's early awareness of documenting his experience led to the preservation of the family's 800 letters from the war years.

Wednesday night [March 24, 1943]

Dear Bernice,

It's tough sledding here.- No snow.

I go on active duty tomorrow, a healed young man. I had a good rest and saw another side of army life.

I got at least some of my letters – The pictures were fine but next time take a couple of mother and dad and grandmother too. Also don't worry about the moods in my letters as they are taking the place of a diary. (save them). Tell mother I got the $15.00 and the cookies. The cookies were very good and not noticeably stale.

The life is dull here and long. We rise at six and have our temperature taken, eat at seven and wait for the doctor's inspection at 8:00. Lunch is at 11:00 and supper at 4:30. Our temperatures and pulse are again recorded just before the lights go out at 9:00. The reading and this writing material are provided by the Red Cross.

I don't know how I'll fit in when I get back tomorrow

but hope to rejoin my old flight and be shipped out soon with them. I'll let you know how things develop and try to reply to all my letters and also write to the new addresses.

Love,
Spinal Meningitis

March 25, 1943

My dear Lee:

I am both glad and sorry to get the news of your sickness, glad because you seem to be in pretty good shape and sorry because you had to have any set-back at all. You have been doing so splendidly that I hoped you would be able to weather this early strenuous period without a kick in the pants. We had an inkling of the trouble from a sentence in Bill Hyde's letter in which he spoke of your being down with measles. I didn't show your Monday's letter to Mother but thought you would be writing again and the news would be more encouraging for her. I hope you won't be too enthusiastic about your flight if there is a question of your health involved. After all, you've got to be in good physical shape and it is better to get in condition than it is to stumble on and at a more important point in your development get a more serious break. I do hope that nothing will interfere with your continuing in your flight but don't let it get you down if you have to be re-scheduled.

Work continues to be plentiful around here at least so far as I am concerned. I can hardly appreciate how any one can live in these times without doing as much extra as he possibly can.

The Athletics [Philadelphia professional baseball

team] are here in training and I just saw Connie Mack over at the Hotel duPont. He is a grand old man. I don't think he would like to have me call him old. We are rolling the diamond at the School today and the boys are going through some of the motions preparatory to forming a team.

Keep a stiff upper lip and don't hesitate to wire or phone if there is any urgency you want to talk about.

As ever,
Dad

Thursday night [March 25]

Dear Dad,

Well I got out [of the infirmary] at last but too late I'm afraid by about two hours. This morning all of old flight 629 from J to Z was placed "on shipping" with all of 612 (a Maryland bunch). I wasn't there and so they took the last H – Hyde, Bill. I lose all my roommates and Springer and Stowell as a result. But then I'll go with the rest of 629 I guess and they should go soon as all the A.C.C.'s [Air Corps Cadets] in B.T.C. # 9 [Basic Training Company] are preparing to leave.

Relay my thanks to mother for this writing paper. It comes in very handy although I won't be able to write after this until I get where I may be going. That rule is for those on shipping (soon me) so don't worry please. (Also don't worry about my comments for I am just writing the situation as it is and certainly you know that I like to criticize.)

My pay arrangement – $50.00 a month minus $6.50 for insurance and $12.50 for war bonds. In five months when I become an Air Cadet my pay will increase to $75.00 *a month and the government will pay my insurance.*

I still don't know what ailed me or what caused the stiffening of my legs but am okay now and will write you as soon as I get resettled. Boy, I'd like to return to Pennsylvania again!

Love,
Lee

An army private's pay of $50.00 a month or $600 a year was in keeping with the general economy which had an average per capita income of $2,000 in 1943. That figure, however, represented the more fortunate, as 40 per cent of the population had an income of less than $1,000. With the mandatory payroll deductions, Lee frequently found himself short of cash during the first months of training and had to write home for money. Shirley and Bernice had great fun teasing their older brother about his military hair cut and sunburn.

Saturday [March] 27, 1943

Dear tall, shorn and moronic,

I received your letter this evening and was amazed to hear from you. Please explain in your next letter home what you were ill from. It might be nice to know.

Last night Walt and I saw "They Got Me Covered." It was funny in parts, but not as consistently amusing as "Road to Morocco." Mother and dad are going to see "The Corn is Green" tonight at the Playhouse, starring Ethel Barrymore. We are certainly getting to be theatre-goers in this house. Shirley and Ben are going tonight to see "Keeper of the Flame" with Spencer Tracy and Katherine Hepburn.

Mother's and Dad's 20th Wedding Anniversary is next Wednesday.

Did you hear about the moron who held the blotter to his ear to hear the Ink Spots? No, Well, I'll tell you some time.

Lots of Love,
Bernice

Sunday evening [March 28, 1943]

Dear Mother,

I wish you wouldn't worry so much about me mother. There is no real need for it really for if anything happens to me the army will let you know about it. As for no news; there is an army rule against writing home during your last week of a specific stage of your training until you have definitely been settled in your next stage. (I hope this gets through!)

I was touched with a severe grippe for a few days and in throwing off the temperature I had some internal hemorages [sic] which showed up as purple spots. Hence Hyde's rumor of the measles. They took me to the hospital for observation on spinal meningitis and released me when they found nothing wrong.

Congratulations to you and Dad on your twentieth wedding anniversary and may you have many more of them.

I was on the beach all afternoon. It sure was a fine day for it.

I'll let you know how things settle so don't worry.
Love,
Lee

After four weeks of marching in the Florida sun, moving from hotel to hotel, and a few days in the infirmary, basic training was over. Lee received shipping orders for the College Training Detachment at Morningside College in Sioux City, Iowa. Sparse belongings crammed into a duffel bag, sunburned Air Cadet Lee Minker boarded the westward-bound train from Miami with the boys of Flight 629 on Saturday morning April 3, 1943. The slow rail trip across the south and then the plains of the mid-west brought them to Chicago, where due to a missed connection Lee enjoyed the wartime hospitality of the city for a few hours.

The movie he saw, *In Which They Serve*, told the story of the surviving crew members of a British naval destroyer as they await rescue in the Mediterranean. Lee thought the movie, which featured actual battle film, was excellent. Early in the war the movie industry mobilized to both provide entertainment and build morale. The Selective Service System declared motion pictures an "essential industry," giving producers access to limited resources such as chemicals for film and exempting actors from the draft. (Lingeman 2003) Throughout Lee's service the family wrote each other about movies, offering critiques and recommendations. After the short break in Chicago, Lee's class boarded the train for Sioux City, Iowa.

Tuesday morning
[probably April 6, 1943]
[Morningside College, Sioux City, Iowa]

Dear Bernice,

Well, we're here. We pulled in about ten and after a brief snack were sent to the gymnasium where the eighty three who came here from Miami Beach will live for two weeks. At that time we will move into regular dorms as a group that is there now is going to move out.

There are about 500 A.C.C's [Air Corp Cadets] here and 5,000 other soldiers at an air base about six miles away. The town seems like a very nice place and so does the college after a very brief look at each but the college does not look as well kept up as Dickinson.

We had quite a trip up! We left at 9:00 A.M. Saturday and that night hit Jacksonville. We then switched from the Seaboard to the Southern R.R. and got into Atlanta in the morning. We really shivered that first night but after that we had no trouble sleeping at all. We then switched to the Frisco Line of the Illinois Central which took us through Birmingham at noon, Jasper, Jackson (9:00 P.M.), Corinth, Cairo, Champaign and Chicago. (9:00 A. M.). First we saw all flat sandy Florida wastes, then hilly Georgia and Alabama red clay wastes. It was dark so we didn't get a chance to see anything of Kentucky or Tennessee. We missed our connections in Chicago so we had a seven hour leave there. It was really grand. Nothing it seems is too good for a soldier there. I saw Noel Coward's "In Which We Serve." It was excellent. And so we arrived in Sioux City this morning on the Milwaukee Road. (Chicago, St. Paul, Milwaukee and Pacific R. R.). The country here is hilly but barren as this is the foothills of the Black Hills.

By the way, could you send me Julia's [Julia Taylor , Lee's high school girlfriend] picture? (the second one) It's lunch time now so I'll sample the new mess.

Love,
Lee

The Miami boys arrived in Sioux City, Iowa on April 6, expecting to be billeted at Morningside College. The Army Air Corps, however, did not know about the contingent, so after a night in the college gymnasium they were sent on to Lincoln, Nebraska. The confusion was not an uncommon event during the massive build-up that began in 1942. A military study on flight training concluded that "often masses of recruits were cooling their heels at every stage of the process, enduring endless boredom, screw-ups, and often difficult physical conditions." (Cameron 1999) Lee was cooling his heels at several points during the rapid Army Air Corps build up which trained nearly 200,000 combat pilots in less than four years. At the University of Nebraska, Lee would experience the exhilaration of his first flight before his nineteenth birthday.

Chapter Two

I Start Flying Monday

April 6, 1943 - June 16, 1943

Dates: April 6, 1943 - June 16, 1943	**Location: University of Nebraska Lincoln, Nebraska**

Progression of Flight Training

Lincoln, NE	Santa Ana, CA	Thunderbird Field, AZ	Pecos, TX	Pecos, TX	Roswell, NM
College Training Attachment	Classification And Pre-flight	Basic Flight Training	Preliminary Flight Training	Advanced Flight School	Transitional
Piper Cub		Stearman	BT-17	Cessna AT-17	B-17

April 7, 1943	Lee arrived in Lincoln, Nebraska for College Detachment Training.
May 6, 1943	General Rommel's Afrika Korp surrendered to American and British forces.
May 8, 1943	An explosion at a munitions plant near Wilmington killed 20 young women.
May 24, 1943	First flight in a Piper Cub at Lincoln Nebraska.
June 3, 1943	Lee Minker passed the check flight at Lincoln Nebraska.
June 16, 1943	Lee celebrated his 19th birthday – the first away from home.
June 20, 1943	The air cadets move to Santa Ana California for testing and classification.

From Sioux City, a local train that stopped in all the small towns across the state took the Miami boys from Iowa to Lincoln, Nebraska. Lee quickly called home to give the family his new address. His parents were out at the time; Bernice, overjoyed at receiving the call, left a typed note about their conversation for her parents. Colleges and universities with a College Training Attachment program had to be creative in the use of facilities. At the University of Nebraska, the brand new Don L. Love Library housed air cadets instead of books. Lee found the campus to be a congenial environment. The university cafeteria offered good food and a busy, if not rigorous, class schedule which he preferred to the boredom of basic training. He wrote home about his schedule, the poor quality of the text books, the wholesome food, K.P. [kitchen police] duty, and the "gig" system of demerits.

"In Recognition of your Army Training,"
Souvenir at The University of Nebraska and its War Training Program
Courtesy University of Nebraska, Archives and Special Collections

---

[Typed note from Bernice]
[Probably April 7, 1943]

Lee called at 8:10 this evening. He sounds swell. His address is:

College training detachment
Air Crew
University of Nebraska
Lincoln, Nebraska

The university is wonderful. They have their own dairy farm and rich milk and cream. They live in a building just built intended for a library. It took them 14 hours to get there and if they had waited a while they could have gotten a through train that took them only 4 hours to get there. As it was they stopped at every little roadstand. Lee wants Julia's picture, ten dollars, he's only been paid ten dollars since he entered, 3 pairs of socks and shorts, writing paper, 620 film. He's going to send a package home the end of the week with pictures, toothpaste tubes, etc. at the end of the week. He expects to be shipped to California after a while or to Texas.

He sounds heavenly,
Bernice

poster advising civilians to save metal

Lee contributed to the war effort when he sent toothpaste tubes home. In the 1940s toothpaste was packaged in small lead/tin alloy tubes which were coated on the inside with wax. Druggists required that old toothpaste tubes be turned in before selling a new one as lead and tin were valuable to the war effort. To alleviate the acute short-age of metal, anything made out of steel, copper, zinc or other alloys was turned into metal scrap for defense plants. Raw materials were not available for consumer goods; consequently items like new bicycles, typewriters or household appliances were nearly impossible to find.

---

undated
[probably April 8]

Dear Lee: -

You are probably welcoming the chance to sit on a seat that isn't moving after a week in transit. Naturally we have been concerned about where you would finally find a bed and a pillow. Mail has been returned from Miami and Sioux City, and we have felt badly because we didn't intend to let two days pass without your hearing from one of us. Now that you seem to be put for a while we'll reestablish the communication chain and keep you abreast [of] the doings here.

Mother, Shirley and I were sorry we were not here last night. It was a treat for Bernice, however, and her lovely and full report of the conversation between you was all typed for us when we got home.

Work at the school is tougher because of the help problem. I have to coach baseball. There is actually no one else on the grounds who can do it. "Jeff" got off the "straight and narrow" again, and I had to let him go. It's a pity—but, as he said, I had given him more chances than anyone else would have given him.

We all join in sending our love to you.

As ever –
Dad

Ralph Minker Sr.'s strength of character was an important part of Lee's growing up years. Dad's sound advice continued in his letters during the war. Lee's departure for the service served as inspiration for his Superintendent's column in the April 1943 issue of *The Ferris Wheel*, the school newsletter. A great deal about Lee's upbringing and his values can be learned from his dad's column.

THE SUPERINTENDENT'S WORD

"You can't beat something with nothing," the late and greatly missed Will Rogers' famous truism that I found thumb-tacked on my son's room door at College the day I went to bring him home for a few days before he left as an aviation cadet, is my theme.

"You can't beat something with nothing." The Bible puts the same truth in this fashion "To him that hath shall be given, and from him that hath not shall be taken away even that which he hath " You've got to have something if you are going to make out anywhere.

Even humble jobs require some things - interest, faithfulness, a desire to please. And greater jobs require just that much more. You've got to have something or you are going to be beaten.

Life is pretty exacting. Jobs are not always as plentiful as they are now - and the better jobs are never plentiful. You've got to have it if you are going to hold that job.

You've got to have it if you are going to build a home. I'm not merely thinking of brick and stones. I'm thinking of love and wholesome living, and healthy as well as fine children.

You've got to have it or else you will always be a bluff.
Now is the time to get it.

This is it:
A Healthy Attitude
A Desire for Self-Improvement
A Development of Some Skills
A Willingness to Work
A Consciousness of your God-Likeness.

Ralph Minker Sr.'s column when Lee left for the service.
Ferris School Archives, April 1943
Courtesy Historical Society of Delaware

Sunday afternoon
[probably April 11]

Dear Mother,

I suppose it's been quite a job for you to keep up with me the last couple of weeks but anyway I'll be stationed here for at least thirty days (I hope) and even up to five months. I'll let you know definitely about that later. Unless I'm in the first thirty day group I'll be able to get ten hours of dual control flying (Piper Cub at the Lincoln Air Base) and four hours of lecture plus my studies in math, physics, history, geography and English and P.T. and drill. Our schedules haven't been arranged yet however so I'm just waiting to see what it will be like.

I was sorry not to find you home when I called the other night but I suppose Bernice told you all about it. This morning we were told to get P.T. equipment, and, as the local supply is nil and the army is getting our shoes, I'd like you to send my gym shorts, T shirt and athletic supporter as quick as possible. Also, because of the great distance between us now, could you send letters airmail so that they won't be out of date when they get here.

Today was the first Sunday since I joined the army that I have had a chance to go to church. The Methodist Church here is very fine. The minister is splendid. The church seems to be about 10% larger than Grace but the choir cannot compare with ours of course.

The town is dominated by the new million dollar state capital which is really magnificent and the university which is also magnificent.

We're living in the Don L. Love Memorial Library which is so new not a book has gotten in. There are about fifty fellows in each dorm with ample study and toilette facilities. We eat in the Student Union building where the home ec department out does itself in feeding us with good wholesome food. Typical Menus:

Breakfast -	*Lunch -*	*Dinner -*
Coffee or 1/2 pt milk	*1/2 pt milk*	*1/2 pt milk*
Cold or hot cereal	*Roast beef*	*Pork chops*
Scrambled eggs	*Boiled Potatoes*	*Baked potatoes*
Sausage	*Peas*	*String beans*
1/2 pt milk for cereal	*White, brown, or raisin bread on the table*	
2 pcs of hot toast	*Fruit cup*	*Salad*
1 thick slab of butter	*Cherry pie*	*Ice cream*
1 orange	*Cookies*	*Cookies*
Unrationed sugar		

The fat in the milk is so great that it floats on top of the coffee. It and a lot of the other stuff come from the university's agricultural school.

That's about all I can think of for now.

Love,
Lee

April 13, 1943

Dear Lee:

I hope that you are settled now and we are able to write to you again knowing where you are. You must have seen lots of country in your travels. Have you seen any cowboys yet? Or, don't they have them there?

Spring has been awfully late in coming this year. We have one sort of lukewarm day, then it clouds over and rains and the next day is freezing again. The trees and flowers have begun to come out several times but are nipped again by the frost.

Our class decided to have the Senior Ball informal as many people were uncertain of transportation. We're going to have it at the University Club and Jay Glover's orchestra is playing.

Have you seen "In Which We Serve" by Noel Coward. It's quite good and the story and photography are interesting. Ben and I saw it Saturday night.

We had a surprise black-out on Sunday night and Grandmother had to spend the night here. Daddy somehow didn't get the yellow signal right away and was quite peeved. He spends most of his afternoons now over at the baseball diamond throwing balls to the boys. I should reduce him some, but it hasn't so far.

Well, write in between classes and let the co-eds alone. Wolf. Call me up sometime!!

Lots of love –
Shirley

Ralph Sr. served as an air raid warden in the civil defense program for New Castle County. In that role, his job was to assure that everyone abided by the black-out regulations. Black-outs required that all lights be extinguished and all windows be covered so that no lights could be seen from the air in case of enemy attack. Blackouts were practiced regularly and invoked when the enemy was spotted along the Atlantic Coast. The wardens were ever on the alert to make sure that every home and commercial establishment had black out curtains or paint and that no automobile lights could be seen from the air.

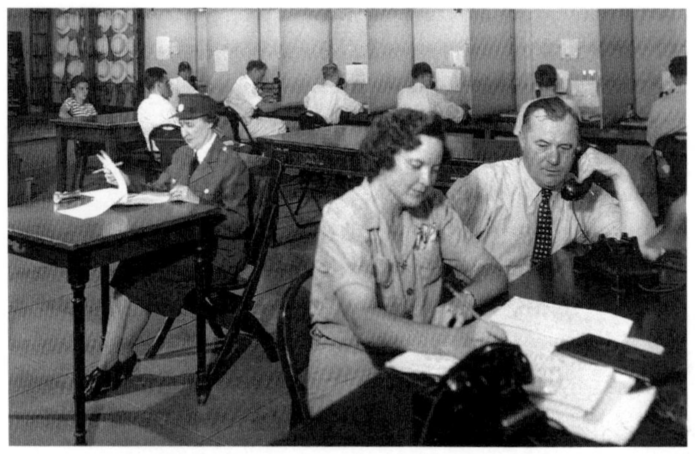

Ralph Minker Sr. at Civil Defense Headquarters
WWII Collection–Courtesy Historical Society of Delaware

Wednesday night
[probably April 14, 1943]
Nebraska

Dear Shirley,

In the third day of zero weather the Miami tomato is gradually turning into a Nebraska snow drop. Those army overcoats really weigh one down.

Today I hit the jackpot -- mother's package and series of letters, Bernice's letter, Mr. Yingst's letter and Julia's.

Also today we got our books- really amateurish except for physics which consists of electricity entirely for us. And for [class] C-1 there is no time for English or history but we have first aid added.

Then we were initiated into the Army Air Corps Weekly Comparative Physical Education Test. This consists of three parts – sit ups, chins and 300 yard shuttle run. The aim is to do the most possible of each type and, for the run, to do it as fast as possible. I was rather lucky and scored a perfect 100 in the sit ups (115 of them) and with that lead proceeded to average 65 which is rated as very good. (second class) There are five classes. Every time I stand up though my stomach feels as if it is stretched to bust.

The sororities are holding a dance in honor of the 103 Miami boys (twenty more came up after us. It's surprising how much better our basic training was then the others at either Morningside or here and we've taught both camps to sing continuously) and for all the cadets. It looks as if we will throw one for the girls, formal and with a name band, in the near future.

Love,
Lee

Families all across the nation ran eagerly to mailboxes, looking for the military P.O. return address on a envelope. Each day the Minkers eagerly checked the post office hoping to hear from Lee. Separated by great distances, letters became the primary link among family members. "What do you hear from Lee?" was the question most often asked when they encountered family and friends. The next letter from Ralph Sr. let Lee know just how much his letters meant to the family.

Friday evening,
The 16th of April, 1943

Dear Lee: -

Mother and I stop at the post office late each night to

bring mail out in the hope, of course, of getting a letter from you. You see mail is just as much an event on this end as on yours. Every move you make means a great deal to us all, and we follow everything you write as closely as we can. You are everything to us and all of us are pulling for you every minute.

Your schedule is a beauty. I had a good laugh over it. They don't leave much time for standing around.

Keep in good shape – and the best to you always.

Dad

Sunday afternoon, April 18, 1943

Dear Lee:-

Dinner is over and while things are reasonably quiet I'll write you. Shirley got your letter when we drove in to the post office last night. Now that your mail has started to come throu I guess you'll be getting something most every day.

Friday I sent you a box with something for Easter. I made the apple-sauce cookies thinking they would not get stale as quickly as some other kinds. By this time I guess you have received the box containing the writing paper, etc.

Is the section you are now in, C-1, being trained for any special thing? You mention that there is no time in it for English or history. If it should turn out that you are sent to Texas in about ten weeks do you think you will have enough time off to come home for a few days, or do they think you fellows don't need furloughs? If they keep sending you further away it will take all of your pay for carfare home, won't it? Have you been paid yet?

I am wondering whether you got to attend church this

morning. Grace [United Methodist Church] was crowded and of course you know what it will be like there next Sunday morning. Do you have to spend your evenings in studying now? I should think you would be quite a physicist by the time you get through this course. I'm glad it isn't me being subjected to all of it.

Are you rooming with the same boys as you were in Miami, or do you have one big dormitory now in the college building? There are so many questions we would like to ask and I guess you don't have time to answer them all; so we do hope you will get home before you are shipped elsewhere.

Love and best wishes from all of us.

Mother

Tuesday night
April 20, 1943

Dear Dad,

I received your letter and mother's package today. I'm going to try to get to church Good Friday evening for communion and to the 11:00 A.M. service Sunday.

I couldn't resist temptation and so I opened the package immediately. I've just sampled the peanut brittle so far but it all looks mighty good. Thanks a lot.

I just finished signing the pay roll. We get paid on the first of the month so maybe I can start staying out of the red again.

Three boys broke out with the measles today so we all have our fingers crossed. I got my second tetanus shot today. The Nebraska R.O.T.C. was mustered into active service today. They live on the third floor of the library. Quite a rivalry has broken out between us – they are "boy allies" and we are "junior birdmen."

Do you think I should wire some flowers to mother for mother's day or let one of you get them for me. If you think it is a good idea to give Julia an Easter corsage can you arrange it?

Lee

Thursday afternoon
April 22, 1943

Dear Bernice,

I just finished a whiz of a physics test on the work that we Miami boys weren't even here to have. I think I got by alright though.

Mother put forth a whole bunch of questions in her last letter and so I'll spend most of this letter trying to answer them.

First of all comes the most distasteful answer of all. I will have absolutely no furlough or stop over time anywhere or at anytime for at least a year unless there is some vital emergency. That reminds me of the latest news on training. I think that our group will either just be the last to go to three months of pre-flight or else be the first to go direct to primary as they are arranging it so that these college courses will take the place of pre-flight. I hope I get pre-flight though (1) for better background (2) because here we are not getting aviation math, physics, meteorology or navigation, have too big classes (45) and don't get any top instruction (a biology prof and a graduate of '41 teach us physics).

Study troubles are developing. With 750 boys there is not enough room and even then you only get at the most – two hours a night.

Did you get my package? Send me a Blue Rocks [local baseball team] schedule. No one has said much about the C.D. [civil defense] any more. Aren't you getting blackouts? I never get to hear any news here. Could you send me weekly summaries of sports and news from the Sunday times and Saturday Journal?

Love,
Lee

When Lee entered the Army Air Corps in 1943, there were more air cadets in the pipeline than the Army had training slots for pilots. The Army Air Corps Flying Training Command had significantly stepped up the number of training airfields and classes throughout 1942. However, they were still hampered by the lack of airplanes and combat experienced instructors. The College Training Detachment in Lincoln was essentially a "holding" action by the Army until the next phase of training.

Thursday noon
April 29, 1943

Dear Bernice,

This is to be a summary letter to get things up to date.

First of all there are some thing I'd like you to send me, i.e. – gym shoes (you can stick another pair of sweat socks in them if you like); developed films; the news and sports summaries for the week from the Saturday Journal and

Sunday Times, a Blue Rocks schedule [Wilmington baseball team], 620 film; two pencils' anything else – like cookies.

Second, the situation here: I should leave Lincoln about June 20 for San Antonio. It certainly seems early to hear of a Delaware Commencement. When is the Junior Prom? I got about a dozen Easter cards this year which is very unusual. (and they all seemed to feature ducks) For about a week now our dorm has been saturated with packages of candies and cakes for Easter. Starting today a new system of bed making goes into effect – my fourth in two months of army life. I have latrine duty for an hour today too. Saturday we will witness a track meet between Nebraska and Iowa instead of having P.T. And last of all, pay day has been pushed back from Saturday to Monday.

Love,
Lee

Friday night
April 30, 1943

Dear Mother,

We had a surprise this afternoon and a very pleasant one too. Pay day! I got $71.17 after I stood in the alphabetical line for thirty three minutes before stepping up to the lieutenant, saluting, sounding off with my name and getting my money. I'm sending (enclosed) fifty dollars home for you to put away for the future. I hope I can keep doing this from now on.

I suppose you have heard or read of the "gig" system which governs aviation cadets. We have it here and for twenty four hours a day, six days a week we have to walk at attention lest we slip up in some way and get gigged. A sample gig list includes about 150 names for violation such as name card out of place, bed wrinkled, out of line or dusty, shoes out of line, untied or unshined, dirty closet, badly rolled clothes, unbuttoned clothes, not singing, talking, out of step, smoking in restricted places, noise after lights out, classroom disorder, study failures, etc. You are allowed six, for each [gig] over that you do one hours work over the week and open post period. This week Mike [Hollihan, Lee's roommate] and I hit eleven apiece so – We'll be well accompanied though.

May 15 we don suntans again and that evening we hold the Military Ball in the Student Union.

Love,
Lee

The gig system, with its adherence to meticulous detail and order, was intended to instill discipline as well as pride in the unit. Learning to follow orders and procedures would help to protect the air crews in combat. Despite the war, life at home continued for his sisters; May is prom time and in June, Shirley graduated from A.I. duPont High School. The festivities are curtailed due to gas rationing, but young people still dance, listen to music, and go to movies, even as every day another friend leaves for military service. Shirley's next letter tells of five departures in just the last week.

May 2, 1943

Dear Lee,

I hope that you will be able to read this letter after I finish, but I feel in the mood to type this afternoon.

Friday night we had our dance and I had a lovely time. The orchestra was the best one that I have ever heard, outside of name bands, of course. We had a six person one, composed of members of George Madden's larger orchestra. He had a soldier in his band who played the trumpet. As he had an air corps insignia on his sleeve, we thought that he might be from the [local] Air Base. He was good, too, and reminded one a little of Harry James looks. [James was a popular trumpet player and band leader in the WWII era.]

Last week quite a few friends of ours went into the Army or Navy. Joe Toomey, Billy Baird, Gordon Lang, and Glade Brendle all went into the Navy and are stationed nearby, at Bainbridge Naval Training Station in Maryland. Clifton Medders went into the Army but no one knows where he is yet. We heard that Jim Buchanan was back in the states, but is quite bad off. He is said to have shrapnel wounds and some sort of tropical diseases.

Yesterday afternoon, the gang went to see "Air Force", and it turned out to be better than the usual airplane and war story. I had never known before that a bomb-sight was so precious. Ruth told me that it was a secret weapon and had to be guarded well.

I don't have anything else to say, but there is quite a collection of clippings and stuff to go with this, so you have plenty to read for a while yet.

Lots of love,
Shirley Minker

The movie that Shirley and her gang saw, *Air Force,* featured the crew of a flying fortress, *Mary Ann*, bound for Pearl Harbor on a training mission on December 6, 1941. After witnessing the deadly air attack by the Japanese, they are assigned to the

Philippines. The drama is created by relationships within the crew as well as the stunning aerial battle sequences. The real *Mary Ann* went down shortly after the film was released in early 1943.

The Norden bombsight shown in *Air Force* was a significant advance for aerial bombing. Developed in great secrecy during the 1930's, the bombsight greatly improved accuracy of the bomb run. The Norden was a complex device, eventually installed only on the lead plane so that all the bombardiers would drop their bombs when the lead bombardier did.

Monday evening
May 3, 1943

Dear Mother,

I'm on guard duty. I went on at 4:30 this afternoon and will be finished at 4:30 tomorrow afternoon. I walk my tour at the rear of the library for two hours and then I have off for four. It's not hard but it is monotonous and I imagine I'll feel rather tired tomorrow night.

I got a nice package of cookies and candy and a postcard from Grandmother Minker today. Call her up and thank her for me will you please. I got your writing paper so I am well stocked at present. Thanks.

Imagine this. My geography professor for the next three weeks is a Dartmouth graduate from Plymouth, Massachusetts, who is a specialist in marketing. We have had quite a chat. Don't ask me how but English and History have been added to my schedule.

Have got to fall out again so, so long.

Love,
Lee

Lee Minker on guard duty at Lincoln, Nebraska
Courtesy Historical Society of Delaware

Saturday noon
May 8, 1943

Dear Dad,

The news of the fall of Africa caused little comment here. The general opinion is that we have at least two years more of war ahead and that we'll get in it anyway so what difference does it make. A big battle for the continent is expected in about two months but everyone seems to regard Japan as our number one danger now.

Love,
Lee

The fall of Africa came at the end of a hard-fought campaign for control of the ports and oil fields of North Africa. After fierce fighting across the desert, General Rommel's renowned German *Afrika Korp* surrendered with 250,000 men taken prisoner in early May 1943. The Africa Campaign was the first decisive victory for the American and British forces. The German failure in Africa was so total that some Americans, like Ralph Minker Sr., hoped it signaled a rapid end to the fighting. Lee's comments from Lincoln on May 8, 1943 turned out to be prescient, "at least two more years of war" was exactly correct. He was able to make another call home on May 11, his dad was deeply disappointed that once again he missed the phone call from his son.

May 12, 1943

Dear Lee:-

My but I'm sorry I was out last night when you called home. Mother did not tell me about the call until this morning. She knew how disappointed I'd be.

I am glad you are feeling a little more at home in the grind. It won't hurt you to see another section as you are making contacts, studying the similarities and differences in people, and matching wits with them.

I had two weddings today. One was a fine young soldier of 25 years from Georgia – a Pottstown, PA boy. I get quite a few such weddings. The men have to have the time waived, and most of the ministers won't do it. I can't see their viewpoint but that's their business.

The boys have done a great job in North Africa, haven't they? When it started caving for us it really did cave in. I think you're going to find this same thing happening all along the line – a month on Sicily – a month on Italy, and a strangle hold on the Mediterranean. A fall of activity will bring some real breaks in Germany, and I'm optimistic to believe substantial progress toward victory will be made by Christmas, 1943. Here's hoping, anyhow.

Keep yourself in good shape, and know that there isn't an hour that I don't consciously move in your direction and say a prayer for you.

As Always –
Dad

Friday, May 14, 1943

Dear Lee:-

It surely was good to hear your voice on the telephone Tuesday night, and I was so glad that I was at home. Of course daddy regretted very much that he was not here, also, to join in. And it tickled Shirley to think that she had a chance to say "hello".

Daddy has just left to pick up the Governor and take him to the opening home game of the Blue Rocks. It is a cool evening, but I imagine there will be a good crowd on hand. I'll send you the clipping later.

Shirley is getting dressed for the junior prom, which is being held at the duPont Country Club. I have been working almost all week to get her clothes in shape.

On Tuesday I went, with two other women from Wilmington, to Elkton, Md. As you may know, hundreds and hundreds of girls and women are employed in the Explosive Plant there. The government has erected dormitories to take care of over 1000 girls, most of whom have come up from the mountain regions of West Virginia. We visited some of the dorms, saw how the girls live, and hope to be able to do something toward making their lives a little more comfortable. There was a terrible explosion there just last week, 20 killed and many more injured. They claim that particular plant is one of the most important in the country in the manufacture of explosives for the government, and everything should be done possible to make these girls happy. Many of them have never before been away from home.

Well, I must stop now and help Shirley get "dolled up". Take good care of yourself and write whenever you can.

Love
Mother

Lee and his dad shared a passion for sports, Edna clipped the sports pages regularly to send him team scores. The minor league *Wilmington Blue Rocks* baseball team was a tie to everything at home. Baseball had to be curtailed during the war when the government imposed wartime restrictions on travel by professional baseball clubs. The Philadelphia *Athletics* conducted their spring training at the Wilmington Ball Park, then the home of the minor league *Blue Rocks*. Ralph Sr. took Governor Walter Bacon to the 1943 season opener, an exhibition game with the Philadelphia *Athletics*. The sports section of the paper reported that the *Blue Rocks* "made an impressive showing against the major leaguers in a 2-0 loss." Reverend Minker and Governor Bacon must have been pleased with such a close game.

In her letter Edna Minker mentioned the "terrible explosion" at the Triumph Explosive plant in Elkton Maryland which made 20 mm and 40 mm shells, grenades, primers and detonators, explosives, fuses, bombs and grenades. Attracted by the war time pay, women came to the plant even though munitions was the most dangerous of the wartime industries. Several deaths occurred at Triumph Explosive prior to the major explosion on May 8 which took 20 lives. The Wilmington papers reported that it took several weeks to identify all the victims of the fire. Edna Minker was one of a group of women who tried to improve the lives of the girls at the Elkton munitions plant.

Undated

Dear Lee,

You really must be angry with me for not writing lately. I'm sorry, but the "Echo" [high school newspaper] came out this week and I've been rushing around. You're getting a issue through the mail, as are all of the soldiers whose picture are in it. The parents are receiving copies too and everyone wants one, so we're making one copy do this time for the family. Sort of rationing.

It certainly was swell of you to send Granny the money for Mother's present. With it she is having her glass set completed. Shirley and I are starting her on plates to set under the sherbets.

Ginger got washed yesterday and promptly went off and rolled in a mud-hole. She stinks like her old self again.

Did you hear about the moron who put his head on the curb to keep his mind out of the gutter? Also about the moron who took a can to the basketball game as he heard they were going to dribble?

The Proms next weekend and Shirley, of course, has a new dress, red and white linen. They're going with Bob Wold and Jean Armentrout.

Well, that completes the news for the moment.
Be Good,
Love, Bernice

May 15, 1943

Dear Lee,

Today is the day after the prom. I slept late and am sitting in my housecoat typing to you this letter. We had a wonderful time, but it seemed like it had just started when it was over. The orchestra was swell and they had two vocalists.

Have you gotten your "Echo" yet? It should be there by now. Don't you think that my picture is horrible? Well, I do. What do you think of it? I know that Mr. Yingst would appreciate it if you could write and tell him what you think. Commencement is coming along pretty good now and it won't be long before I am through at Alexis I. [duPont high school] I hate to think of my Physics and Trig exams but I guess that I'll get through.

If you don't hear from me next week you'll know that I'm studying hard for exams.

Lots of love,
Shirley

Monday night
May 17, 1943

Dear Mother,

Yesterday I joined the Lincoln Public Library and I

hope to squeeze some good reading in now and then. A good book on the training I am to get is "He's in the Air Corps Now" by Graham and Kulack. Of course the pre-flight part has been changed so much that it is out of date on details although the general objectives still hold. Eight boys leave here for San Antonio and classification on Friday by the way.

We're having tests in all our subjects this week so I'll have to keep "on the ball." I'm sorry but I can't seem to think of much more news.

Love,
Lee

Wednesday night
May 19, 1943

Dear Dad,

Here is the biggest news that I have had since joining the Air Corps. Two boys of the D section have been transferred to the engineers. As a result Captain Whiting selected the two top men, academically as well as militarily of section C, and placed them in section D-1. Those two were Minker and Stilwell.

I have had my training advanced by almost a month. We will have ten hours of dual control flying in Cubs by the way.

That's all I have time for now as I am cramming for finals in all my subjects here. Today's mail contained letters from Uncle Marion, Grandmother Minker, Julia and Shirley. The telephone number here is 27788.

Love,
Lee

Saturday noon
May 22, 1943

Dear Mother,

I suppose you were surprised by my letter saying that I was to start flying Monday. Well it's all true and in the future my mail should be sent to Section E-1. As things are at present we are scheduled to fly until June 18, 1943. Then we will go to Nashville, Tennessee, San Antonio, Texas, or Santa Ana, California for classification. After that we will either go to pre-flight or primary training school although some of us might flunk out during the two weeks of tests at classification.

We are in the San Antonio district but the E section which left last night went to Santa Ana. It was a night which I will never forget—last night. At 9:00 P.M. the word came that E [section] was to ship, the very day they had finished flying, and you can imagine the hustle and excitement mixed with envy and hard good-byes. They all marched off to the station at 11:00 P.M., taps were pushed back, after we had all sung the Army Air Corps song and Auld Lang Syne. Jim Ham [close friend of the family] went with them.

Enclosed you will find my driver's license. I wish that you would renew it for me even though I have almost forgotten what a car looks like.

There isn't much more new news. The weather here is turning hot as Nebraska weather does, we are told. Today we are to shift rooms so that each section will be quartered by itself. The E section is moving down to the first floor I think.

Sunday noon

I was interrupted by the moving yesterday. I'm in dorm 1-A now. Not a thing new has happened since. I went to church this morning. I like Dr. Kennedy's sermons more every time I hear them.

Love,
Lee

The first flying experience for many Army Air Cadets was in the open cockpit of a Piper Cub. The Piper Aircraft company modified their J-3 two seater monoplane for military use, the resulting L-4 model earned its fame as a trainer. With its light weight, low maintenance, and easy maneuverability, the dual control cub was the ideal aircraft for introduction to the basics of flying. A highly dependable airplane, four out of every five pilots in WWII got their start in a Piper Cub. In the cub, young pilots could feel the thrill of flight – even on a windy day— as Lee discovered.

Monday night May 24, 1943

Dear Shirley,

I've flown! This morning at ten I was the second of the new E section to go into the air. For forty five minutes I experienced a sensation that differed from anything I've ever experienced before. It's hard to describe, but there seems to be nothing at all around you – you're floating in midair, but with the awful roar of the Franklin 65 H.P. engine in your ears. The ground looks just as if it were a picture by Stephen Curry.

We rode out to the Lincoln Airfield on a rickety old bus at 8:00 A. M. Then the 84 of us of Sections E-1 and E-2 were sorted out and given instructors. Mine is a Minnesota Swede – Jorgenson - and seems to be a swell fellow. He has three other pupils in section E-1 and four others in section E-2. My three companions from section E-1 are quite a cross section – Henry Lee, a San Francisco Chinese boy, John Schneider, from Washington, Edwin P. Doughty, from Philadelphia.

I went up in cub number seven and after climbing to 300 feet headed off to practice area number four where the instructor leveled out and explained the elements of flying. After that he gave me the controls and I flew the Cub for a while. It differs from driving a car in that there is no surface to ride upon and wind blows you around. The wind was going at fifteen miles from the west and so it was very bumpy. As a result I had an attack of airsickness.

At 4:00 P.M. in the afternoon I went up again, with some premonition, but felt good the whole time. Jorgenson said that the first bad feeling might have come from first time nervousness and that if it wasn't so necessary to get us through our course they wouldn't even have sent us up in such rough weather at the beginning of our course. Jorgenson showed me 90 and 180 turns when flying level or gliding or climbing with 30° or 45° banks. He also put me through rigorous coordinate exercises so that after forty five minutes I really began to get the hang of it all.

Rechange my address. They have now decided to let old addresses stand so send my mail to section C- 1 again. My birthday is coming soon but there isn't much in the line of presents that I want this year. Maybe the family could send me a good watch though. That is one thing that I will need soon – water proof, luminous dial, unbreakable crystal and accuracy plus so that it can take a beating and still be reliable.

Love,
Lee

Lee with Piper Cub at Lincoln, Nebraska
Courtesy Historical Society of Delaware

Saturday noon
May 29, 1943

Dear Bernice,

I've got four hours in the air now so I'm quite an ace. P-38's are next! I was supposed to get a check flight from the C.A.A. [Civil Aeronautics Authority] inspector yesterday but they wouldn't allow anyone up – too much wind. I will be the first to get a check flight and so far I am the most advanced student. Next week I'll go up for an hour at a time instead of 45 minutes. I have now done everything that I will be allowed to do in a Cub except spins. I have taken off and landed by myself and have done turns, eights, S's, stalls, coordination exercises, forced landings, rectangular courses, glides and climbs, etc.

Monday we get paid! It's time for a parade so I'll have to quit now.

Love,
Lee

Lee's reference to flying a P-38 in his letter to Bernice was a bit of brotherly humor. The Boeing P-38 Lightening, a long-range escort fighter had a maximum cruising speed of 422 mph, saw action in Africa in 1943 and nearly every major campaign of the war. Lee had to spend time in slower, simpler aircraft before taking on a plane such as the P-38. The Army Air Corps training carefully transitioned students to successively heavier and more complex aircraft.

Tuesday morning June 1st

Dear Lee:

We got almost as much thrill as you did after reading the description of your first flight. I liked your description of it so much I took the letter with me to the Governor's [Governor Walter C. Bacon] apartment last Friday night and read it to him. He enjoyed it also, and sends his best. There has been a blank so far as letters are concerned since the one written last Monday night – so we are anxiously awaiting the news of the second and third trips into the air. Mother thinks you may be on the move somewhere. I scouted the notion. We'll wait and see.

I called Mr. Hyde the other evening and read him your letter. Bill hasn't flown yet – but expects to move from where he is to some spot soon.

As ever,
Dad

Friday night June 4, 1943

Dear Dad,

I had addressed this letter to you on Friday night only to stop there and attempt to put in a long distance call home to you. It didn't get through so I'll write and hope that you are not worrying about the lack of news from me. You must forgive this and learn to expect it more and more as I get further along in my training. If anything should ever go wrong, the army a friend or myself will let you know all about it.

Yesterday I had my check flight, after a weeks delay due to high winds, and went through spins. I did fair on my check flight after the layoff but in the afternoon did much better. Layoffs seem to hurt. I went through a half dozen spins in a row, three turns each. First I just held on while Jorgensen flew one; than I followed through on one to the right and one to the left; then I flew the spins, with Jorgenson holding his stick, and his breath. It seems funny but I hardly felt the spins. What gets you is the pull out. In a real plane you black out for a second when you pull out of a spin but in the Cub all that you feel is your stomach being pushed in and your cheeks feeling flabby and deflated. I have trouble counting the number of turns we made as we spin except for that a spin is relatively simple. First you cut off the motor and pull the nose up to a point about six inches above the horizon. Then, just as she stalls, you push the stick hard forward and hit the rudder, right or left depending on whether you want to make a right or left spin. You just topple over to a side and head down, all of the time rotating in a small circle. When you've had enough you hit the opposite rudder hard and pull back the stick. As you level off you put on the motor and climb back to 3000 feet so that you can do it over again.

I'll be shipping out sometime between the eleventh and the twenty first, it seems now. Where?? When that happens I'll have letters, magazines, camera and incidentals shipped home.

I'm sending Julia a gardenia corsage by wire for her graduation. I only got $30 pay this month so I am keeping it all but next month I will get $ 75 (flying pay) plus $25 (for flying this month) plus $6.50 (maybe $13)(the U.S. furnishes flying insurance). 7 hours in the air.

Love,
Lee

In her next letter, Edna tells her son that she is now a "working lady". Her experience was repeated across the country as three million additional women entered the workforce during WWII. The defense plants, with their voracious appetite for workers and promise of healthy pay checks attracted significant numbers of women. They produced bombs, bullets, tanks, planes, trucks, rifles and guns. Women joined the ranks of newly formed military units such as the WACS and the WAVES, further contributing to the shortage of office workers. When she became the Ferris School secretary, Edna Minker joined the millions of women who for the first time worked outside the home.

Monday, June 14, 1943

Dear Lee:

Maybe you will be surprised to learn that your mother is a "working lady" now. Miss Horner, you know, left last week to become a WAVE which left daddy high and dry as far as a secretary is concerned, so for a while at least I am trying to hold down the job. Of course there are some things she did which I cannot do, but maybe we can struggle along somehow until the proper person is found. I reported to work a little after 8 this morning. When I went over home for lunch you should have seen your two sisters. You might have thought they had lost every friend they have in the world. They seem to think it is terrible for me not to be around the house every minute they are, but I guess they will get used to it.

I saw Julia yesterday and congratulated [her] on winning the scholarship. She was wearing your gardenias. Shirley was thrilled to death with hers. They surely were lovely. I am not sure whether she wrote you before or after she got them.

Shirley has not found anything to do yet. Bernice is working on Saturdays at Crosby & Hill's [department store].

I sent you off a box of cookies, candy, etc. on Saturday in hopes it will reach you in time for your birthday. It did not seem much to send for your birthday. Daddy intended to get a letter off but I don't believe he has found time yet. Of course you know without my telling you that we wish you the happiest possible birthday and hope next year you will be able to celebrate it at home.

I do hope that the rain has let up by now and that you are able to get in some training in the way of flying every day. Do you think you will be shipping off somewhere else this week, or must you get in a certain number of hours flying before you leave there?

Lots of love from all of us.

Mother

Lonely on his 19th birthday, his first away from home, Lee quietly observed the occasion with a box of goodies sent by his mother. War-time separation from family was particularly difficult on birthdays and holidays, celebrating alone became yet another reminder of the loss of normalcy in everyone's lives. Women baked cookies, cake and candy to send to the servicemen all over the country and abroad. Recipes for cookies with rationed ingredients that would "keep" for several weeks in the mail were featured in the newspapers. The box from home brightened many a soldier's day.

Wednesday evening June 16, 1943
[Lee's 19th birthday]

Dear Dad,

This is by far the strangest birthday I have ever had – away out here in Nebraska just biding time until the government is ready to take me for further training. The box from home meant more than any birthday cake ever has.

Today I spent in the sun playing football. I'm trying to get into the best possible shape before our two week lay off at classification and, I hope, the grind of pre-flight. I'm worried about my eyes. If I wash out I'll probably have to go to A.M. school (Aviation Mechanics) which is a disheartening outlook to say the least.

I'll have my suitcase sent home Saturday with my camera and letters, etc. I'll let you know my address as soon as possible. Grandmother Minker and Grandmother Jones both sent birthday greetings. Please thank them for me because I am not going to write much more until I know where I am. I'll have to cut down on my correspondence too because at present I write regularly to twenty five persons. You all can help by spreading my news around Wilmington.

Yours,
Lee

Lee spent nearly three months in Lincoln, Nebraska where he completed the first milestone in flight training, 10 hours in a Piper Cub. He called his parents on June 14 to let them know not to write as he was leaving Lincoln in a few days. Shortly after his birthday on June 16, Class 44–C of aviation cadets shipped out to Santa Ana Army Air Base, where Lee would endure testing and classification, one of the toughest hurdles on the long road to becoming a combat pilot.

Chapter Three

I Was Classified as PILOT this Morning!

June 20, 1943 - August 29, 1943

Dates: June 20 1943 to August 29 1943	Location: Santa Ana, CA

Progression of Flight Training

Lincoln, NE	Santa Ana, CA	Thunderbird Field, AZ	Pecos, TX	Pecos, TX	Roswell, NM
College Training Attachment	Classification And Pre-flight	Basic Flight Training	Preliminary Flight Training	Advanced Flight School	Transitional Flight School
Piper Cub		Stearman	BT-17	Cessna AT-17	B-17

June 22, 1943	Lee's class arrived in Santa Ana for classification.
July 6, 1943	Lee was classified a pilot after several weeks of testing.
July 12, 1943	Pre-flight training began.
Aug. 1, 1943	Lee and army buddy Charles Hammel are on pass in Hollywood.
Aug. 29,1943	Lee received shipping orders for ThunderBird II in Arizona.

A three-day train ride from Nebraska across the arid southwest brought Lee to the Santa Ana Army Air Base (SAAAB) in Costa Mesa, California. One of the nation's largest certification and training sites, more than 200,000 men passed through Santa Ana during the war. The primary function of the base was classification: the rigorous physical, psychological, and classroom tests designed to match men to a position as a pilot, navigator, or bombardier. The grueling selection process yielded the best candidates for the investment of training resources. Lee's growing anxiety over classification came through in his letters; he worried over his eyesight and other tests. One by one, the family members encouraged him while allowing for the possibility that he might not pass the tests for pilot.

Ferris Industrial School of Delaware
Box 230
Wilmington, Delaware

Monday, June 21, 1943

Dearest Lee:

We all stayed around the house all evening yesterday in the hopes that a phone call would come through from you, and I awoke several times in the night thinking of you. In this morning's mail I received the snapshots of you in the plane and notice they were mailed on Friday. When you called us last Monday night you said to hold up all mail, which we have been doing; but I am sending you this morning in the hopes it will be forwarded in case you have left Lincoln.

I am still alive after one week of work as daddy's secretary, and think I will like it. This week will be a little more difficult because grandmother Jones went to Aunt Grace's on Saturday to be gone a week or more, which will mean that your two sisters will have to arise before I leave for the office in the morning. Shirley has an application in to work in the office of American Aviation (duPont airport people), but I don't know whether anything will come of it. She has also answered several ads. She doesn't want to work in any store, and of course there is little she can do in an office for she can't type, etc.

The roses are blooming beautifully just now and we are hoping the Japanese beetles will not be very plentiful this year. Strawberries will be over this week. Delaware berries have been selling this year at $.50 a box, so we are glad we did not have to buy any.

Well, I must get down to some office work now. I did want to say, however, that I hope you do not get yourself worked up about classification school. I know you have your heart set on being a pilot,--for your sake I hope that things turn out that way. But remember it is no disgrace if, because of eyes or something else, you cannot make the grade. Daddy has something in mind which he will write you about later.

Love and best wishes from all of us.

Mother

In her next letter, Shirley referred to an "awful mess" at home; with zoot suiters, race riots, and coal strikes in the headlines. On the west coast, riots broke out when a group of sailors attacked Hispanic and black youth wearing "zoot suits." With its wide legs and lapels that required yards of extra fabric, the public saw the flamboyant garb as an unpatriotic gesture. The military consumed much of the supply of suit fabric, a rationed commodity since 1942. Over 1,000 youths were caught up in the violence that lasted two days; similar attacks on the zoot-suiters occurred in San Diego, Long Beach, Chicago, Detroit, and Philadelphia.

The worst race riot occurred in Detroit, a major wartime production center that drew thousands of new workers, both black and white, from the south. The jobs were plentiful, but housing was not. The crowded and unsanitary living conditions for the blacks contributed to the tension which erupted on June 20, 1943 between teenagers of both races. As the outbreak escalated, the police were unable to contain the crowds or the violence, which killed thirty-four people. Federal troops had to be brought in to quiet the city; they occupied Detroit until January 1944.

Shirley also asked her brother what he thought about the coal strike. Union leaders had made a "no strike" pledge at the beginning of the war; nevertheless, scattered strikes had occurred in 1941 and 1942. In April 1943, the coal miners stopped working to protest rising prices and limits on wages, shortages of meat, and deplorable housing conditions. President Roosevelt promptly ordered government seizure of the coal mines. The wartime economy ran on coal: railroads, electricity, steel, and shipping all required coal to operate. The miners went back to work under a thirty day cooling off agreement. Two more strikes occurred during the summer; finally the union leaders and the government reached a contract agreement in October. The coal strike was portrayed in the press as unpatriotic and a threat to war production.

June 23, 1943

Dear Lee,

I thought that I would take a chance on writing you, and maybe you will get it, maybe not. We got your pictures of you in the plane and you look like you mean business, but pictures can be touched up, can't they? I thought your instructor would be older than that. How old is he, he seems young for one?

I haven't gotten a job yet, but I've answered several ads and filed several applications. This morning I got an answer from one ad, but it seems the place is in Philadelphia, so I don't know yet. The news on the world front has been good for us lately, but here at home we've had an awful mess – race riots, coal strikes, and zoot-suiters – what do you think?

Sunday morning Bernice and I stayed home from church and took a long sun-bath in the yard. We got so hot sitting there we turned on the hose and sprinkled each other like we used to when we were all little kids.

Did you like the caramels for your birthday? We thought they would send better than chocolates. Well, I hope you get settled soon and call us again. I'll write soon.

Lots of love –

Shirley

From the time of arrival on June 22, 1943 at Santa Ana until departure at the end of August, the air cadets had a busy schedule. This was the first base where Lee thought that the Army was organized in the business of training for war. The number of airmen in training often exceeded the Army Air Corp's capacity of instructors and planes, resulting in wasted time and occasional confusion. At the outbreak of the war the Army Air Corps had only 9,000 pilots, graduating about 1,200 a year from pilot training. Clearly an inadequate supply to fight an air war in Europe and the Pacific, pilot and crew training had to be stepped up – quickly. (Cameron 1999)

President Roosevelt had called for the production of 50,000 planes a year in the fall of 1940. Given that in the prior fiscal year the Army Air Force actually received only 886 new airplanes, the production goal was an astronomical jump. The country also suffered from a shortage of officers, military flight instructors, air bases, and training equipment. Lee did not write home during the move from Lincoln to Santa Ana, finally on June 24 he gave the family details of his new assignment.

Thursday night June 24, 1943

Dear Dad,

They are really putting us through the mill. We are on the move from reveille [sic] till 7:00 P.M. But at last I have hit a post which has a system about it, and what a gigantic place it is too. Our C.O. is a fine fellow. We have a good mixture of boys from the Pacific Coast, Texas and the East Coast – 240 now. The food is grand and plentiful. But even still that queer tension that this military life brings gets ever more intense. Cadet classification, pre-flight and P-38 advanced training are carried on here and they waste no words in telling us to forget all except killing Japs and Huns.

By tomorrow's end I will have finished my tests and information interviews on every type of subject. These take three days of solid work and are designed to measure aptitude. Then will come that day for physical G4. We have settled in our new barracks, had gas and fire drills, marching drills and lectures galore.

The ride from Lincoln took three days – for two the Southern Pacific gave us a day coach and for all three [days] the food stank. Kansas looked like a nice farm state – well kept and rich but flooded at the time. From there on, except for occasional oil wells, the land was flat, 110 F. and barren to the extreme. California is refreshingly cool and rich looking but gives one the appearance of having grown up too quickly. The boys from there show signs of class prejudice against Japanese and Mexicans.

I don't know how often I'll be able to write but I'll do it as often as possible. I won't be able to call for at least two weeks. Wish me luck and write soon.

Love,
Lee

P.S. Because of the distance send letters by air mail. Send me some stamps.

Monday evening June 27, 1943

Dear Mother,

I think I'm in! Having finished my psychological, mental, aptitude and physical tests at 3:00 P.M. this afternoon without any hitch I'm feeling rather cocky. Three of us came bounding out of the test building right into a curtain of smoke which set us coughing and choking. Then a big top-sergeant bawled at us to put on our gas masks as this was a practice raid. Two parts troubled me a bit. Night vision – this test is new and was used for the first time as a requirement on squadron six. Depth perception. I'll just have to wait about a week now before I know for sure whether or not I am to be an Aviation Cadet – Bombardier, Pilot or Navigator.

I haven't much news as we have all been living under the terrific tension of a week of tests. At least nine of our 84 have washed. Feet and eyes get most credit.

Every Sunday afternoon we march in a big review for Colonel Robertson. Although not as big or as perfect as Miami it was quite a spectacle. Approximately 15,000 men marched. By the way, among the notables stationed here are Joe Dimaggio, Merle Hapes (All American of Mississippi State who out hits Joe on the ball team), and Larry Adler (the great harmonica player).

Julia has a birthday July 8. As I can't get out of here for 42 days could you get her something? Get something a little different and lasting. Say hello to everybody for me.

Love,

Lee

The New York Yankee star, Joe DiMaggio, stationed at Santa Ana when Lee was there, set a record in 1941 when he hit successfully in 56 straight games; he won the American League MVP award in 1939 and in 1941. Like many other ball players, such as Ted Williams, "Joltin' Joe" DiMaggio missed several seasons to serve in WWII. Nearly 3,000 of the 4,400 players in the major and minor leagues went into the service.

Ferris Industrial School of Delaware
Box 230
Wilmington, Delaware

Monday morning, June 28, 1943

Dear Lee:

Maybe my boss won't fire me for getting off a letter to you before I do any office work this morning.

We had the mail picked up on the 9 o'clock trip last night and in it were your two letters,- the one to me and the one to daddy. Up to the time of receiving the letters we had been listening for the telephone to ring, thinking you might be calling us from somewhere, for it had seemed a long time since we heard from you. We read your letter to the guests who were in the house [that] evening, and they all enjoyed it, almost as much as we.

We had a blackout Friday evening from 9 to ten, and an air-raid test yesterday afternoon shortly after 2. Daddy and Mr. Blaine were attending a flag-raising service at Brookland Terrace. Of course daddy had to leave and the crowd had to disband until the all-clear.

You do seem to have a full schedule, but I image you would rather have it that way than have to sit around with time on your hands. I want you to learn to fly, --not to kill; if the time ever comes when it is necessary, to get planes, not murder. Every Sunday morning daddy prays in church for the boys in the service and of course we send up a special one for you, not only on Sunday but every day.

Your suitcase has not come thru yet, but I remember that it took your laundry case and clothes a long time to get from Miami. Julia sat in front of us in church yesterday morning. She has a job for the summer in the duPont company.

The Blue Rocks have been slipping some lately. The clippings I have are over at the house so that this letter may go off without them if I find someone going in town who can mail it this morning. I know you are anxious for mail.

Love from everyone one of us and of course we are always wishing for you the very best.

Mother

June 29, 1943.

Dear Lee:

You can't imagine the lift your letters Sunday night gave us. I asked Mr. Van Brundt [staff for the Ferris School] to pick up the mail on the last trip, in the hope there might be a letter from you, -- and there were two. As mother told you, three Reverends (Johns, Colona and Bond) and their wives were visiting us, and shared the news from our main front.

You've certainly seen the country. Possibly I should drop the "the" and say "you've certainly seen country." There is plenty of it between the Atlantic and Pacific, the

Gulf and the Lakes. Stretches of waste, cultivated acres, towns, cities, -- you've gotten the feel of it. It used to be something to say at twenty-one that one had been to Chicago or Washington, - but at nineteen you've checked the country from Maine to Mexico. I think it is rather fortunate that you landed in California. The climate ought to be better than Texas, and the training the best.

From what you intimate the going is pretty strenuous. I guess it can't be otherwise. You used to think you worked for Wing, [Lee's professor of Ancient History at Dickinson College] but I suppose that was tame compared with your daily assignments now. Do the best you can and don't worry. Luck to you in your exams and tests. We're waiting anxiously the results of the classification period.

I am of the opinion that if you do not come up with something you like it would be better to try to place yourself somewhere more to your liking. I've had in mind the Intelligence Division as rather important and good groundwork for the law. Keep it in mind.

The Rocks [Blue Rocks, local baseball team] are having a tough time. Lost again last night to Hagerstown. Clippings enclosed. Must close. Keep in good shape and the best to you.

Dad

Wednesday, June 30, 1943

Dear Lee:

At the present moment I have the weight of the whole school upon my broad shoulders, so I'll write you and relieve the tension. Daddy went to N.Y. this morning; Mr.

Hamm is taking a few day's vacation and expects to be back this afternoon; Mr. Briggs has gone into Juvenile Court; Can't say I've done such a good job so far for a boy ran away from Ball cottage this morning and I had to report it to the state police. Today is a red-letter day, for I got my first pay check.

The circus was here yesterday and Monday and the girls and I had thought something of going last night, but when we found that reserved seats were $2.35 per we changed our minds.

Thursday morning

Your suitcase arrived just a few minutes ago,--looks like it's been thru the war.

Yesterday afternoon between 4:30 and 5 three negro boys got away, so you see I had quite a hectic day. Here's hoping today is an improvement. Daddy and Mr. Hamm will both be here, so maybe it will.

Love from all of us, and of course you know we are pulling for you always.

Mother

Thursday night July 1, 1943

Dear Shirley,

They are continuing to run us ragged even though we have finished all our tests and are just anxiously awaiting classification.

One morning we spent on chemical warfare – gas mask drill, smelling of different types of gas, and gas chamber session (thirty minutes in a chamber of tear gas). That afternoon we took a eight mile hike during which trucks came along and sprayed gas at us so that we had a practical gas mask drill.

Another morning the Chaplains of the base talked to the Protestant, Catholic and Jewish groups. I didn't think too much of their background. That afternoon we had motion pictures and lectures on diseases.

Today we spent seeing movies and hearing lectures on military intelligence (secrecy, camouflage, [sic] information) and "Why We Are at War". That last named picture was a masterpiece of news, travel and commentary on the Axis Countries and what they stand for.

The news of Macarthur's new offensive caused a lot of excitement today. The son of Colonel Robertson, C.O. at S.A.A.A.B. [Santa Ana Army Air Base], is flying a P-38 out there somewhere.

Tomorrow will be spent on the manual of arms followed by guard duty tomorrow night. We should get M.M. (Mess Management, the glorified name for K. P.) soon. Aviation Cadets do not have M. M. by the way.

Next Monday our two week quarantine inside the classification area ends. That will mean only thirty more days before we can go to L.A. on Saturday night. I don't know when we'll begin pre-flight. Today I got a two week old package of cookies from Julia. Write soon.

Love,
Lee

MacArthur's new offensive in New Guinea was welcome at a time when there was little other news for the Allies. The Army had yet to establish the western front in Europe and the invasion of Italy had not begun. After the loss of Bataan in April 1942 and the retreat to Australia, MacArthur launched the New Guinea Campaign in 1943, a slow and costly movement up the north coast of New Guinea against the well-entrenched Japanese. By the time Lee wrote his July 1 letter, the Americans and Australians had gained some ground on the march to re-take the Philippines.

Jubilant in his July 6 letter that he made it through the first round of classification, Lee reported that nearly 40 per cent of the cadets "washed out". The aptitude and physical tests behind him, he was rewarded with a pair of gold air cadet wings and the knowledge that the Army Air Corps thought he had the ability to become a pilot.

Tuesday noon July 6, 1943

Dear Mother,

I was classified as PILOT this morning at the auditorium and immediately took the oath of an Aviation Cadet: "In the presence of Almighty God ..." Of course all of us are feeling mighty happy about it all even though there is pity for the unlucky. About 200 of us were classified pilots, 20 as bombardiers and 20 washed. Charles Hammel of whom I have written before is forced to have a recheck though. If luck comes we will get to pre-flight soon because they are really speeding up training. We are now taking P.T. from 5:30 A.M. to 6:00 A.M. and from 2:30 P.M. to 4:00 P.M. so you see that they are really whipping us into shape. Last night we finished our two week classification quarantine but we will have post quarantine for thirty more days. The Cadet Specials at the P.X. are really the greatest concoction I have ever eaten – and for only twenty cents too. Please excuse the lack of paragraphing but I am in a hurry to get off the good news to a few others before our too brief rest ends.

Love to you all,
Lee

July 8th, 1943

Dear Lee,

Today I didn't work at the hospital and had a grand time just loafing after this morning's session of bible school.

Last night Shirley, (defense worker), Sissie and I went to see "Coney Island." It was one of the best musicals I've seen in a coon's age. The special academy award short, "Theatre Business at War" was at the theatre and was grand.

Billy is coming home Saturday night and we're going out to paint the town "hot pink." It's the first time he has been home since he left after the prom and I can hardly wait.

I hope your classification business is straightened out soon and I wish you all the luck there in your tests.

July 9th, 1943

Just got the news about your pilot rating. Yippeee! Bang Bang! Hip, hip, hurrayyy! Fly home as soon as you can.

Lots of Love,
Bernice

Pre-flight instruction, consisting of military, ground, and physical training was held at Santa Ana. The classes were often boring, taught by pilots who preferred to be in the action of the war. The amount of time in pre-flight tended to be expanded or condensed based on the need for new pilots. Often the delay in pre-flight could be traced to the lack of available planes for the next phase of instruction.

Monday July 12, 1943

Dear Mother,

From now on you will have to expect letters at infrequent intervals for from now on we are supposed to talk, breathe and eat military aviation – and so they leave little time for anything else. I am now to start a six-week pre-flight course consisting of what C.T.D. [College Training Detachment] should have taught us plus aircraft identification and code (a regular nine week course). Then we go to primary flight.

Right now we are marking time until the squadron is filled up. 125 from squadron 6 are here at present. We spent all morning G.I.-ing the barracks. Yesterday we all had M.M. I received $5.71 in tips as a waiter. Cadets tip as officers and gentlemen. Friday night we went to a broadcast of "Wings to Victory" at Santa Ana. Last night I had my picture taken in my cadet uniform but will not be able to get the pictures for some time yet.

The English pilot training system is being put into use bit by bit. In brief – it eliminates primary as we now know it by using Basic Trainers in primary and A.Ts [Advanced Trainer] in Basic. Thus time is not wasted with low power planes.

Our new schedule:

5:15 A.M.	*get up and prepare for inspection*
5:30 A.M.	*official revielie [sic]*
5:40 A.M.	*fall out for inspection*
6:00 A.M.	*Class*
7:00 A.M.	*Breakfast*
8:00 A.M.	*Class*
9:00 A.M.	*Class*

10:00 A.M.	*Class*
11:00 A.M.	*Class*
12:00	*Lunch*
2:00 P.M.	*P.T.*
4:00 P.M.	*drill and retreat*
5:30 P.M.	*Supper*
8:00 P.M.	*Study*
10:00 P.M.	*Taps*

Gigs [demerit points] are now given out and strict record is made of each squadrons marching in parade, care of area and general attitude each week. The lowest of the ten in a wing gets M.M. the next Sunday.

Love,
Lee

The new schedule prevented Lee from writing to the family and friends, prompting Shirley to write, "your letters are scarcer than butter." One of the foods rationed by the government, butter was nearly impossible to get. Milk, the basic ingredient of butter, was used to make cheese and in canned or dried milk production, most of which was shipped overseas. A week's ration coupons were needed to buy just a half of pound of butter – when it was available. Birthday cakes and other desserts, which used butter and sugar, were one of the causalities on the home front.

There are few complaints from the family about shortages. The Minkers, along with millions of Americans, learned to make do. One of the most popular campaign slogans of the home front encouraged everyone to: "Use it up, Wear it Out, Make it Do or Do Without."

July 18, 1943 Sunday

Dear Lee –

How's everything? Your letters are scarcer than butter and that's going some. We understand though that you are very busy so we don't mind too much. Have you started your flying again, yet? My job is keeping me up on aviation. They're now going to start training pilots with gliders over there. I think it's the first school of its kind. Some fellows fly over from the Air Base in long, two-seater silver ships. They call them PT's, I guess that means pilot trainer, or does it. They have a large C-47 over there now being repaired. That's quite a big ship. There was a big Navy ship over there the other day with a group of officials in it. All the big shots.

Today in church they dedicated an honor roll plaque, It's a lovely plaque in the front vestibule. Your name was all wrong though. Guess what they had on it! R. Lee Minker Jr. I've never seen it printed that way before, have you? It'll be fixed up; though so maybe by the time you get home it'll be fixed up.

Yesterday Bernice and I heard Glenn Miller in person! No kidding! He's on with a soldier band on Saturday afternoon from 2:00 – 2:30. He really sounded swell and his band had the same large group of saxophones in it. He must have the same arranger, or something. We were tickled to death just to hear his voice though. What do you think of Frank Sinatra? Didn't I tell you last summer when I heard him that he was wonderful? He's really in the big time now and sounds just as wonderful. Maybe you don't hear much about him but he's really going strong according to all the New York reports.

Well, papers running out. I'll write soon, so do you if you have time.

Lots of love –
Shirley

Shirley listened to the Glenn Miller Orchestra along with much of the rest of the country. One of the best of the big bands of the swing era, Miller's hits included *Little Brown Jug, Pennsylvania 6-5000*, and *Moonlight Serenade*. The Miller Orchestra played engagements all over the country and appeared on a CBS radio show. When the popular bandleader went into the Army in 1942 he formed the Glenn Miller Army Air Force Band, continuing his unique big band sound in front of the troops. Tragically, Miller was killed on Christmas Eve, 1944 when his plane went down over the English Channel.

Shirley first heard Frank Sinatra sing in the summer of 1942 when he was the vocalist with the Tommy Dorsey Orchestra, one of the biggest acts of the early 1940s. In 1943 Sinatra began working solo and soon became a teen idol, with hysterical "bobby-soxer" fans screaming and swooning during his performances. The war time years were the beginning of the rise to stardom for the singer known simply as "The Voice." Sinatra was drafted by the Army, but was 4-F (unfit for service) due to an old ear injury. He had the adoration of thousands of teen-age girls, along with a fabulous salary and 4-F status – Sinatra was not popular with servicemen.

Wednesday morning (July 20 1943)

Dear Lee:-

Daddy received your letter this morning, and of course we are always glad to hear from you even though you think you haven't much news to write.

Thieves broke into the Ration Board office in Wilmington over the weekend and stole gas coupons for more than 10,000,000 gal. together with some oil coupons. They broke into a concrete and steel cabinet. So far they have not been found.

The pictures which we took will not be ready until next week, but I'll let you have them as soon as they come. How soon will yours be ready?

Love from everybody.
Mother

The theft of ration coupons was not uncommon during the war. Gas coupons were especially valuable; the average driver was allotted only three gallons of gas a week, war workers, truckers and other essential drivers had higher allotments. Families no longer took a "Sunday drive" as driving for pleasure was banned in early 1943. The coupons missing from the Wilmington Ration Board most likely turned up on the Black Market where bogus or stolen coupons were freely available for a price. (Lingeman 2003)

Tues. night July 27, 1943

Dear Lee –

I got your grand long letter on Sunday morning and we passed it around the breakfast table. Maybe you will get into Los Angles this week-end. Can you go in swimming anywhere near there? How far are you from the Ocean?

I'm so glad you wrote Granny Jones a letter. I guess by now you've gotten hers. She was thrilled that you wrote to her. It means a lot to her, you know.

Yesterday and today they were picking up gliders over at the airport. That is what they do, by the way. Install units for pickup up gliders in airplanes. It doesn't sound like much but they have to take almost the whole floor. They were giving people rides in the glider. You had to be twenty-one or have a written consent from your parents. I didn't know in time or I would have gone. They all enjoyed it and I'm going to go when they do it again.

There are only about five boys in our class now who haven't gone [into the service]. They certainly took them awfully fast, don't you think?

I'll be writing again soon, so until then,

Lots of love and kisses,
Shirley

Sunday afternoon
August 3, 1943

Dear Shirley,

I am writing to you as I am climbing to 5,000 feet altitude in the S.A.A.A.B. altitude chamber. We are now coming down lickety split after only one minute at 5,000. This is just to test our ears – to see if the ear drums will normally adapt themselves to quick changes in altitude. As yet I have felt no more than when I would go underground on the train to Philly.

We are now starting a climb to 18,000 feet – still without masks. In two minutes we arrived at 18,000 and we are now sitting here for ten minutes to notice the effects. Everyone of us is belching and passing gas as the pressure is so reduced; one boy had to leave because of ear trouble; one boy vomited but is sticking it out. My pulse is now 96 compared with 80 before flight.

I have just finished putting on my mask. I have the old type continuous flow while about half of the others are using the new type demand flow. The old type furnishes and uses more oxygen but that is all that is different. I had to adjust a dial which regulates the flow of the oxygen but now I am all set as we are climbing up to 38,000 feet for an hour flight.

In preparation for this altitude flight squadron 64 has been on special diet and no exercise for two days. We will return to normal on Thursday. Fats and starches were the main banned items. While in classification we went to Post Theatre Number 1 for three hours of films and lecture about high altitude flying and we had another half hour lecture before coming into the high pressure chamber today.

We were led to a big white tank after the last lecture and twenty of us filed into the seats against the wall. It gave me sort of a gold fish feeling for there are big portholes in the walls through which we are being continually watched for signs of anoxia or the bends.

Two boys have had to leave already because of the bends by the way. We couldn't bring watches or pens into the chamber because of the pressure and I had to take thirty minutes off just before starting this page to please the sergeant by reading a pamphlet on high altitude flying. It's a rule of the A.A.F. that oxygen masks must be worn above 10,000 feet during the day and on all flights at night.

We have started down now. We are taking a thirty second halt at 20,000 feet so that bends will not set in from too fast a change in altitude. It took us five minutes to come down from 38,000 feet and get out of the tank. My temperature was 99 before and after flight; my pulse was 80 before flight, 96 after ten minutes without mask at 18,000 feet and 80 at 38,000 feet and sea level. I am feeling fine and am eager to take a B-25 up there in reality some day. I hope you like the account of the high altitude chamber. I cannot think of much other news.

This week we have started trying to take code at eight words a minute on tape transmission.

I am finishing this up in the barracks. Tell Mother that we are getting Golden Bantam corn and succotash regularly. As for M.M. – all cadets must serve on M.M. guard, C.Q. and other such details. We are rated on these duties and the rating will go on our service record thus helping to decide whether we are to be Flight Officers or Second Lieutenants.

Love,
Lee

Air Cadet Lee Minker with buddies at Santa Ana.
Courtesy Historical Society of Delaware

The grueling pace of training in the heat of southern California was relieved with the occasional weekend pass. Like nearly every G.I. stationed at Santa Ana, Lee used his weekend pass to see Los Angeles. Only 35 miles north of the base, a soldier could tour the sites, catch a glimpse of movie stars, have a bite to eat and if he was lucky – get back to the base without being A.W.O.L. (away without leave). A favorite stopping place for the servicemen was the Hollywood Canteen, where a boy from Delaware could dance with the beautiful Hedy Lamarr and be served a sandwich by movie star Patricia Morrison. The stars, directors and production people of Hollywood served sandwiches, coffee and doughnuts and presented shows with musicians, singers and comics in an effort to create a gay mood for the servicemen. A bit dazzled by the sites and the stars, Lee delightedly sent home autographs, mementos and a detailed report of his taste of glamorous Hollywood.

Sunday evening   August 8, 1943

Dear Bernice,

You have no doubt already examined the trophys from my first weekend pass to L.A. Here's the story. After P.T. Saturday afternoon we showered and reported for inspection by Lieutenant Kemp. At 4:15 we were heading (Charles Hammel and I) for the buses at the Baker Street Gates. These busses [sic]take three hours or more to get to L. A. because of the demand on Saturdays but taxis or station wagons or even army trucks cannot be used for transportation instead. Therefore the permanent party men on the base get a carload of cadets, charge $ 2.00 and head for L.A. I took a clipper and got at the Biltmore Hotel in an hour. It was full; every hotel was full. In fact there *were only Y or Elks dorms in all L.A., Beverly Hills or Hollywood. So at 3:00 A.M. I returned to the L.A. Pacific Electric Station and caught a ride back to the base in much the same manner as I had coming in.*

I ran up a $5.00 taxi bill looking for lodging but at the same time got a general idea of what the mushroomed mass of the three cities was like. It is every bit as congested as Washington and servicemen are everywhere. At 8:30 we grabbed a milkshake and entered the Palladium. It was breathtaking. One gets an impression of a big and tasteful hotel – the appointments blend perfectly with the living room furniture and rugs; there are two dining balconies completely surrounding the big dance floor; but the lighting is the real distinction, they play with it like they do at Longwood [duPont estate outside of Wilmington]. It is the best place I have ever seen or heard of for a dance hall of distinction. Jimmy Dorsey played in great style.

Next I went for refreshment at the Brown Derby. Gene Tierney and George Raft were there at the same time. I went to the Hollywood canteen. In reality this is just a floor show of an hour and a half during which time you can eat, drink, dance, and be merry. I got Ish Kibible's autograph for you. I danced with Hedy Lamarr to the tune of "Stardust" and got a sandwich from Patricia Morrison. Other places of interest and entertainment were filled or closed by now so I headed back. Other places of interest I saw were – Grauman's Chinese Theatre, Chinatown, Earl Carol's, Ciro's, Trocadero, Morocambo, Beverly-Wilshire, Fox Studios, N.B.C. and L. A. City Hall – however.

There is a lot to do but passes are such that you have to start back to the base by 9:00 A.M. Sunday morning in order to make parade.

Tell Dad that I mailed the insurance policy. Talking of furnace shortages. Every barracks here has a wonderful furnace but except for a very few instances none of them have been used during S.A.A.B's first seventeen months.

I'll send my picture sometime this week.

Love,

Lee

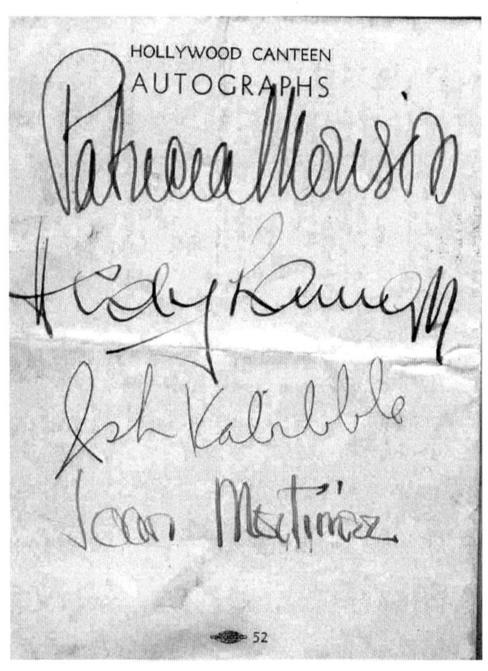

Autographs from the Hollywood Canteen, July 1943
Patricia Morrison, Hedy Lamarr, Ish Kabibble, Joan Martinez
Courtesy Delaware Historical Society

Sunday evening
August 15, 1943

Dear Mother,

The mail is really piling up on me these days and I owe letters to almost everybody. Because of various details etc. we are three days behind in our studies. Tomorrow we all get M.M. [Mess Management] and Thursday exams start for our pre-flight finals so I don't know how I'll come out on code, physics or aircraft identification.If anyone flunks a subject he stays for nine additional weeks of pre-flight. Ten percent usually stay for studies or sickness. All through our training they subject us to West Point super discipline and confinement; they change regulations endlessly to nettle us (six ways to fold blankets).

Last night I heard Frank Sinatra with the Los Angeles Philharmonic at the Hollywood Bowl. He was really good.

Los Angeles and Detroit have probably grown faster than any city of recent years. L.A. is over populated to the extreme and will soon probably equal New York as a center of culture, finance and industry.

That's about all the news for now. I'll write again as soon as I can.

Love,
Lee

Saturday afternoon
August 21, 1943

Dear Mother,

Yesterday we had finals in all our subjects so you can

see what a strain we have been under the last few days in trying to squeeze some study time out of our already overcrowded schedule. I think I did rather well in all except Aircraft Identification. My second test in Aircraft pulls the average for the course to about 68 I'm afraid but we get a recheck so I will come out okay. As yet we can only speculate on the future: 1. we may ship anytime from Monday to a month from Monday. 2. we will not have an over abundance of details until we ship. 3. Blythe is our rumored destination (California – Arizona dessert [sic] border).

We are still going to classes but allowed to do what we wish. I'm writing this letter in code class. Tonight is the night of our party. I'm taking a U.C.L.A. coed. I'll write more about it latter [sic]. I'll be sending home old letters, etc., soon and also a package of V620 film that I managed to pick up at the P.X.

Three boys washed [out] yesterday because they fainted in the pressure chamber. Last night Squadron 64 was defeated by Squadron 35 for the S.A.A.A. basketball championship. It was an excellent game, 37-34, but they had the taller average squad and two of our first team were invalided. [Squadron] 35 had a bunch of Big Ten stars.

Love,
Lee

P.S. I passed Aircraft!

Friday afternoon
August 27, 1943

Dear Dad,

They are to announce our primary schools in an hour

but I have already seen my shipping orders – I am going to Phoenix, Arizona – Thunderbird Field II.

I have rather mixed feelings on it all. I don't like the idea of being stuck in the Arizona dessert [sic] and being separated from most of my friends but Thunderbird is the best primary in the country as well as the hardest. It is an army school in contrast to most primaries which are civilian run. I believe that I will fly bi-wing Stearmens. Approximately 100 of [flight #] 64 are going to Thunderbird but only a couple from Nebraska or Miami.

This afternoon we are to have our graduation ceremonies on the main drill field. Yesterday we heard an interesting talk by Colonel Hans Adamsun who was lost in the Pacific with Rickenbacker.

Don't send any mail until I let you know my new address.

As ever,
Lee

Colonel Admunsum, who spoke to the graduating class, had quite a story to tell. Admunsum served as aide to Eddie Rickenbacker, World War I Fighter Ace. In October 1942, on a secret mission to see General Douglas MacArthur, their B-17D and its crew disappeared over the Pacific. They spent three weeks on life rafts without food or water before being rescued. The story was a major news event in the early days of World War II, their rescue a boost to morale and testimony to the courage of American fighting men against tremendous odds.

Sunday evening
August 29, 1943

Dear Mother,

I have just finished cramming my belongings into two stenciled brown barracks bags. Everybody is running around full of excitement – some are showering, one playing a sax, radio blaring and many in bull sessions.

I have to get my bags to 8th and K streets by 8:00 A.M. tomorrow morning and I have to be on the truck at 9:00 A.M. Last night I saw Ken Murray and Betty Grable in "Blackouts of 1943". It was pretty good.

There is a California law which cleans all liquor out of sight at midnight. At that time everything then closes and soldiers are left with nothing to do and no place to sleep. I've been lucky on sleep but most just go without.

I'll write as soon as I get settled in Thunderbird. Oh yes, there are four Thunderbirds, The original, Thunderbird I was shown in the movie of the same name. I am to attend Thunderbird II.

Love,
Lee

By the end of August, pre-flight was over and Lee was on the move again, assigned to Thunderbird Field II in Phoenix, Arizona for primary flight training. The pressure for more pilots and crews intensified in the summer of 1943. The Eighth Air Force pursued a policy of daytime precision bombing of German industrial targets that required a large force for each mission. The raids on Germany were accompanied by dramatic losses.

Daytime bombing was especially hazardous. The British had tried it and abandoned the concept as too costly. The Eighth's B-

17s and B-24s suffered heavy losses over Europe, especially after the bombing of Germany started in January 1943. The heavy bombers had the range to reach almost any target in Germany, but in the early months there were no Allied fighters that had the range to follow. Once the Allied fighter escorts turned back, the Eighth's bombers were vulnerable to attacks by German *Luftwaffe* fighters. ". . . During the spring, summer, and fall of 1943 the Eighth Air Force losses of planes and men sometimes reached 12% for a day's raid. One in four airmen were being lost. At one point it became statistically impossible for a bomber crewman to survive a 25-mission tour of duty." (www.mightyeighth.org)

Against these horrific odds, thousands of young men like Lee Minker eagerly continued training to join the ranks of the Eighth Air Force. The Santa Ana Base Commandant, Colonel W. A. Robertson, sent each family a congratulatory letter after classification, noting the attributes which their son had shown: ". . .sound judgment, a keen and alert mind, and the ability to perfectly coordinate mind and body in the flying of an airplane." The letter assured the Minkers that their son's training would be " ... the best our country can give."

HEADQUARTERS
SANTA ANA ARMY AIR BASE
OFFICE OF THE COMMANDING OFFICER
SANTA ANA, CALIFORNIA

13 July 1943

Dear Mr. Minker,

It is with great pleasure that I notify you that your son, Ralph L. Minker, Jr., has been selected by the Classification Board for Pilot training in the United States Army Air Forces. I congratulate both you and him on this achievement.

He will soon be transferred to one of the Army Air Forces West Coast Training Center elementary flying schools and will then begin his flight training. The course of instruction which he will pursue throughout the flying schools is thorough, intensive and the best that our Country can give to fit him for his future duties and responsibilities as a member of the Army Air Forces. Upon successful completion of his flying training, he will receive his wings and the rating of airplane Pilot.

In either war or peace, a Pilot occupies a position that requires sound judgment, a keen and alert mind, a sound body and the ability to perfectly coordinate mind and body in the flying of the airplane. It is imperative that the men who fly our military aircraft possess these qualifications, for upon their skill will depend in large measure the success of our war effort.

It is my hope that you will derive great satisfaction from your son's selection for Pilot training, and that his future career in the Army Air Forces will be one of continuing success and service.

Sincerely yours,

W. A. Robertson

W. A. ROBERTSON,
Colonel, Air Corps,
Commandant and Base Commander.

Congratulations letter from Santa Ana Commander
Courtesy Historical Society of Delaware

Chapter Four

Flying Training is Perfectly Safe

August 31, 1943 – October 31, 1943

Dates: August 31, 1943 – October 31, 1943	**Location: Thunderbird Field, Phoenix, Arizona**

Progression of Flight Training

Lincoln, NE	Santa Ana, CA	Thunderbird Field, AZ	Pecos, TX	Pecos, TX	Roswell, NM
College Training Attachment	Classification And Pre-flight	Basic Flight Training	Preliminary Flight Training	Advanced Flight School	Transitional
Piper Cub		Stearman	BT-17	Cessna AT-17	B-17

August 30 1943	Air Cadet Minker departed Santa Ana, California for Thunderbird Field, Arizona for primary training.
September 6, 1943	Lee took his first flight in a bi-wing trainer.
September 29, 1943	Lee passed all of the solo checks.
October 14 , 1943	Lee passed the 40 hour civilian flight check.
October 31, 1943	Lee completed primary flight training. He was assigned to Pecos Field, Texas for basic flight training.

The train ride from Santa Ana to Thunderbird took the air cadets through the barren southwest to Phoenix, Arizona. From there they traveled by bus to reach Thunderbird Field II, north of Scottsdale, where Lee had his first glimpse of the desert. The Army preferred southern locations for pilot training because the climate allowed more flying days than other parts of the country. The heat, wind, and dust, however, presented their own problems to young fliers.

Primary training at Thunderbird Field – where 40% of the cadets washed out – was the first flight school for Lee after classification as a pilot. Here the instructors quickly weeded out candidates who wouldn't make the grade, or simply couldn't learn fast enough to meet the quotas for fighting an air war on two fronts. The Army Air Corps had a well thought out, methodical process for transforming recruits into pilots. After classification and pre-flight school, the training progressed from primary, to basic, to advanced flight school. With the growing demand for pilots, the Army Air Corps condensed each school from ten weeks of instruction to nine weeks. Students had to demonstrate proficiency with a series of skills before moving on to the next stage: take off and landings, maneuvers, controls, and instruments of the aircraft. (Cameron 1999) The cadets at Thunderbird flew the Stearman PT-17 as they learned the fundamentals of flight: take offs, landings, basic turns and maneuvers.

Tuesday evening
August 31, 1943

Dear Mother,

Monday morning I rose at the regular time, handed in my bedding, lugged my barracks bags five blocks, said good-byes for an hour and then fell out at the main parade ground. Trucks took us to the Southern Pacific R.R. station in Santa Ana and after an hour we moved out with the boys.

The easiest way to tell you how being a Cadet has raised me in army eyes is to compare my train rides. Before we have always had two to a berth or day coaches. Yesterday we had air conditioned compartment cars, three to a compartment. Before our food was sparse and of low quality ($.48 a meal) but yesterday for lunch and dinner we had magnificent lamb and chicken dinners ($1.00 a meal).

We arrived in Phoenix station at 8:00 A.M. We just waited around for an hour and then found out that we would get no breakfast. Instead we piled into tourist busses and started for Thunderbird II. As we drove through Phoenix I got the impression that it was a sprawling slow moving Southern city. Green was everywhere but a depressing though dry heat hit us hard. And then as we reached the country I saw the dessert [sic].

Small ranges of desolate black erosion riddled hills and mountains rose abruptly from the dirty barren soil which supported occasional [sic] bushes or cacti. Then we saw columns of dust reaching skyward and small whirlwinds of dust racing along the ground and we saw what was the dread of all pilots – violent upward air currents, thermals.

After twenty miles we turned in toward a group of low and colorfully painted buildings – Thunderbird. It looked mighty desolate there at the foot of the mountain in Paradise Valley. First we had lunch – cafeteria style and all we could eat. We drank more than we ate though for the heat was really heating us. (We take salt tablets at each meal). Then we went through the usual routine – physical, draw bedding, unpack, get beds, get goggles, listen to commandant's talk. Twelve of us are in a room which is filled with fans. Three rooms make a flight; two flights make a squadron. There are now twice as many cadets here as ever before.

We are to spend most of this week getting acclimated. Saturday we will get our schedules, planes and instructors. Monday we fly!

That's the news for now but don't expect too much more because after we start flying we will have even less spare time than we had in pre-flight.

Please send my sunglasses quickly as well as that shoe equipment. (add liquid brown polish.)

Say hello to everyone for me.
Love,
Lee

September 3, 1943

Dear Lee:

Your letter from Phoenix was waiting for me here at the office this morning and I hasten to get off one to you before starting my day's work.

Your picture arrived only yesterday and were we proud of it. I like it so much better than that snapshot for it is now so severe. It looks just like we remember you. I displayed it on my desk here all morning and then took it home for the girls to see. We are all thrilled with it. Of course your sisters are very critical and think your lips are colored too much, but you know them.

The box with letters, sunglasses, etc. arrived only Wednesday. I will try to get the glasses in today to be fixed. I did not think you wanted them back so thus far have done nothing about them. If they cannot be fixed I'll let you know.

We saw "This is the Army" one night last week and liked it very much. It is being held over for the third week. They say "Watch on the Rhine" with Bette Davis is very good. It is playing at Warner's now.

I know you will be glad to be in the air once again and we shall be thinking of you on Monday, as you start again.

With lots and lots of love,
Mother

Air Cadet Lee Minker, newly classified as a pilot. Santa Ana, August, 1943
Photo arrived in the mail on September 2, 1943.
Courtesy Historical Society of Delaware

Watch on the Rhine, another film with a war message, dramatized the threats Americans would face if we did not fight the Nazis. Based on Lillian Hellman's 1941 award winning play, the film starred Paul Lucas and Bette Davis as a couple who come to America from Germany in the late 1930s. Bette Davis, as the American born wife of a German anti-Nazi leader, tells her mother and brother, "The world has changed, it's time you knew that." In the end, the main characters face heroic choices just as would be asked of American families: "We will be in for trouble . . . but we are not made of paste."

The first flight at Thunderbird brought a spirited description of the Stearman trainer from Lee. The Stearman P.T.-17 was everything a novice pilot could want, an extremely stable aircraft known for its easy handling. With its bright yellow bi-wings, and welded steel frame covered in blue fabric, the "wing tip to wing tip" line of Stearmans at Thunderbird was an impressive sight. Adapted from a civilian design, the Army had the Stearman's top speed of 300 mph reduced to about 100 to 120 mph for military training purposes. Also known as the Stearman Kaydet, Boeing produced 8,584 of the two-seater biplane to train the pilots who would take command of bombers, fighters, and troop transports. Lee's civilian instructor, a former stunt flyer, showed off the spins, snap rolls and Lazy 8's that cadets had to master.

PT-17 Stearman
Courtesy of Collings Foundation

Monday evening
September 6, 1943

Dear Dad,

I went up today for forty minutes but the ride was as different from a ride in a Cub as a ride in our Packard is from a ride in a Model T. It was wonderful! I flew in 324, one of the big 225 horsepower Stearman bi-wing blue P.T.-17's, with my instructor, Mr. Ray Newton, an Oklahoma stunt flyer and one of the original Thunderbird instructors. Mr. Newton is a grand fellow who believes in starting from the very beginning and mastering every maneuver in its turn before attempting something new. He also believes in letting his students do most of the flying. But getting back to our Stearmans – these ships are capable of going 300 m.p.h. but the Army has had Boeing cut them down to 100 m.p.h. and build in heavy torque (propeller tendency to pull the ship hard to the left), easy stalling and high landing speed. Thus there will be hardly one ship which we will fly latter which will have any feature harder to cope with. Besides that Stearmans are the most powerful and most rugged of our training ships and exceeds most of our fighters in size. She responds instantly to the controls and so is easy to fly.

I guess you can tell that I am well pleased with the Stearman and you wonder why more washout on Stearmans than on Ryans. For one thing a Ryan has only half the power, size and bad performance characteristics but if you look farther you see that 90% of those who wash in basic training are Ryan men – the jump is too much. 40-% of our class will wash here at Thunderbird, 20% will be voluntary eliminees who haven't the will power, the desire or the push to stick. Air sickness of course contributes heavily to this group. The other 20% will wash for various reasons: violation of safety rules, ground school flunks, violation of cadet conduct and mostly on insufficient progress. Everyone can fly but few can learn as quickly as the army wishes or acquire the precision needed. Of course, checkitis (my trouble of tightening up when being tested) will get quite a few. The boys in the second 20% may have a chance to be navigators or bombardiers, the others can never become officers nor leave the Air Corps unless they join the paratroops.

Today I just did elementary turns, climbs and glides. Tomorrow I will begin take-offs, landings, stalls, and spins.

Sunday I tried to call home but couldn't get through. I'm going to try again this coming Sunday though. I'd just like to talk to you all again.

We started ground school today with Air Navigation and Engines. Both cram a lot of material but it doesn't look hard. This is the only time that we will ever study engines by the way. I'm really tired tonight after our first full day.

Sunday morning most of [class] 44-C attended religious services. I went to the Protestant service which was held on the shady lawn by the swimming pool. I really enjoyed it, especially the sermon by our flying Chaplain. (he serves all Thunderbirds). He spoke on the Lords Prayer and its meaning for all men.

I think that I have rambled through most of the news. Do you think that Mother might have something good-to-eat which she could send me? Please send nothing that heat affects, like icing.

Yours,
Lee

With each Allied victory, the families on the home front hoped that the war was coming to an end. The news of the surrender of Italy on September 8 was but one of many false hopes. The Italian government signed a secret agreement with the Allies on September 3, 1943. By the time the Italian armistice was announced a few days later, the American and British invasion to drive the Germans out of Italy was well underway. Edna's next letter is both hopeful and cautionary.

September 10, 1943

Dear Lee:-

Yesterday we were sweltering almost and today is a typical September day, - sun shining brightly and a cool breeze. Yesterday I was out of the office all day to take care of the District meeting. Shirley sang "The Lord's Prayer" in the afternoon meeting, accompanied by May, and I think she never sang more beautifully.

Last night we had the big rally for the third war loan. There was a parade at 7:30 and although I was pretty tired after a full day I did go in town with Shirley to see the parade, for Bernice marched in it, all dolled up in her A.W.V.S. uniform [American Women's Voluntary Service]. They looked very nice, too. Some soldiers from Ft. duPont and the air base were in the parade, as well as the band from Aberdeen.

How much news do you boys get to hear? Do you have any time to listen to the radio? I suppose you all heard with joy the news about Italy surrendering. Of course we are being cautioned not be too optimistic, but it does seem as though things are beginning to break for us and I do hope the end cannot be too far way.

Were you to walk in your room now you would find it full of Shirley's clothes for that is where we are putting them as we get things finished.

I must stop now, for with being out of the office all day yesterday I have plenty of work to do today.

Love from everybody.
Mother

Sunday evening
September 12, 1943

Dear Bernice,

I tried to get a call through to Wilmington again today but failed so I'll try again next Sunday. Friday afternoon the package from home arrived. The articles inside were just what I needed and the whole room appreciated the Krispy Krunch, which kept excellently by the way. There is only one more thing I wish you could get me – a glass case. My sunglasses broke in my pocket last time and I don't want it to happen again. Thanks a lot for the writing paper. I was just running out of it.

I have four hours of flying in now and have had all the fundamental maneuvers but I am nervous about my lack of precision and take offs.

Rumor: We are expected to get 1/3 of our primary flying in BTs [Basic Trainer].

We are being pointed for the Asiatic Theatre in all our studies, lectures, etc.

It's almost time for taps so I'll have to close. I can't

seem to think of much to say so let me know what you want to know.

Love,
Lee

The Minkers' hopes for an early end to the fighting were quickly dashed as news reached the U.S. of the German counter offensive. On September 9, 1943, the American 5th Army landed at Salerno, south of Naples, joining the British 8th Army which had invaded Italy on September 3, 1943. For six days German armor units savagely attacked the Allies. The U.S. infantry was thinly stretched along the coast near Naples while the Germans had just received fresh reinforcements. The Nazis unleashed a counter attack on the weak U.S. lines in an effort to push the U.S. Army back to the Mediterranean Sea. Only timely support from naval gunfire and close air support helped the U.S. infantry to break out of the beachhead on September 15. The next day the U.S. forces joined the British 8th Army coming from the south; the invasion was a success, but the fierce German resistance at Salerno was a preview of the long Italian campaign to follow.

After Salerno, the Germans reinforced their positions in Italy and pulled their army back from the invasion beaches to the strongly fortified Gustav Line, south of Rome. By early October the combination of rain, snow, flooding and German resistance brought the Allied drive northward to a halt. In spite of the surrender of Italy in early September 1943, the Italian campaign would last almost two more years, until the end of the war in Europe.

Tuesday, September 14.

Dear Lee:-

I hope you will not think I am neglecting you. I thought

I would get time here at the office to write you a letter today; but it is now 5 o'clock and no letter written. Before going to the house to get dinner ready I'll send off a few lines.

Daddy and Mr. Boykin went to the ball game last night, and is was so exciting that daddy could not sleep half of the night. I enclose clipping about the game.

I guess you have heard of Richard duPont,- the one who has done so much with gliders. He was killed Saturday while testing a glider at March Field, Cal. The glider went into a spin, he with two others jumped, but his parachute failed to open. The other two landed safely. Two others remained in the glider and were killed. He was a special assistant to Gen. Arnold of the Army Air Force, in charge of glider experiments.

The news from Italy doesn't sound very good today, - with the Germans reported driving back the Americans and English and a reported 10,000 of our boys caught. I guess we were all too jubilant last week.

Grandmother Minker came out this afternoon to help me with Shirley's sewing and will stay a few days I guess. I think she is making apple dumplings for dinner tonight. Shirley went over to school this afternoon to get her vaccination certificate and took your picture to show Mr. Yingst [high school science teacher]. She was also to give him your new address, for he called just about the time you were leaving Santa Ana and asked how to reach you, so I guess you'll be getting a letter soon.

Is it possible for you to try to put a call thru any time except Sunday afternoon? If so, let us know what day or night and we will be waiting for you. It would be nice if you could call before Shirley leaves. We are not sure yet whether she will have to go on Tuesday or Wednesday. Lots of love and I'll try to write more later in the week.

Mother

Monday
September 20, 1943

Dear Lee –

I haven't written for quite a few days, so when I have a moment or two now, I thought I'd write to you. Yesterday the operator called and said that Phoenix was on the line. It was about 1:30 our time and we got the Phoenix operator finally. She said someone answered out there and went to get you but after waiting about twenty minutes she said she'd call us back when they located you. We never got called back though, so I imagine the line was cut off or something. We were terribly disappointed.

I'm sorry to hear that you don't think you're making out so well on your flying. It is just because you're serious and tense? I hope so. Maybe because it's so different from flying one of those cubs which you started on. I certainly hope you get the feel of it. Don't worry too much about it and relax a little. I can remember when you were first learning to drive a car, you become more sure of yourself and gained confidence. I'm sure it's the same here. Good luck on your solo. We're rooting for you!

Lots of love and luck –
Shirley

Saturday morning

Dear Lee:-

Your letters to daddy and Shirley came this morning. That was a fine letter to daddy, - I haven't read Shirley's yet. Her letter did not come air-mail, having some kind of notation on it that there was not room for it to come that way. I am getting some airmail stamps at the post office this morning and hope to have them in time to put in this letter for your use.

We are glad you are enjoying the flying, etc. at Thunderbird and hope that soon you will get over that tenseness so that you will feel perfectly at ease. In Wanamaker's [department store] last Saturday they had a bomber but we were too rushed to examine it thoroughly. It was in three sections, and we did look at the part in which you would be seated. They seem such huge things for you to be able to take up and handle, but I guess it is all in knowing how.

We hope you will be able to put a call through this Sunday. I shall plan to be home all day after church in the morning.

Lots of love,
Mother

Wednesday evening
September 29, 1943

Dear Dad,

No, I haven't washed out yet although I am being run ragged. In fact rumor has it that we will spend this weekend in flying. The upper class leaves this week and so we will attempt to pull ahead of schedule by using all of the planes on the post.

I have passed all of my solo checks and so can now check out a plane for myself. I must concentrate on mastering fundamentals for my twenty hour check now. Counting today's time I now have a total of fourteen hours flying time, one hour solo time, six practice forced landings and sixty five regular landings.

Phoenix provided little except a good steak dinner last Sunday. Bob Dowling and I walked around, bowled and saw movies "Valley of Fear" with Orson Welles and "Behind the Rising Sun." The Indian curio shops looked interesting for souveniers [sic] but none of them were open. Did Mother get the package of cactus I sent her?

Is Shirley settled at college yet? If so, what is her address? Say hello to everybody for me.

Yours,
Lee

September 30, 1943

Dear Lee:

Before I close my desk and call it a day as far as the office is concerned I'll write you.

We received a letter from Shirley yesterday morning, written Tuesday morning after she had two classes, - typing and biology. She took your biology book with her in the hope that it would be of some help. She seemed to be getting settled alright, but her first night was not a very restful one I guess. There was a pajama party scheduled for 8:30 and it had hardly begun when the air raid siren sounded, so they sat in darkness for about an hour. She was very tired then she finally got to bed and then at six o'clock reveille for the air cadets woke them. But after she has been there a while and got used to the sounds of the city, campus, etc. I expect she won't hear anything until she is called. She had 8 o'clock classes every morning.

Delaware, Pennsylvania and New Jersey had its first real air-raid scare about 2 a.m. this morning. The yellow signal came through, a complete surprise to daddy, who usually knows in advance at least the day or night when a practice is scheduled. When he got to the Wilmington control center no one knew anything except that the army had sent the signal. After about 2 hours the all-clear was sounded. Unidentified planes had been spotted somewhere and reported to Governor's Island by Washington. The sky was full of searchlights. Not many people knew of it at the time, of course, for there was no audible signal,- only the key ones in each sector knew.

Have you made any more solos?

All our love.
Mother

The Wilmington evening paper reported that "The Army First Fighter Command sounded a genuine "yellow" alert in five states and the District of Columbia. The alarm was sent out because unidentified planes, later determined to be friendly were sighted off the Atlantic Coast. Time was lost in Wilmington because the city control center was unmanned when the yellow signal was flashed at 2:10 o'clock.". The newspaper reported confusion and failure to respond in several towns. Outside of Wilmington the county system was manned and the 30 sub-control centers responded promptly, "according to county defense coordinator, Ralph L. Minker." (Journal-Every Evening September 30, 1943)

Sunday evening
October 3, 1943

Dear Mother,

Your son is a might weary boy tonight. But I am also happy for today Mr. Le Friece passed me on my twenty hour check.

Starting with last Friday and continuing up through tomorrow we have been and will be on the flight line seven hours a day. We have been held in over this weekend but we still had to rise at 5:30 A.M. and a special stand by clothing, barracks and personal inspection was held for our benefit at 9:00 A.M.

I had just finished making up my time after two hours of solo and one hour of dual flying when Mr. LeFriece tapped me on the shoulder and said to get into silver 394 for a progress check. I was worn out then and at the thought of a dreaded check ride my heart stood still. However I took off without mishap and climbed to 4,000 feet. There I proceeded to do my stall series – power on and power off stalls straight ahead, to the left and to the right. Mr. Le Friece showed me how to do Chandelles and rudder stalls and I practiced them. (A Chandelle is a climbing turn of 180. Rudder stalls are more complete than the others in that you hold the stall until the nose of the plane passes down through the horizon.) Then Mr. Le Friece took over and gave me the works – slow roles, snap rolls and loops and upside down flying. The only thing that worried me was "where was I?" However, I will get them in due time. Then I did a power on spin after clearing myself with 360 steep bank turns. He really chewed me for using too steep a bank in the steep turns. Finally I returned to the field. It wasn't too bad but it wasn't good by a long shot.

Oh yes, five packages hit our room yesterday so we have been feasting. The applesauce cookies seemed to taste better than anything else though.

I now have six hours solo time, sixteen hours dual time, ten forced landings and eighty four regular landings.

Say hello to my Grandmothers for me. I wish I had time in which to write them.

Love,
Lee

Monday noon

P.S. Taps came too early last night.

This morning I spent an hour in the Link Trainer. You just climb in and shut the hood so that all you can see is the instrument panel. Then you try to fly by exerting pressure on the delicate controls. But it just doesn't seem the same as contact flight and nine times out of ten you will end up 8,000 feet below ground.

An early flight simulator, the Link trainer consisted of a fuselage with wings mounted on a turn table. The instructor used radio communications and beacons to create problems the student had to navigate around, flying only by instruments. The Link trainer provided an important lesson that would be needed by a combat pilot – to fly around and above obstacles. With its black hood pulled up, the pilot could only see the instruments by the cockpit lights. The resulting blind flying gave the student limited experience in flying through cloud banks with no visual landmarks or horizon line. Within a year, the lessons of the Link trainer would prove to be invaluable, in bad-weather take offs and flying through the dense smoke of German flak.

The Link Trainer, an early simulator.
Courtesy Historical Society of Delaware

Sunday afternoon
October 10, 1943

Dear Shirley.

I think that I will have my roughest check this week – the Army Forty Hour Progress Check. I hope my luck holds out. I'll have a lot to practice in preparation for I now have acrobatics [sic] loops and slow and snap rolls. Too much precision is not expected but I must know the how of it in preparation for future training. A favorite trick of check pilots is to call a forced landing when you are on your back in a slow roll. I am using a new pen for this letter because my old one fell from my pocket during a loop. Last week we concentrated on accuracy landings. We had to make five solo landings for grading of 90 stage, 180 stage and 90 power stage.

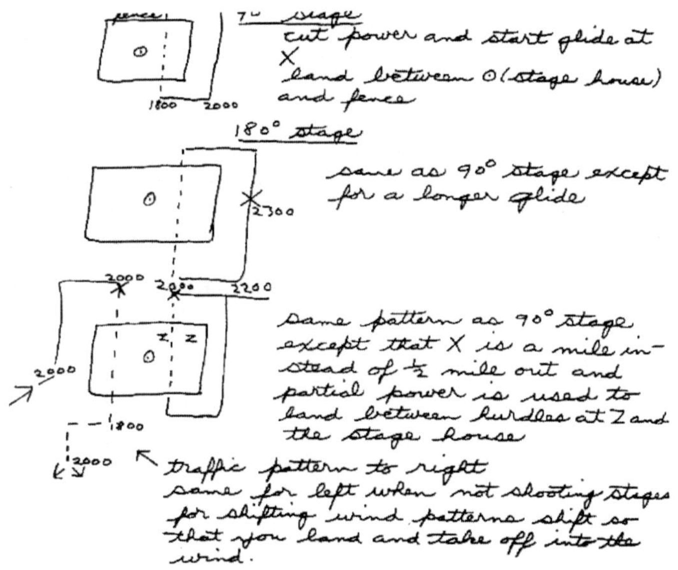

I wish you would exchange my letters with home and vise versa unless we are discussing something personal. That way I hope to send more news.

Love,

Lee

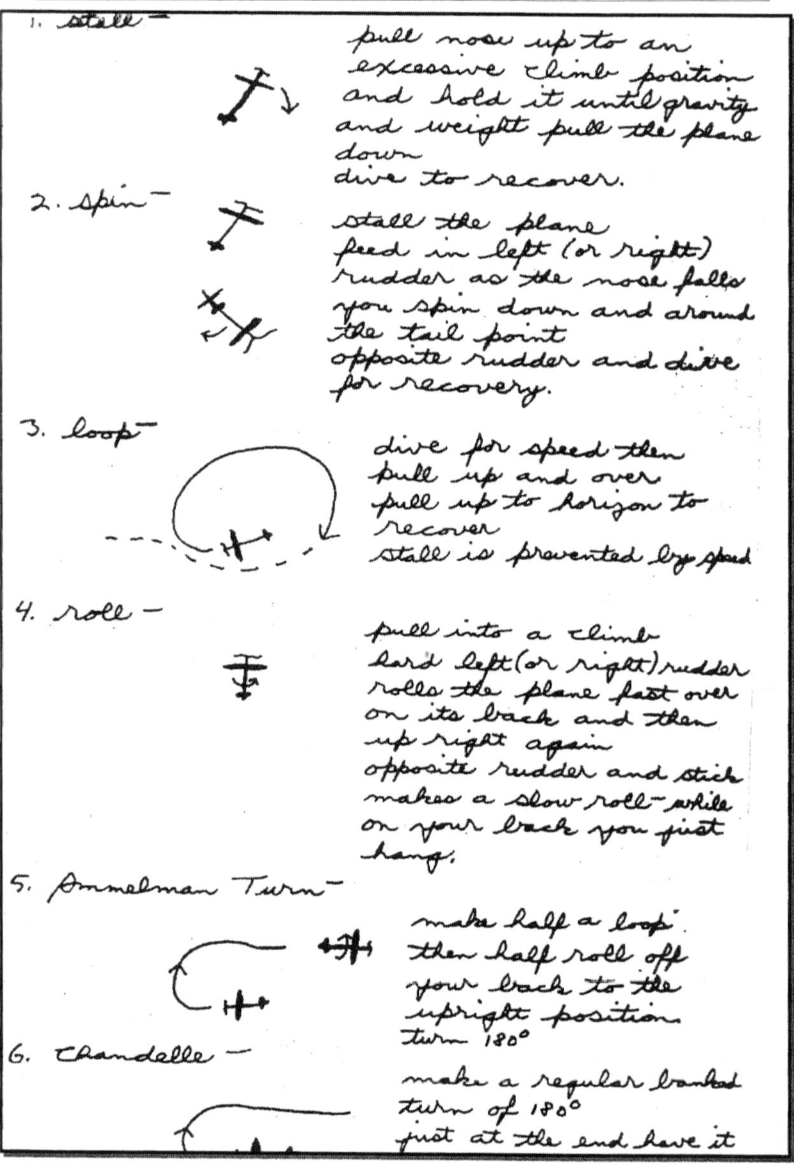

1. stall —

pull nose up to an
excessive climb position
and hold it until gravity
and weight pull the plane
down
dive to recover.

2. spin —

stall the plane
feed in left (or right)
rudder as the nose falls
you spin down and around
the tail point
opposite rudder and dive
for recovery.

3. loop —

dive for speed then
pull up and over
pull up to horizon to
recover
stall is prevented by speed

4. roll —

pull into a climb
hard left (or right) rudder
rolls the plane fast over
on its back and then
up right again
opposite rudder and stick
makes a slow roll — while
on your back you just
hang.

5. Immelman Turn —

make half a loop.
then half roll off
your back to the
upright position
turn 180°

6. Chandelle —

make a regular banked
turn of 180°
just at the end have it

Drawing of flight maneuvers. Undated letter from Lee, 1943.
Courtesy Historical Society of Delaware

Wednesday evening
October 13, 1943

Dear Dad,

I have a moment in which to write before falling out for navigation class. We will be filing mock cross country briefs every night now in preparation for the short fifty mile hop and back which we will make while in primary and for the many longer hops further in our training.

Quite a few of the Stearman's are being overhauled this week and as a result my hours are building up slow. Total hours: 35:25; solo: 12:20. At present I am in the midst of one of those periods in which maneuvers [sic] seem to become worse instead of better. Some of the reason may be that I have become overconfident after proving that I could fly; some may be because of the normal leveling out of the progress check curve; most of all though the disease of flight fatigue brought on by homesickness after eight months and the ever stricter monotony of military life tends to make me, and all Cadets, sick of it all.

A financial explanation:

An Aviation Cadet receives $75.00 a month pay plus $1.00 a day food allowance and $1.25 a day lodging allowance. The government keeps up a Cadet insurance but bond purchases and miscellaneous other charges, if any, are deducted from his pay. (I spent $12.50 a month on war bonds.) It so happens that Hayward and Conneley (contractors to Southwestern Airways for Thunderbird) charge only $1.15 a day for lodging. Thus I make $3.00 during a thirty day month on my lodging allowance. Various other discrepancies [sic] will occur during my training so that as a cadet my monthly pay will average $83.30 without deductions. I purchased the last bond as a *part of the Arizona campaign for the third bond drive. I spend less here than I did at Santa Ana, near L. A.*

Say hello to everybody for me.

Yours,
Lee

Friday, October 15

Dear Lee: -

The box of cactus arrived this morning. The package was stamped "received in bad condition" but I think the plants are O.K.- only the box was battered in. Thanks so much for thinking of me. I'll get them arranged in pots this evening and hope I can keep them all in good shape for you to see when you come home.

We enjoyed your letter with the drawings. I think you did very well for a person who can't draw. Daddy was proud of the letter, - read it in the Board meeting here at school yesterday. It seems almost incredible that you can do such things in a plane. You must get a great thrill over mastering such things. Here's to your continued success.

Our plans are to drive to Williamsport [to see Shirley] if it is a nice day Sunday. Should it rain I don't think we will go. On the way up last time we passed what must be a camp for war prisoners, in the wilds of Pa. We did not see any prisoners, but there were large signs telling us it was government property and that no one should stop along the road or enter, and it was barb-wire enclosed.

Love,
Mother

On the drive to see Shirley at Dickinson Junior College the Minkers most likely passed Camp Hill, one of several POW camps in Pennsylvania. Because of the shortage of farm workers, the prisoners helped with the chores for many German speaking farmers in Pennsylvania. The first of the German POWs were transferred to the U.S. after the fall of Africa in 1942. Other POWs were survivors of sunken U-boats, and later in the war, thousands were transported to the U.S. after capture in Germany. By the end of 1943, there were 123,440 German POWs in U. S. camps scattered across the country.

Sunday afternoon
October 17, 1943

Dear Mother,

Another crammed week has ended. Thursday I passed a forty hour civilian progress check; Friday I made a dual cross country trip to Casa Grande. At weeks end I have a total of 42 hours 7 minutes flying time – 16 hours 45 minutes solo and 153 landings.

I had been expecting an army check but received the civilian instead. That is bad for now I will probably have the army check as my final check probably at about fifty hours, maybe at the end of this week. I hope my luck continues.

The one dual and one solo cross country trip that is made during primary training is very simple but good sound training for future and longer trips, ultimately bombing missions over enemy territory. The trip to Casa Grande (population 2,500) is fifty miles almost due south of Thunderbird II. We fly by contact navigation, i.e. from land mark to land mark. After taking off we climb to 4,500 feet and fly over Scottsdale (a store and a garage). On our left is Falcon Primary, on our right is Phoenix. We fly between Mesa and Tempe and over Chandler (5,000 population). This district is green because of irrigation but soon we are flying over the desert again with Williams Advanced twin-engine [plant] three miles to our left. Next we fly between two surprisingly huge square Japanese relocation camps. Finally we start gliding down as we fly over the Sacatan Mountains for Three Point Auxiliary [sic] field is just beyond. We land then take off again for the journey back over the same route but at 3,500 feet. At cruising speed of 85 miles per hour the whole procedure takes about an hour and three quarters. There is no excitement although occasionally a P-38, a P-40 [both were fighters] or a formation of AT-10s [advanced two engine trainer] fly haughtily by. I am occupied in remaining on course, in holding a constant altitude, in looking out for other planes and at noting the time at which I pass over the different landmarks.

Enclosed is a picture of my flying group. You can see several Stearmans in the background and the Macdowel Mountain six miles away. To the left is the mile square field; front and rear extends our mile flight line; to the right is the field proper.

Love,
Lee

Lee's flight path took him took him over the Gila River Relocation Center, situated about 50 miles south of Phoenix. Located within the Gila River Indian Reservation, over 13,000 Japanese-Americans were interned at the camp for the duration of the war. Shortly after the attack on Pearl Harbor, President

Roosevelt signed Executive Order 9066 which resulted in the round-up and internment of 120,000 Japanese-Americans. The reason for the order was the mistaken fear of an imminent attack on the West Coast by the Japanese fleet and the perceived likelihood that the Japanese would spy on American activities.

The two square camps that Lee observed from the air were most likely Canal Camp in the eastern half of the Relocation Center, and Butte Camp in the western half. Gila had the most extensive agricultural programs of all the camps with 7,000 acres in production which accounts for the "two surprisingly huge square Japanese relocation camps" he reported seeing from the air.

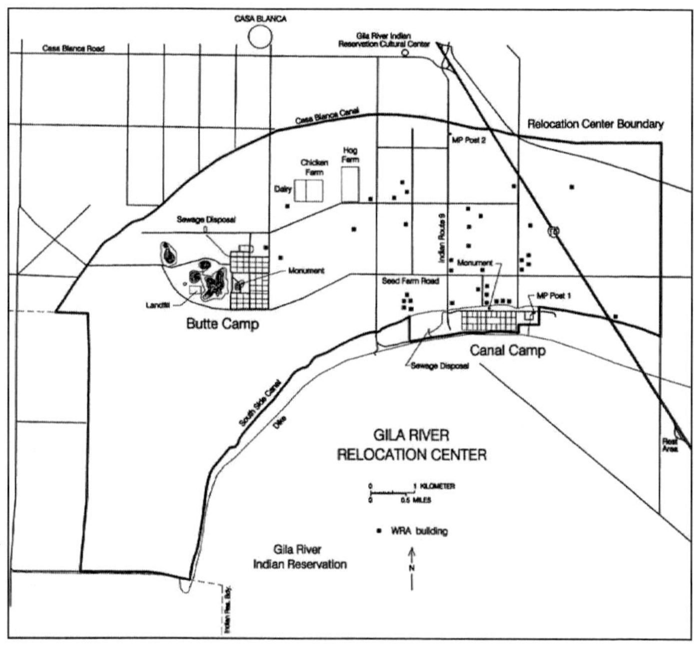

Map of the Gila River Relocation Center,
Gila River Indian Reservation, Arizona.
National Park Service

Flying buddies in front of Stearman P.T.-17, Thunderbird Field, October, 1943
O. P. Canant, Anthony E. Paratore, Ralph L. Minker Jr., Instructor Ray F. Newton, Paul E. Perry, Robert Casey. Enclosed in October 17, 1943 letter to Edna Minker.
Courtesy Historical Society of Delaware

Tuesday, October 19

Dear Lee:-

Your letter to daddy, written Wednesday, did not arrive until this morning, although sent air-mail. Of course there are days when you are down in the dumps,- that happens to almost anyone. There are days when things are so hectic around here and so little good seems to come out of my effort to help that I am ready to give up and quit. Life is like that. We just have to keep going. The fact that you boys are not allowed home must make it much worse for you and I imagine your spells of being sick of it all come more often as a result. Does the rule still hold that you won't get home until your year is up?

I am going to try to locate one of those glass shelves to windows to hold the pots of cactus which you sent. I have them all planted and am keeping them in the garage until the painter gets thru inside and I am straightened up. I guess I'll give grandmother Minker one because I think it would please her to have it from you.

Love from all of us, and lots of it.
Mother

October 26, 1943.

Dear Lee:-

We have been having a real old-fashioned northeaster today, - pouring rain and the wind blowing a gale, and getting much colder. I am getting ready to leave the office and go over to school to get our NO. 4 ration books which are being issued today and up through Thursday. They are supposed to be good for two years, I believe, I certainly hope we won't have to use them that long. I won't object to using them for a good many years if necessary, if only the war is over.

We were thinking of you all day yesterday, when you were supposed to get your army check, and of course we shall be looking forward to receiving a letter within the next day or two. On Thursday I made some cookies and got them and a box of caramels off to you Monday. I guess they will reach you before you are shipped somewhere else.

There were quite a number of service men in church Sunday morning, a Chinese soldier sat in front of me. He was with a flyer with an overseas stripe. Saturday night we had "Thunderbirds" here at the school, and grandmother Jones and I went up to chapel to see it. I was so glad that I had a chance to see it, for it gives me some idea of the country you are in and the difficult tasks you boys have every day. By the way, do they really "duck" you after you make your solo, or was that just a "Hollywood" touch?

The United War Fund campaign is now on and I have been asked to secure subscriptions from those on the staff here at the school.

Love and our very best wishes always.
Mother

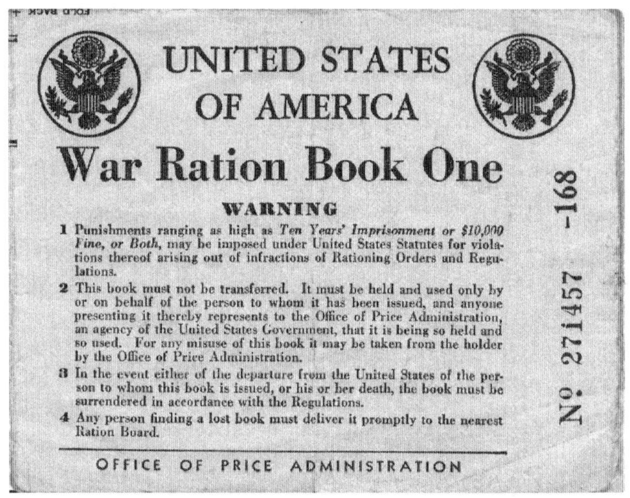

UNITED STATES
OF AMERICA

War Ration Book One

WARNING

1 Punishments ranging as high as *Ten Years' Imprisonment or $10,000 Fine, or Both,* may be imposed under United States Statutes for violations thereof arising out of infractions of Rationing Orders and Regulations.

2 This book must not be transferred. It must be held and used only by or on behalf of the person to whom it has been issued, and anyone presenting it thereby represents to the Office of Price Administration, an agency of the United States Government, that it is being so held and so used. For any misuse of this book it may be taken from the holder by the Office of Price Administration.

3 In the event either of the departure from the United States of the person to whom this book is issued, or his or her death, the book must be surrendered in accordance with the Regulations.

4 Any person finding a lost book must deliver it promptly to the nearest Ration Board.

OFFICE OF PRICE ADMINISTRATION

No. 271457 -168

Ration Book similar to the one Edna Minker used.
World War II archives, Historical Society of Delaware

"Thunderbirds: Soldiers of the Air," a 1942 production of the USAAC, tells the story of a love triangle with a flying instructor

(Preston Foster), a local ranch girl (Jean Tierney), and a British flyer (John Sutton). The army's real message spoken by the base commander, is the challenge of "training baby faced boys to be pilots . . . We need fliers and we need them quick." Experienced pilots dreaded the assignment to a training unit; instructing was as a routine task, far removed from the action of combat flying. At the close of the film, the narrator asks that we "pay homage to the instructors," because "We can't win unless [these boys] know their job." Love interest and army messages aside, the appeal of the film for the Minker family was the stunning Technicolor footage of Stearman PT-13s and Vultee BT-13s soaring over the Arizona desert. Now mother and grandmother could easily imagine where Lee was and the daunting work he was doing.

Friday evening
October 30, 1943
Williamsport, Pa.

Dear Lee: --

We just got in from the movies and I just washed my hair. We saw Nelson Eddy in "Phantom of the Opera." It was quite spooky in parts and everyone chewed their fingernails but it was still very good. Claude Rains was in it too.

Well, we're through with Freshman Week. Boy, we really got it from the sophs too. I guess it wasn't as bad as some of the things that you had to do but you know how the freshmen get kicked around.

I hope this letter reaches you before you leave Thunderbird. I had no idea you would move again quite so soon. How many more parts does your training have? All the cadets here yell "Thunderbird" at me when I wear my raincoat as that is where I've got the insignia sewn.

Well, I'm about ready to fall asleep right now, so I hope you won't mind the scribble and wanderings. Write as soon as you get where you're going so I'll have your address. You wouldn't by any chance be coming East, would you? I hope, I hope!! Be good and have fun.

Lots and lots of love –
Shirley

The Thunderbird Field 2 insignia patch won by the AAC cadets (and Shirley Minker). The insignia was red and black on a crème background.

Courtesy Historical Society of Delaware

Sunday evening
October 31, 1943

Dear Dad,

Another phase of my aircrew training has been completed. At the end of my eight months in the Air Corps I have seen service in Florida, Nebraska, California and Arizona and have had basic military training, college pre-pre-flight review training, pre-flight training and primary flying training. To my credit is ten hours of flying 85 horsepower Piper Cubs and 65 hours of flying 165 horsepower Stearman PT-17s.

This has been a grand experience. I have been trained along heretofore undeveloped lines, have seen much and have made many new friends. In many ways I have grown a little more mature. Naturally at times this life has not been easy but there is a job to do and this life is preparing me to help complete the job.

But my training is only fifty percent completed. From what I know now the following is what is in store for me from November till March. At 1400 Wednesday, November 3, 1943, roughly 200 cadets will leave Thunderbird II for basic training at Pecos, Texas. (Rumor has it that some may go to Morono Field, Tucson, Arizona, for two engine fighter training) Pecos is in the midst of nowhere but is supposed to be tops as a flying field. At Pecos we should fly about thirty hours in BT-13s and the rest of our eight hours in two engine AT11's or 9's. Then at advanced we should be able to choose our ship – B-25, B-26, A-20, B-17, B-24, B-29. Our instructors will now be army flyers. Basic will consist chiefly of step ups to more powerful ships, reviews of primary fundamentals, formation and navigational flying.

I wish that you and Mother wouldn't worry about me. My schedule leaves little time for letter writing so please excuse the lack of news. I am in great shape; flying training is perfectly safe. The only accidents in primary have been minor wing scraping ground loops. Our planes are tops; Mr. Newton put a Stearman into a spin, put his feet up in the air and his hands over the sides and after one more turn our ship leveled into cruising flight.

I am glad that my PT [Primary Training] was a Stearman for comments of boys who fly Ryans and Fairchilds say that they are hardly more than Cubs—safe, but not powerful, not capable of all maneuvers, [sic] not requiring much skill to master and a huge jump to BTs

[Basic Trainer].

I'm studying weather now so I'll close. Give my best to everyone.

Yours,
Lee

With the self-assurance of a nineteen year old, Lee assured his parents that ". . . flying training is perfectly safe." In fact, the army reports show that flying training was not safe. In 1943 alone there were over 4,000 accidents in primary trainers, with 226 fatalities; by the end of the war, 439 students were killed in primary trainers. The combined statistics for Primary, Basic, and Advanced Trainers show just over 3,500 losses in training. This figure is not the total of training fatalities, as other losses occurred in operational and specialty training. *(Army Air Forces Statistical Digest, World War II, Table 213)*

The agile yellow and blue Stearman at Thunderbird Field introduced the fundamentals of flying, the first step on the way to flying a multi engine bomber. Even as Lee progressed to the next phase of training at Pecos Field in Texas, the bomb group he would eventually join, the 447th, was preparing to leave the United States for their new base in Rattlesden, England. Eleven more months of training in three different planes were needed to prepare Lee for his job in England.

Chapter Five

The Flying Hours are Beginning to Pile Up

November 3, 1943 - December 31, 1943

Dates: November 3, 1943 to December 31, 1943	**Location: Pecos, Texas**

Progression of Flight Training

Lincoln, NE	Santa Ana, CA	Thunderbird Field, AZ	Pecos, TX	Pecos, TX	Roswell, NM
College Training Attachment	Classification And Pre-flight	Basic Flight Training	Preliminary Flight Training	Advanced Flight School	Transitional Flight School
Piper Cub		Stearman	BT-17	Cessna AT-17	B-17

Nov. 3, 1943	Lee arrived in Pecos, Texas for basic flight school.
Nov. 5, 1943	Instructor Lieutenant Nolan took Lee up for his first flight in the BT -17.
Nov. 8, 1943	The 447th Bomb Group began departing for England.
Nov. 20, 1943	Two aircraft from the 447th Bomb Group are lost over the North Sea en route to England.
Dec. 6, 1943	Pecos Field is designated as an Advanced Flight School.
Dec. 24, 1943	The 447th B. G. flew their first mission from Rattlesden AFB.

When Lee arrived at Pecos Army Air Field in early November, he found a hastily built army air base with the long runways needed by novice pilots. Originally the Pecos Municipal Airport, the runways were carved out of the semi-arid fields in West Texas. The 1,800 acre base had one runway of 7,200 feet, and two others at 6,200 feet each. The living quarters and mess hall were hurriedly built structures covered in tarpaper, barely adequate for the task of housing and feeding several thousand soldiers. Pecos Field eventually had over 4,300 personnel, at any given time half were students. Seventeen classes of pilots (a total of 3,367) were trained at Pecos Field, completing the course in one-month intervals.

Lee Minker's class, # 44C, was double the size of the previous class of young airmen. The expansion in class size can be attributed to the need to replace the losses from the first months of daylight bombing in Europe. The Eighth Air Force needed thousands of planes and tens of thousands of pilots and aircrews to carryout this strategy of daylight precision bombing of military and industrial sites. The early raids did not have the benefit of fighter escort into Germany, consequently, the bomber losses were appalling. For example, during the last week of July 1943 the USAAF lost over 100 bombers and 1,000 men. For some targets, the results were considered meager, given the investment of planes, pilots, and crews. The size of the training pipeline had to grow – as quickly as possible.

Sunday morning
November 7, 1943

Dear Dad,

I arrived here at Pecos late Thursday afternoon after an uneventful ride on the Southern Pacific and Texas and Pacific railroads. I had a chance to look over the business districts of Tucson and El Paso during short stops and saw the Rio Grande "Creek" and Mexico on its far side.

All through my air crew training I have been warned, "Wait till you get to Blank if you think this is rough." Usually I have been rushed like mad for a month and then forgotten; every training program has been full, some trouble is experienced in tackling new experiences – but probably the administration of the air crew trainer program causes much unnecessary trouble.

1. *The quick and huge expansion of the Air Forces without adequate preparation.*
2. *Limited competent personnel*
3. *Class 44-C is just slightly more than double the size of class 44-A*
4. *Equipment limitations.*

Pecos Army Airfield then is hit hard by these

limitations as far as equipment, cadet numbers and preparation. But the officer personnel seems to be extremely adequate. Because of one officer acting as flight instructor for every six cadets, because of numerous ground school officers and because of quite a few student officers supplementing the normal tactical group there is much more contact between officers and men. Because of the teaching aspect and the importance of polishing men for combat, officer quality is high.

This is a big field. The flight line of two miles is filled five deep with wing tip to wing tip BT-13 [basic trainer] and AT-17 [advanced trainer] planes. Besides cadets there is an equal number of permanent party. We stand formal retreat every night. Food is good, but sparse because cadet allowances have been cut to G. I. in an effort to cut food consumption. Athletics strikes me as being especially fine. Teams of fifteen compete in leagues of touch football, softball, basketball and volleyball for squadron, group, class and post championships during the nine week stay here. The aim is to develop judgement, coolness and coordination. Our flight practice area extends about thirty miles in every direction and includes four auxiliary [sic] fields. Ground school subjects consist of radio, radio code, air craft identification, instruments, navigation and meteorology. Cold nights, high winds, flat dustlands are features of this part of Texas. We are on Central War Time.

My flying instructor is Lieutenant Nolan of Trenton, New Jersey. He seems like a very nice fellow. I was disappointed in my flying however. Too many asked for multi-engine training so I was one of the boys transferred to single engine. This may have its benefits later on however for I will have more experience before I step up to bigger stuff. At present I must concentrate on the first half of my training in BT-13s – transition and mastery of fundamentals.

We sleep one hour more here but spend most of our evenings in ground school so letter writing is going to be harder. I'll write as often as I can but the family will have to relay much of my news to others.

Yours,
Lee

The BT-13 flown in basic training at Pecos introduced the combat pilots-to-be to a more powerful and complex aircraft than the Stearman. The single engine, two-seater enclosed cockpit plane was extremely agile and stable, but less forgiving than the Stearman bi-wing Lee flew in primary training. The BT-13 earned the nickname "Vibrator" due to its tendency to shake when approaching stall speed. The BT-13 had a maximum air speed of 180 mph and a range of 725 miles. In this intermediate stage between basic and advanced training, students were introduced to formation flying, instrument and night work. Ground school, not nearly as exciting as flying over the vast expanse of Texas, covered radio code, navigation, and air craft identification.

Vultee BT-13/BT-15 trainer flown during Primary Training in Pecos, TX.
Courtesy Historical Society of Delaware

November 10, 1943

Dearest Lee:

Needless to say we were glad to get your Jumbo card this morning, letting us know that you had really landed in Pecos, Texas. I don't worry when we don't hear from you, but we do miss you terribly and every time we hear by letter it helps a little.

We read in the papers that there were blizzards in several of the western states and snow was predicted for us today, but none has come yet. Did any of it reach you, or don't they have snow in the part of Texas in which you are?

I'll have to get out a map and get your location in my mind.

Don't forget to let us know as soon as you can what you would like [us] to send for Christmas, for we don't want to load you up with things which will be useless and just in your way. Christmas shopping will be more hectic this year than last and I would like to do what I have to do this month if possible.

Take good care of yourself and let us know all about your new set-up as soon as you can.

Lots of love from everybody.

Mother

Thursday evening
November 11, 1943

Dear Mother,

I have fifteen moments for a brief note. Maybe this schedule will help explain why.

0545 – first call – 0615
0615 – breakfast – 0645
0700 – flight line – 1300
1315 – lunch – 1345
1400 – athletics – 1500
1500 – showers – 1530
1530 – ground school – 1730
1730 – formal retreat – 1830
1830 – dinner – 1900
2030 – ground school – 2130
2200 – taps
x – this doesn't include time for G.I.ing equipment or self, for going to and fro, etc.

Yesterday I took the required practice parachute jump. I leapt head first from a thirty foot tower only to be jerked terrifically about two feet above the ground as the rope attached to the parachute attached to me came to its greatest extent.

I now have three and a half hours in the BTG-13 and am just beginning to get acquainted. The complicated procedures required for each different maneuver [sic] in changing prop pitch, fuel mixture, gas tanks, instruments, throttle, radio, trim tabs and flaps are the chief bottleneck.

Believe it or not, every day on the flight line I wear sweatsuit, flying suit, leather jacket and gloves to combat the cold. Write soon. Could you send me some cookies for Thanksgiving. I wish that I could be home with you all then but I will be thinking of you anyhow. Nine weeks of basic, nine weeks of advanced, and then maybe I can get home to see you all.

What should I do about getting Shirley a birthday present? What do you all want for Christmas? I would like a good flying wristwatch from the family. The Army takes care of most of my needs.

Love,
Lee

Thursday morning
November 17, 1943
Williamsport, Penna.

Dear Lee: --

I've just come out of a horrible biology test! She only gives us a few questions but we have to write about a whole book on each one of them.

That flying field certainly must be of a pretty big size to have such a flight line. The funny thing is that we haven't heard much about it but we do [hear] about lots of other fields in Texas. I guess we're just ignorant here in the East!

I wonder if you could ever call me from Texas. Maybe you could on Thanksgiving Day or sometime, but you'd have to let me know beforehand.

I won't be getting home for Christmas until December 22nd. We have to come back the 3rd or 4th too. Mother said I'd have to do my shopping up here. I'll have an awful time getting home with all my stuff, I'm afraid.

Well, I really don't have too much news. I'll try to keep up on my weekly letter too and don't you worry too much if you don't get yours off. Remember how you spent last Thanksgiving Day. In the infirmary at Dickinson College. That seems like a long time ago, doesn't it. Ever since last year in high school seems like eons ago to me now. I'll write sometime again soon.

Lots of love –
Shirley

Thursday, November 18

Dear Lee:

I mailed your Thanksgiving box on Tuesday and do hope it reaches you by Thanksgiving Day. Let me know how the gingerbread arrives. We are being urged to get off all Christmas mail in November if possible, but I hate to make you cookies so far ahead. I know I'll not get yours off this month. Don't forget to tell us about the kind of watch you want when you write, if you haven't already done so.

Last night daddy and I went to see "For Whom the Bell Tolls". It's fine acting, but terrible of course, although it did not take as much out of me as "Bataan". I suppose that is because Bataan was a picture of our fighting forces and what is going on from day to day, while the Spanish civil war now seems far away, and to some really was fought by the Germans, Italians and Russians as a testing ground for their weapons in this present conflict.

Do you remember Roy Wilson who used to go to Silver brook [church] when we were there,-sang in the choir? He moved to Centerville, Md., you may remember, and visited us in Crisfield. The morning paper announces he was killed in action.

Daddy got a letter from Senator Bridges this week and he was asking for you. He has a boy in the South Pacific.

Of course you know without saying that we shall all be thinking of you even more than ever on Thanksgiving Day, and praying that this time next year we shall all be together once more.

With all my love,
Mother

Understandably, Edna Minker had a difficult time watching the movie *Bataan*, the story of U.S. troops trapped on the Bataan Peninsula in the spring of 1942. The film depicted gruesome, hand-to-hand combat as a dozen soldiers die of malaria and battle wounds during MacArthur's retreat from the Philippines. Few movies released during the war were as grisly and realistic in staging death as *Bataan*. Lee's mother must have felt the tension between the accepted necessity for the war and the threat to her only son during every moment of the film.

Thursday noon
November 18, 1943

Dear Dad,

This letter will have to substitute for me in wishing you a very happy birthday. I wish that I could be home to personally wish you and Bernice happy birthday and to spend Thanksgiving with the whole family but I will be thinking of you as I am flying my BT and looking forward to the day when I can see you again.

By the end of this week I will have finished two weeks of flying; I will be soloed out; I will be perfecting the fundamentals and be ready to start on instrument flying next week. To date I have six hours and twenty minutes of flying.

I finished instruments class with a grade of 93% and communications class with a grade of 95%. I am just beginning radio code class and navigation class. I suppose that code and aircraft identification will again be the most troublesome subjects.

This morning I went to the dentist to have the stitches removed from my gum. While I was in the chair he decided to look at the other wisdom teeth which he was to pull. He found out however that [they] had not even started growing as yet and that the other was too small to grab. So I will have a reprieve.

This morning we were lectured on new developments in army aviation. Next spring look for:

1. *the new super-bomber modeled from the Flying Fortress and B-19: the B-29.*
2. *the new fight modeled from the P-39 air cobra.*
3. *the new Wright super-light and efficient aircraft engine which when installed in a Fortress will increase its bomb load from three to ten tons.*

4. the recently tested and most sensational of all – a rocket propelled plane.

This Air Corps is fast becoming the worlds greatest in manpower, machines and training.

How is everything at the school these days? Has the number of boys been decreased by the draft or the boom or has the lack of sufficient and experienced workers both at the school and in the field resulted in a decrease in juvenile delinquency. I suppose the budget is rather tight these days but is there a prospect of a modernization program at war's end so as to provide transitional work for returning men and future security of their children?

Believe it or not, I had oysters fried for lunch. They were small and flat tasting, not at all like the Crisfield variety, but at least they were oysters. I can remember the first time we three children tasted oysters— raw, over the kitchen sink in Crisfield [Maryland].

Professor Thompson [Dickinson College] once said in Psychology class, that a child's character developed most from imitation of its parents. I can truthfully say that my highest ambition is to pattern myself after you.

As ever,
Lee

While Lee was learning to fly the BT-13 in basic training, the unit he would join in October of 1944, the 447th Bomb Group, prepared to leave for England. After months of training and processing in the U.S., the first 447th crews arrived in England in July, 1943. Ground personnel and several combat crews of the 709th squadron sailed on HMS *Queen Elizabeth* on November 2, 1943. They disembarked in Scotland, then went by train to Rattlesden, Suffolk England, arriving November 31, 1943. The air echelon departed from Goose Bay, Labrador on November 20,

1943, arriving at Rattlesden on November 24. Two planes were lost en route, one piloted by Captain Lester S. White of the 710th squadron, and a second plane piloted by Lieutenant Leonard J. Theison of the 708th squadron. It was believed that the plane piloted by Captain White iced up and went down in the North Atlantic after take-off from the frigid landscape of Goose Bay. Lieutenant Theison and his crew also disappeared after take-off. There were no distress calls from either plane. (Warfle 2004) By the end of November, the bomb group came nearly to full strength (minus the two crews lost en route) with four squadrons, each with 18 authorized crews. The men of the 447th had three weeks after their arrival to get ready for the first mission.

Nov. 24, 1943

Dear Lee,

I am now sixteen. I don't look any older, I don't feel any older, and I certainly don't act any older. To all my knowledge I didn't grow an inch which I shall rue from this day forward.

How's the old wisdom teeth coming along, or should I say going? I don't think I have any. Perhaps that explains my report card. Hm?

Shirley called Sunday night to wish Dad a happy birthday. We really had a crowd out for dinner. Both Grannies, all 3 brothers and wives.

Mom probably told you about our excursion to New York. What a place! We had a Swedish dinner at The Stockholm. We helped ourselves from a Smorgasbord and you could go back as many times as you wanted for seconds.

Listen, Bum, write home and tell us <u>explicitly</u> dat watch youse wants fer Xmas, see? Make, etc.? Also include *a couple of things you need that Granny could get, like hankies, etc. Right away!*

Do you want me to get anything for mom for you for Christmas? I could order her some Spode or glassware for her set; 'cause she would like them as well as anything. Better write me soon about this 'cause its hard to get stuff around here at short notice.

How d'ya like me new writing paper. It's me sister's present ter me. Mom gave me a white sweater. Wal, pard, guess I better go ter mess as Mammy is callin!

So long!

Love,
Bernice

In his 1943 Thanksgiving Day Proclamation, President Roosevelt gave thanks for the contributions of those on the home front. "Our forges and hearths and mills have wrought well; and our weapons have not failed. Our farmers, victory gardeners, and crop volunteers have gathered and stored a heavy harvest in the barns and bins and cellars. Our total food production for the year is the greatest in the annals of our country. For all these things we are devoutly thankful, knowing also that so great mercies exact from us the greatest measure of sacrifice and service."

Despite the record farm production, preparing Thanksgiving dinner in 1943 was a challenge in most households. Ration stamps were required to purchase meat, canned fruit and vegetables, butter, and sugar – if they could be found on the grocers' shelves. Housewives had to save sugar and butter coupons if they wanted a pumpkin pie on the Thanksgiving table. On the Sunday before Thanksgiving the Minker family celebrated Ralph Sr.'s November 22 birthday and Bernice's coming 16th birthday on November 24. On Thanksgiving Day Edna, Ralph, Bernice, and Walter, a friend of Bernice's, had a quiet dinner of leftovers. In her Thanksgiving letter to her son, Edna did not comment on rationing, rather on what was important to her – the lonely holiday with two of her children away: Lee in the Army Air Corps and Shirley at college.

Friday, November 26, 1943

Dear Lee:-

Well, Thanksgiving day is over. As Bernice said this morning, it didn't seem much like Thanksgiving Day to us. I guess it takes more than a turkey to make a Thanksgiving dinner. We had enough left from last Sunday for daddy, Bernice, Walter and I. We ate about 2:30, listening to the Penn-Cornell game meanwhile.

It was a relief to us to receive the letter saying you would not have any more wisdom teeth out. It all seemed rather foolish to us, but I suppose the authorities know best.

If I keep on sending you notices of weddings you will soon begin to think that you are the only "bachelor" of your crowd left. How some of these boys will make a living, enough to support a wife, when this war is suddenly over and they are thrown back into civilian life, and many of the wives now working lose their jobs because jobs will not be so plentiful, I do not know.

Shirley's report came yesterday, and she again got 4 A's and 1 B. I've got a lot of work piled up, for of course I was not in the office yesterday, so this letter must be a little shorter than usual. Don't forget to let us know about that watch if you have not already done so.

Lots of love,
Mother

Friday evening   November 26, 1943

Dear mother,

An early morning Texas cloudburst turned Pecos Field in a quagmire and caused the canceling of flying. Yesterday a heavy fog caused all ships to be grounded.

I now have had four hours of instrument flying and am able to take off, climb, glide, turn and regulate my speed. I get the queerest of sensations at times of climbing, diving, or turning. Then I look at my artificial horizon, altimeter or directional gyro and find that my inner ear and my muscle sense are wrong. I fly under a black cloth canopy in the rear cockpit while my instructor, Lieutenant Nolan, sits in front and keeps me on an even keel. By December 5, we are supposed to have 37 hours of transition and instruments. My time is average – fifteen hours to date.

If I go to twin engine advanced training I will probably go to Marfa, near El Paso, have a ten day furlough and go to operational in Texas. If I remain in single engines I will probably go to Luke, near Phoenix, get a ten day furlough and then operational training in P-47s in New England or in P-51s in the mid west. So I should be home about March 15, 1944.

The dentist could only find one wisdom tooth so the agony is postponed. Really I didn't feel a thing on the first one. The doctors, dentists and nurses are all tops.

Love,
Lee

Thanksgiving weekend of 1943 marked the first meeting of the three Allied leaders during World War II: President Franklin D. Roosevelt, Great Britain's Prime Minister Winston Churchill, and Premier Joseph Stalin of the Soviet Union. President Roosevelt announced after the conference, "We agreed on every point concerned with the launching of a gigantic attack upon Germany." The strategy would begin with the invasion of France, named "Operation Overlord" in mid-May 1944. The appointment of General Dwight D. Eisenhower as the Supreme Allied Commander accelerated the preparation to invade Europe and destroy the German forces. Eisenhower began to apply considerable pressure on the leadership of the Eighth Air Force for direct air support of the ground troops in Operation Overlord. The leadership of the Eighth Air Force, convinced of the value of strategic bombing of transportation and communication targets, was reluctant to divert its resources. The discussion of the role of the air force in the invasion continued throughout the winter and into the early spring of 1944.

Sunday morning
November 28, 1943

Dear Dad,

Due to inclement weather for Thursday, Friday and Saturday I must fly this afternoon. (It even snowed a bit Friday.) To date I have only fifteen hours of flying time and I must have 37 hours by December 6.

On December 6, 1943 Pecos Field will cease to be a Basic flying training school and will become instead an Advanced two engine flying training school. All students now at Pecos will remain to fly AT-9s, 11s and 17s and, maybe, 322s (small P-38s and B-25s) I will graduate from

Pecos in February or March with my pair of silver wings.

That is all of the definite news at present. Probably our whole training program will be revised because of this sudden accent on offensive bombardment for next year's offensive. Before the change over they will cram BT time in transition, solo, instruments, acrobatics [sic] and formation flying.

Please tell Mother to add a half dozen handkerchiefs to her list.

Please note the new address on the envelope.

Yours,
Lee

High school students were also immersed in the war; they conducted paper drives, recycled scrap metal, and sold war stamps and war bonds. The war stamps could be bought for a few cents, pasted into a book and when the value reached $18.75, be traded in for a $25 war bond. Bernice wrote to her brother about the airmen who came to A.I. duPont high school to speak at a bond rally, one of them had flown on the Ploesti Raid on August 1, 1943. The Ploesti oil fields in Rumania, estimated to supply 30 per cent of Germany's liquid fuel, were the target of a daring Allied raid. Although the Allies inflicted heavy damage, the cost was high. Of 177 planes and 1,726 men who took off on the mission, 54 planes and 532 men did not return. A survivor of the Ploesti raid would have been a glamorous hero to sixteen year old Bernice as she listened to him at the bond rally.

Poster encouraging Americans to buy war bonds.

Undated

Dear Lee,

Well, I've been set on my heels again! I'm in bed with another cold. It hangs on and on so I kept snifflin' and blowin'.

The other day we had two fellows at school to talk to us. One, a staff sergeant, tail gunner in the air B-17s, was on the Ploesti oil fields raid and had the distinguished service cross. He was from Boston, Mass. The other, a first Louis [lieutenant], was all of 6'2" and a navigator in North Africa. He was from Hanover, Mass. They were both good speeches and talked in typical New England dialect. They had a lot of fun ribbing each other but their message was serious and of course, given to urge us on to buying more bonds.

Shirley called home Sunday night. She was very tired, what with exams and all, but is going to catch up on her sleep this weekend when two of her numerous boy friends go home on leave. She seems to be doing a good job of keeping up the morale, what?

Well, gotta stop and close-up. Be good and don't land upside down.

Love,
Bernice

P.S. Was out at Tatnals [long-time family friends] yesterday. Nancy was asking for you, Romeo.

The second anniversary of Pearl Harbor brought a reflective letter from Lee. He had a clear memory of the moment on the Dickinson campus that "changed the whole course of my life." He optimistically wrote his mother that the war will be over "by this time next year." His life in the Army Air Corps was totally different than anything he could have imagined in Carlisle, Pennsylvania as a college freshmen in 1941. For Edna, the day had another meaning, for it was Shirley's eighteenth birthday.

Sunday afternoon
December 5, 1943

Dear Mother,

Two years ago, on a sunny and yet snappy Sunday afternoon, I was returning to Conway [Hall] after a good roast beef dinner and an hour of rearranging the fraternity furniture from the pledge formal of the night before. As Bill Virgin and I came up the walk Professor Fink [economics professor at Dickinson College] rushed from his house next door and shouted, "The Japanese have bombed Pearl Harbor."

That moment changed the whole course of my life. At first there was a period of intense excitement and anxiety –What was going to happen? After the New Years a nervous calm prevailed but war became more real. Shocking defeats hit the U.S. and her allies, coffee, sugar, gas and oil were rationed, bond drives and civilian defense organization, the draft, the college acceleration program and college reserve brought the war close by December, 1942. Then I was called in February, 1943, for basic training as an A.C.C. Pvt. In Miami Beach, Florida. I passed through College Training, Pre-Flight and Primary training and December, 1943, finds me in Basic Flying training at Pecos, Texas, with the future looking bright for a U.S. victory by this time next year.

I have been putting this letter off all week in the hope that I could get some definite news on the course of my future training. As it looks now I will probably get a full eight hours in BT-13s for a bunch came in today from Morano Basic School and they will be the first advanced students in AT-17s this month and in B-25s next month. I will be one month behind them. Rumor has it that we are in line for instructing or air transport upon graduation in March. I hope that I don't have to instruct.

Irony: We got paid Tuesday evening but then had to pay back fifty cents for our Thanksgiving dinner. Some inspecting brass has been here lately and so the quality of the food has increased amazingly.

Thanks for digging for my Christmas list. I am going to address some cards this afternoon. Enclosed you will find some money with which I wish you would get something for Shirley and Julia for Christmas. And don't forget Grandmother Minker either. Fruit cake, cheese, crackers, peanut butter, toll house cookies, etc.— I like them all. Nothing but white in handkerchiefs please. Socks, underwear, writing paper and a watch are all I can think of in the line of gifts for myself. (or a writing paper pack.)

Say hello to everybody for me.

Love,
Lee

The walk in front of Professor Fink's house on West High Street (circa 1941), Carlisle, PA where Lee first heard the news of the attack on Pearl Harbor. Courtesy Archives of Dickinson College.

December 7, 1943

Dearest Lee:

This is Shirley's birthday, Pearl Harbor Day and Delaware Day! The sun is shining brightly and it is not very cold here, - quite different from the day 18 years ago when I journeyed to the hospital in the wee small hours, with the snow piled high and the temperature way down. This is the first birthday Shirley has ever been away from home. I sent here a white sweater for a birthday present and baked her a chocolate cake. The cake won't last long I imagine, with all those girls to help eat it.

Lee, I am going to try to get your box off with at least some Christmas things in it this week. There will be nothing in it which will spoil, so please do not be tempted to open any Christmas boxes before December 25 if they arrive early. We do want you to have a little bit of the Christmas spirit on that day and something to remind you of home.

I suppose last week was filled with flying hours, if you made up all the hours which you said were necessary. When do you enter "advanced" training? Is it still the plan that you will remain there for it?

With all my love.
Mother

Tuesday night Dec. 14, 1943
Williamsport, Pa.

Dear Lee:

I'm over in the chapel and we're getting ready to go on, but you know how plays are. We'll probably have to wait an hour or so, so I think I'll be safe in writing you. This week is supposed to be test week but most of the teachers are being swell and aren't giving us any because of the pageant.

I got your money safely last week. I'll try to get something for everyone you mentioned, so don't you worry about it. I've got all of my own shopping done and the stores are packed here all the time.

These last few days have been icy cold. The air is so very clear but so sharp it almost hurts to take a breath. They flooded over the tennis courts and it's frozen solid. Some of the cadets were skating on it tonight but most of our skates are at home. We're all going to bring them back at Christmas time. I think the cadets want to play ice-hockey on it.

Last night about 11:30 we had a blackout. It's only the second we've had since I've been here. We had one on the first night I was here and that was on September 27th!

The moon was out so brightly that we sat by the window and ate during the blackout. I don't know whether or not they had one in Delaware too, or whether it was just this state.

This time next week I'll be home, everyone is saying. I think I'll try to write you a letter on the way home and tell you what is going on.

With all my love –
Shirley

Wednesday evening
December 15, 1943

Dear Dad,

Cold clear weather has come to Pecos and the flying hours are beginning to pile up. It is interesting to note that weather had grounded planes at Pecos only one day in fifteen months until 44-C came along; 44-C has lost ten days of flying in six weeks. However solo, cross country, night flying, good weather and the fact that class 44-C is the only class and using all the planes at Pecos are reasons for the excellent progress.

Tuesday I took my 250 mile three hour cross country from Pecos to Salt Flat, (land), to Intermittent Lake to Van Horn, (land), to Pecos. There isn't much to tell for I just flew the course I had marked out in Navigation class to the El Paso sectional chart. Mountain peaks, highways, railroads and salt lakes provided check points along the route. I cruised at 8,000 feet at about 130 miles per hour. I passed two speeding Hellcats [Navy fighter planes] at Salt Flat and a big C-46 [Army transport plane] over Van Horn.

Night flying consists of one hour dual time, five hours of solo local time and two hours of solo cross country. For my money nothing can top the beauty of night flying with a full moon and a sky full of stars. It takes awhile to adjust to the different perspective on landing but it comes, with a few bumps. There are three periods at night – 7:30 till 9:30, 9:30 till 11:30 and 11:30 till 1:30. I fly last tonight.

I passed my basic instrument check and so have finished instrument training for Basic. I am now ready to take up airobatics [sic] and formation. Then after filling out my time in solo flying I will enter my advanced training. I hope to see you all in March. I now have 45 hours of flying and will probably be finished or be so high in time that I will have two or three days off to spend in El Paso at Christmas time before beginning Advanced.

Yesterday everyone on the base took four huge Sulpha-Diazine pills. The pills are supposed to ward off the flu which has stricken quite a few. I feel fine so don't worry.

Say hello to everyone for me.

Yours,
Lee

When a mild flu epidemic swept through the country in the winter of 1943, Sulfa-Diazine, thought to be a preventive, was widely administered to the troops. The Army Air Corps could not afford to lose pilot training days. Lee managed to escape the flu, but could not get all the flying time he wanted as the boys who did get sick had priority on available planes.

Monday evening
December 20, 1943

Dear Bernice,

Today we cadets were permitted to indicate our choice for Advanced Flying Training. These choices will be weighted with recommendations by our instructors and the army needs-of-the-moment in assigning us for future training. I asked for B-26 medium bombardment, B-25 medium bombardment and Air Transport, in that order. I will soon know the result for Basic training ends January 7, 1944, and Advanced training begins on the ninth.

But then I am not yet through Basic notwithstanding my 54 flying hours; only seventy hours are necessary. I have yet to pass my transition check and [have] one hour more of dual instruction formation and acrobatics. But I should get by okay. I had an hour of formation yesterday (Saturday) and I must say that it is the most exacting as well as the most fun of any of my flying so far. Never must your eyes waver from the leader and always you must keep the formation intact from the moment you take off to the moment you land.

I am afraid I won't have my full time in by Christmas as I had hoped for I am being held down while flu patients and others catch up in their time. In fact, I have had time to tackle "Building the British Empire" by James Truslow Adams.

No package has come yet but that is probably because of the late mail rush. I'll try calling on Sunday. Until then have a good time at the formal and on Christmas.

Love,
Lee

Tuesday [December 21, 1943]

Dear Lee,

Well, I've caught something. . . I am going to get up tomorrow come Hell or high water. You're not catching me in bed another Christmas!

Shirley gets home about 8:00 tomorrow night. Daddy says that while she's home we're all going to take another excursion to New York. That is going to be lots of fun.

Sinatra is up at the Earle this week. The first night there the crowd booed him off the stage. He got mad and said whoever wanted to could come up and fight. Nobody did. Walt says he used to an amateur boxer. Maybe that's why.

We aren't going to have a very big tree this year and it's just as well, 'cause I know I could never untangle all those lights. Do you think you could go A.W.O.L [away without leave] just one night to get them straight?

Well, bub, have a nice Christmas and don't eat too much. You know we'll all be thinking of you, so don't feel lonesome. I hope your presents are just what you want and that Santa fills your stocking up to the top with love and kisses and happiness.

Merry Christmas,
Bernice

As Lee completed the first phase of pilot training, the 447th Bomb Group flew their first mission against Nazi Germany, joining a force of B-17s and B-24s dispatched to France Christmas Eve, 1943. The target was the launching ramp at Drionville for a new weapon (V-1 bomb) aimed just across the English Channel at London and Southampton. The British learned of the V-1 bomb, an early version of a cruise missile, from messages intercepted when they broke the highly secret German code, Enigma. There were no losses that day for the Eighth Air Force. Lee was lonely on his first Christmas away from home, his letter to his mother was sadly prophetic: "Maybe my next Christmas will be spent with you all, and then, maybe I will be across doing a job."

Christmas Day, 1943

Dear Mother,

I must admit that I am a little blue on my first Christmas day away from home. Maybe my next Christmas will be spent with you all, and then, maybe I will be across doing a job. But wherever I may be, you will be in my heart.

Because of rain yesterday we must fly on Sunday and are limited to a 100 mile radius from Pecos. However, flying will be finished this week as well as ground school so maybe we will have some time off around New Years.

I slept late this morning but finally got up to open my gifts. I am sorry to say that your package and that of Uncle Marion has not arrived as yet but I expect it soon as the mail gets caught up.

I hope you all had a good Christmas. Some photographs are coming as belated gifts. I wish that you would distribute them. My dinner was much like the old ones at home – good, and I had two drumsticks. I'll try to call you. Until then – Merry Christmas to you all.

Love,
Lee

Tuesday evening
December 28, 1943

Dear Dad,

It did me a world of good to hear you and the rest of the family over long distance last night. I hope that I didn't call after you had gotten into bed. I thought that maybe you would all be staying up for a call anyway, and I did want to wish you all a Merry Christmas, no matter how late. I placed my call to the base exchange at 6:47 P.M. so you see that there was quite a delay. The delay was accented by the fact that about thirty cadets were trying to get calls through on two phones. At 10:00 P.M. most of the boys had either completed their connection or yielded to the call of taps.

I opened your package this morning and am still wondering how in the world I will ever eat all of the cookies and candy so attractively packaged. But I must admit that the watch from you and Mother is my favorite gift. Thank you very much!

I finished my formation flying today and now have a total of 63 hours and 30 minutes. I will finish up by Friday. We finish ground school Thursday and go to the range Friday to fire the Colt 45 Caliber pistol and the Thompson Sub-Machine Gun.

That is the news from here. I hope you have a good time in New York.

Your son,
Lee

December 31, 1943

Dear Lee:-

Your pictures arrived this morning and they are fine. I think I like them even better than the ones sent from Santa Ana, for they look so natural. You do look so well and happy. It was the nicest thing [that] could have happened to us on the last day of the year, with the exception of having you in person with us.

I do hope everything we sent reached you in good condition. It surely made me feel badly that our box did not arrive for Christmas for it was sent two weeks before. But the damage can't be remedied now. Was the watch the kind you wanted, and did the gifts from your sisters arrive for it was sent a week later than my box? I do hope and pray that next New Year's eve we can all have a celebration together, -not only us but the whole world; that this war will be over and we can think of other things. Our very best to you, dear, and all my love.

Mother

On the last day of 1943 the 447th B.G. flew their third mission, suffering their second combat loss in two days. The first happened on December 30, 1943, when A/C # 42 31173 *Maid to Please*, piloted by Lieutenant Julian Y. Schrero, was observed 30 miles northeast of Paris, spinning down with one or more engines smoking badly, the result of a flak burst. Just after bombs away on the next day's mission to Cognac, France, A/C #42 31125 *No Regrets*, piloted by Lieutenant Milton R. Moore, spun down in flames evidently the result of a flak burst, and broke up in the air. Five chutes were reported, both crews were from the 711th squadron.

1943 closed with uncertainty – about the progress of the war and Lee's future. In Europe, 1944 would be a year of decision; the year of maximum effort on the part of the Allies. Lee finished basic flight training early in January, he didn't know which type of plane he would be assigned to fly. Advanced flight school and transitional flight school lay ahead of him, as did assignment to the European Theatre of Operations. Maximum effort would require more pilots than the Eighth Air Force could put in the air in 1943.

Chapter Six

A Pair of Silver Wings

January 4, 1944 - March 26, 1944

Dates: January 4, 1944 to March 26, 1944	**Location: Pecos, Texas Wilmington, Delaware**

Progression of Flight Training

Lincoln, NE	Santa Ana, CA	Thunderbird Field, AZ	Pecos, TX	Pecos, TX	Roswell, NM
College Training Attachment	Classification And Pre-flight	Basic Flight Training	Preliminary Flight Training	Advanced Flight School	Transitional
Piper Cub		Stearman	BT-17	Cessna AT-17	B-17

Jan. 2, 1944	Lee graduated from basic flight school. Advanced flight school training at Pecos Field.
Jan. 18, 1944	Ralph Minker, Sr. began work on the 4th War Bond Drive.
March 12, 1944	Lee Minker received his wings and a commission in the U.S. Army Air Corp.
March 13 – 22, 1944	The family celebrated Lee's brief furlough in Wilmington, Delaware.
March 22, 1944	Lee left Wilmington for Pecos, Texas to begin transitional training.

Early in 1944, the air war expanded with the relentless bombing of Germany and the creation of new air bases in England, leading to the buildup for D-Day and the invasion of France. With the availability of increasing numbers of P-51 Mustang fighters, for the first time the B-17 bombers could be escorted all the way into Germany. The fighters successfully defended the heavy bombers over the targets, aggressively shooting down *Luftwaffe* fighter planes. For Air Cadet Minker the new year started with a brief graduation ceremony from primary training; he stayed at Pecos Field when it was redesignated an Advanced Pilot School in early 1944. During this third phase of training, students flew the Cessna AT-17, the transition plane to two engine aircraft, a major step in learning to fly any of the military bombers.

Sunday noon
January 2, 1944

Dear Dad,

I have just finished lunch and just dressed in my Class A uniform in preparation for the graduation festivities of the last and largest Basic class of cadets. We are supposed to fall out at 1300 and march to the ramp. There among the old BTs we will listen to Colonel Barrett speak and then pass in review.

It scarcely seems possible that I am ready to start Advanced Flying Training –

That only two months away are a ten day graduation furlough, a pair of silver wings and an officer's commission in the United States Army Air Forces.

But there is plenty of hard work ahead of me before graduation day. I must fly over 100 hours in the AT-17. The big battle will be in the transition from single engine to double engine operation; half of my time will be as co-pilot in the comfortable five place cabin; night, formation, instrument and cross country flying will be accented along with fifteen hours of Link trainer.

Early in our Advanced training we will take mental exams. The results of these exams plus the material from each cadet's service record will determine who is to be commissioned a Flight Officer or a Second Lieutenant.

Sometime next week we are to be given another G4 physical examination. During the first week of Advanced we are supposed to order our officer's clothing at the Post Exchange we are measured and then asked which articles we wish to purchase. When the order is finally placed the ordering cadet gives the P.X. a promissory note which will be paid for in full out of the $250.00 uniform allowance of *each cadet. The uniforms are delivered just before graduation; if a cadet is eliminated the contract is torn up. The uniforms here are of serviceable, but not the best, quality and the selection is poor. As a result most of the boys are purchasing a minimum of clothing here. The rest they hope to buy while on furlough or at some future base. I don't know too much about the requirements but a complete outfit is supposed to cost up to $350.00 Pink and Green shirts and pants, officer's blouse and cap, coat, white silk scarf, shoes and accessories [sic] are required. It might be a good thing if you sort of kept an eye open around Wilmington. One article – the coats sold here are short coats. I would like a regular length grey topcoat (maybe reversible) which would be serviceable in civilian life. Please do not buy anything without checking with me first at least.*

Say hello to everybody for me.

Yours,
Lee

The Cessna AT-17 two engine trainer, Advanced Flight School.
Courtesy Collings Foundation

The two-engine Cessna advanced trainer transitioned student pilots from the single-engine planes of primary and basic training to the multiple-engine aircraft used for combat. In the AT-17 he would master a two-engine plane, increase his instrument flying skills, and be introduced to night and formation flying.

Tuesday Jan. 4, 1944

Dear Lee,

Gee, it seems funny to write 1944 at the beginning of a letter.

Today A.I. [Alexis I. du Pont High School] played its first [basketball] game with Ferris [Ralph Minker Sr. was Superintendent of Ferris School]. We really got a run for our money for the first time in years. We only beat them by about 10 points. At one point in the game the score was 25-23 in favor of Ferris.

Sunday night mother and Daddy had Dr. Betty and Edgar, Mr. and Mrs. Maxwell and the Herrings out for a get together and feed. Of course when they walked in the hall they admired the picture of Shirley and I which we gave Dad for Christmas. Then they saw yours and Shirley and I might as well have been dead for all the attention they paid to us.

Well, gotta go now, as I can't concentrate on Bob Hope and you both.

Lots of Love,
Bernice

Bernice, like much of the country, listened weekly to Bob Hope's radio show. Airing on Tuesdays from 10:00 – 10:30 p.m. and sponsored by Pepsodent, it was radio's highest-rated series during the war years. Hope's self effacing and easy going humor from Vaudeville days made him a star in the 1940s. On the show, Hope did a monologue and exchanged scripted barbs with guests such as Jack Benny and Judy Garland, concluding the program with a skit performed with Jerry Cologna, his sidekick with the handlebar mustache. In 1941 the *Bob Hope Show* aired from an Army Air Force Field for the first time. The show in Riverside, California was the beginning of a lasting relationship between Bob Hope and the U.S. fighting forces.

Shirley and Bernice Minker, photo from Christmas 1943.
Historic Society of Delaware

Thursday night
January 13, 1944

Dear Lee:

I've just got back from attending the graduation service of a Squadron of cadets over at the chapel. This is the first time that I have been able to go and I liked it very much. It sounded great to hear three hundred and fifty cadets joining in singing the Army Air Corps song. Tomorrow night a graduation dance is being held at the Acacia Club which is the Service Mens Club here in Williamsport. I'm going with a boy from Squadron D. It's the first time that I have been out with him so I don't know how it will work out. I'll probably have fun though because I'm going with Mimi McCloskey who is my "big sister" and lots of fun besides.

Last night I called home to ask mother about some important things. It feels so wonderful to pick up the phone and hear Bernice, mother, dad, and granny on the other end of the line. Are you going to call home this month at all? The connection when you called during Christmas vacation was so clear, it seemed even better than when you called from Carlisle sometimes.

Three of the girls from our house were engaged over X-mas holidays and so we don't feel like we are all deserted. When are you going to be engaged? I guess it will be when you get your wings! Heh! Heh! Have you met any really nice girls in all your travels around this country?

Well, Lee, this isn't such an interesting letter but there isn't too much interesting going on here. Take good care of yourself and write if you have a moment or two.

Lots of love and luck –
Shirley

Lee tried to call home once a month – as did millions of other stateside soldiers. The technology of the 1940s required that an operator manually make the connections needed to place a long distance call. With several hundred boys placing calls from Pecos, the wait at the base telephone center could take several hours. Telephone traffic was so heavy across the country during evening hours that the telephone company ran ads asking customers, "What's the Rush?... give 7 to 10 to the servicemen."

Bell Telephone Ad circa 1944

Sunday noon
January 16, 1944

Dear Dad,

Believe it or not we had six inches of snow fall here Thursday night. It was the first snow that I have seen in eleven months and it came as quite a surprise for the early part of the week had been spring like. But it vanished by Saturday noon before a warm west wind.

Group II is flying this afternoon in an attempt to get everyone soloed out as soon as possible. I will shoot landings today – regular, single engine and cross wind and tomorrow and should solo (with a student co-pilot) Tuesday or Wednesday. Then I can really bear down and master this plane.

The AT-17 is manufactured by Cessna of fabric and wood construction with two Jacobs 225 horsepower motors. It cruises at the very good speed of 160 miles per hour and does not stall until it falls to 40 miles per hour. It cruises on one engine at 90 miles per hour. A new feature to me is the retractable landing gear. The interior is richly furnished and has accomadations [sic] for three besides the pilot and co-pilot. It seems much like a family car and, in fact, the controls are worked by a steering wheel.

I can get no news at all about graduation. Maybe I can learn something from 44-B when they graduate in about two weeks but as for cutting time, the only thing to do seems to be to catch a plane out of Dallas on the thirteenth of March. This field is not so fortunate as to have Air Transport of Tactical ships, upon which I might get a hop, stop here. There is one very, very slim chance that the one other Eastern boy here (from New York) might have his father drive out for graduation and then the three of us would exchange shifts driving back. But an individual cadet can find out nothing yet.

As soon as possible I will send you my measurements and I wish that you would purchase a suitable long grey topcoat. That type coat will last for use after the war. Keep it in Wilmington for me though.

Say hello to everybody for me.

Yours,
Lee

The Fourth Bond Drive, mentioned in Edna's next letter, began on January 18, 1944 with a goal of raising \$14 billion. Ralph Minker Sr. was among the half million citizens who volunteered for war bond drive committees; he successfully led the bond drives in New Castle Country, Delaware. At the end of the campaign, \$16.7 billion in war bonds had been sold across the country. The eight bond drives conducted during WW II raised a total of \$185.7 billion to finance the war. Fifteen million Americans bought the U.S. Treasury Department bonds which paid 2.9 percent and matured in 10 years. (Samuel 1997)

Throughout WWII, posters were used to arouse strong emotions as the designers linked the home front with the military front to persuade Americans to buy bonds. Well known illustrators such as Ben Shahn, Norman Rockwell and others were recruited as illustrators for the government. Civilians such as Ralph Minker, Sr. were recruited as salesmen for the most successful mass marketing campaign in history.

Government poster urging citizens to buy war bonds.

January 28, 1944

Dear Lee:-

These days are crowded for both daddy and me. The

4th War Loan drive is now on and that means more activities for him. We are trying to get someone interested in coming out Sunday evenings to help put on worthwhile programs of handicraft, etc. in the cottages, especially for the younger boys. Our leadership is not what it should be and it worries him when things do not go as they should to help improve the boys who are sent here.

How is your advanced training coming along? According to the papers many flying schools are being closed up, as well as other army camps, because the peak of the training has been passed. I guess you have heard no more about the possibility of your getting a ride home with that boy from N.Y., have you?

It is now after 12 and I must stop for lunch. Take good care of yourself and write whenever you can. I'll try to get a box of cookies, etc. off to you sometime in the near future.

Lots of love,
Mother

Sunday evening
January 30, 1944

Dear Dad,

At this moment I am seated at a small maple writing desk in the Cadet Day Room writing letters to you, to Shirley and to Julia. At the same time I am hoping to complete a long distance call home to Wilmington.

Last evening I was best man at the wedding of Donald Harold Sites and Wilma Wittenberger. I have been with Hal ever since CTD at Nebraska and we have paled [sic] around together. Both he and the bride are from Boise,

Idaho, are alumni of the University of Idaho and are twenty years of age. They were childhood sweethearts and so the moment Mr. Sites decided to take a vacation from his lumber business it was also decided that Mr. And Mrs. Sites and Wilma would come to Pecos and that Hal and Wilma should marry. But don't worry; I have no definite plans along this line, as yet.

Early this morning the Cadet Area was fleeced – waletts [sic] were taken from pants of nearly everyone. Because of the Cadet Honor Code suspicion centers on some enlisted man, and even more so since a G.I. was apprehended at this same type of job about two months ago. But pay day is tomorrow. I only have about five dollars in my walett [sic] and so I wouldn't have missed it so much but the thief only lifted one pocket – the pocket containing my photos – with my complete address book, pictures and clippings. Maybe it will be thrown aside and found but in case it is forever lost I wish that you would:

1. *Send me my Christmas card list and any others that you can think of.*
2. *Search for old film negatives and have retakes made up.*
3. *Try to get three or four packs of film for new pictures for use when I get my graduation furlough.*

Have you been able to get any new slant about my graduation furlough or transportation home? Last week I contracted to purchase my minimum uniform at the Post Exchange. The total charge will be around $125.00 out of my $250.00 uniform allowance, about a third below outside prices. It is all good standard but I will need to add to it quite a bit.

Because the planes had to be overhauled last week I didn't fly many hours. I now have fifteen hours and have started formation and instrument flying. I will not fly at night this week as previously scheduled but will instead fly transition, cross country, instruments and formation. Two boys washed out last week by the way.

It doesn't look as if my call east will come through tonight. Maybe some future week night would be a better time to call.

As always,
Lee

P.S. One of the planes on the base flies all mail to El Paso hence the El Paso postmark on my letters.

Tuesday
February 1, 1944

Dear Bernice,

It has rained here in the western desert of Texas for two days without a letup. Naturally all flying has been called off but it was quite a surprise when Major Strayer announced an open post from noon Tuesday to noon Wednesday.

This afternoon I made final arrangements concerning my officer's uniform. Pertinent data:

Dark Green Blouse (Model Shop)	*$ 52.50*
Dark Green Trousers (MS)	*$ 22.50*
Dark Green Shirt (Post Exchange)	*$ 10.00*
Pink Shirt (PX)	*$ 10.00*
Pink Trousers (PX)	*$ 12.00*
Dark Green Crusher Cap (PX)	*$ 6.00*
Dark Green Flight Cap (PX)	*$ 1.75*
Grey Trench Coat (MS)	*$ 65.00*

Misc (Bars, wings, insignia,
Ties, belt) (PX)
Total for basic Winter Uniform $189.75

The prices are outrageous but there is no choice but to buy. That is why I have asked Dad to look around for summer uniforms. You may tell him that he can forget about looking for a trench coat or a dark green blouse. I will need a summer suntan blouse though, socks and the complete summer uniform. When I get home we can take inventory but I believe I am just about set for underclothes, shoes, flying equipment, toilette articles, etc.

Class 44-D will graduate from Pecos Advanced Flying Training School on Tuesday afternoon, February 8, 1944. I will study carefully – 1. Various assignments; 2. Furlough lengths; 3. Transportation facilities; 4. Number of Flight Officers; 5. Etc.

Monday I was paid $63.43. I had exactly $3.00 at the time. At graduation time I will receive of approximately $125.00 plus a $250.00 uniform allowance from which I must pay out almost $190.00. Between now and graduation I will spend $10.00; Today I spent $15.00 on a new walett [sic] and various toilet [sic] articles. If I have laid aside a surplus since purchasing my last war bond that surplus will be refunded as officers must buy bonds under another plan than that used for the men. (more paper! More work!) I should have about $225.00 from which to purchase transport home, have a furlough, buy a summer uniform, purchase transport to my transition base and last a month, until pay day.

Take care of yourself and study hard.

Love,
Lee

February 4, 1944

Dear Lee:

We were sorry to learn from your letter that you were not able to get a call through to us last Sunday night. I think Sunday is the safest night to call if you can. How about trying on February 13? So far as I know we will all be there,-- in fact if you say you will call then we will make it a point to be.

Too bad about the loss of those wallets. Over the weekend I will look around the house to see if we have any negatives which you would want developed. I was about to ask you to bring some films home when you come, for we haven't been able to get any lately. But I will try again and I've also written Shirley to be on the lookout. Sometimes she can get things in Williamsport which we cannot get here in Wilmington.

I would have liked to have looked in on the wedding last Saturday. Who was the more nervous, - the groom or you?

Lots of love,
Mother

Sunday noon
February 6, 1944

Dear Mother,

I hope that all of you at home will excuse me for not writing more often but it seems as if there is never any time, never a moment of my own. The ample amount of work seems to make the days fly by though. Although today is Sunday a regular full day schedule is being followed: Reveille [sic] at 0800; breakfast at 0805; ground school at

0850; physical training at 1150; lunch at 1300; flight line from 1345 till 1820; supper at 1830; night flight line from 1900 till 0030. I hope this will help to explain why I will not be able to call you this month.

But it won't be long before I will be home to see you all again. Class 44-b graduates in the morning of February 8, Class 44-C should graduate in the morning of March 12. So apply the evening train schedule for March 12 to your plans. It seems that as soon as the graduation ceremonies finish furloughs may be begun but that the army records show that the furlough begins March 13, an extra day is gained for the furlough. It also seems that several boys are getting the jump on the crowds and in time on Dallas by attempting to get reservations on an airliner at Big Springs on the thirteenth. It only costs $ 28.00 to fly from Big Springs to Louisville, Kentuckey [sic], by the way. There really isn't much new news from here on graduation, furlough, commission, uniform, etc.

I have twenty hours of co-pilot and twenty hours of pilot flying time to my credit now in every phase of flying. Yesterday I flew at 500 foot cross country—200 miles at 500 foot above the ground. Low navigation is quite different: you don't see an object until you are on it and then it whizzes by; radar cannot detect a low flying plane.

You know that I am always thinking of you.

Love,
Lee

Tuesday noon
February 8, 1944

Dear Mother,

Because of class 44-b graduation festivities I have quite a bit of free time today between marching in review and listening to speeches. However I will fly tonight.

I bought the trench coat because I must either have it or a short coat before leaving this field.

Please forget the long distance call this month. With my schedule I really don't have the time. I'll see what I can do about extra furlough time. Could you send some red roses to Julia for Valentine's Day.

Yours,
Lee

Thirteen months of writing letters, watching for the mail, and waiting for telephone calls were about to be over. In mid-March, their son would arrive home. As the days in February went by, anticipation filled the household like the flowers that would soon bloom in their spring garden. Pilot graduation (everyone hoped) and a furlough were now only a few weeks away. Lee remained uncertain about passing all the final tests, he would not know for sure until shortly before graduation.

February 11, 1944

Dearest Lee:-

I received a very lovely valentine this morning and want to thank you for taking the time out to send it. One arrived from Shirley, also. I did not get one off for you. The one you received from Bernice was what I intended to send, but she wanted it to go in her name, thinking I would get in to town to get another. But I have had no time off this week. I am sure you do not need to be told, however, that I am thinking of you on Valentine's Day and every other day of the year.

I find myself getting more excited each day as the time approaches for your coming home. I hope that most of the winter weather is over by that time so that will not interfere with any of our plans.

Love, from your valentine,

Mother

Monday noon
February 14, 1944

Dear Mother,

I have so little time for letter writing that often I forget to thank you and the rest of the family for your letters and packages. Please excuse me for truly there is nothing that I look forward to any more than mail from home.

Your proposed trip to New York sounds like a lot of fun but I would like to be in Wilmington most of Sunday so that I may see friends who may get home over the weekend and friends in church. And I really would like to attend a beautiful church service at Grace again. Maybe Dad and I can visit Dickinson and Williamsport one day. But most of all I just wish to live and rest with you all, visit old friends, see the Blue Bombers [basketball team] maybe and so on.

Yesterday we spent an hour in selecting and ordering graduation announcements, officer's cards and personal 201 files. I ordered twenty announcements at ten cents each and *one hundred cards at $ 2.75. The 201 file costs five dollars and contains a complete and official record of each officer's army career – service, duties, achievements, flying time.*

Saturday night we flew a cross country of three hours from Pecos to Midland to Wink to Salt Flat to Pecos. As soon as we returned we went up for an hour pilot and an hour co-pilot night formation. Finally we finished at about five in the morning. We slept until two Sunday afternoon, got up, ate and went to the flight line. There was a dust storm raging though and as we couldn't fly we just sat and talked in the ready room. Finally at nine Sunday evening, we were allowed to leave. The overabundance of such stupidity in the army is disgusting! It will take us most of this week to finish night flying but then we can concentrate on instruments, the one difficult phase of Advanced Flying Training.

Love,
Lee

Army Air Forces
Advanced Pilot School
at
Pecos Army Air Field
Pecos, Texas
announces the graduation of
Class 44-C
Sunday morning, March twelfth
Nineteen hundred and forty-four
at ten o'clock
Sub Depot Hangar

Announcement of Advanced Flight Training graduation
Courtesy Historical Society of Delaware

Tuesday noon
February 29, 1944

Dear Mother,

I have been in active service with the United States Army Air Forces for one year and four days. In twelve days time I hope to graduate from aircrew training. The past year has been quite an experience. If and when I graduate I will be commissioned a Second Lieutenant.

This morning a ground fog blew into Pecos just as flying was scheduled to begin and so there was no flying. Everyone is beginning to wonder if we will ever get our flying in. I must fly ten hours more of instruments, three hours of day navigation and four hours of night formation before March twelfth.

This morning I was paid $89.75; March twelfth I will be paid a $250.00 uniform allowance and about $20.00 cadet salary for March. I now have $23.25 in my walett. [sic] All this money totals up to $383.00. From this total I must pay for uniforms, transportation home and miscelaneous [sic] expenses. I believe that I can make ends meet but it would be smart to play safe. You will receive no more war bonds for a while, by the way. But I will explain my new financial status in detail when I get home. I have no news about travel time or transport home. I will only buy two sets of suntans (cotton) here.

Love,
Lee

Sunday
March 5, 1944

Dear Lee: --

Well, I guess this is the last time I'll be writing to you while you are out there. I can't really believe that by this time next week you will be graduated and starting on your way home. I do want you to know that I'd give anything to see you get your Wings next Sunday, but even if I can't be there I'll be thinking of you. I want you to know that I'm so very proud of you and that all of us are! I know that when you started out in the Air Corps we knew you would be up against some tough work, but even though you have had some tough going you've come through fine. I'm so darn proud of you that all I do is boast about my brother around here 'til all the girls are sick!

I'm hoping that I'll get a phone call from home tonight because I usually do after marks come out! I'm so glad that you were able to get a call through last week but I wish I had been there!

Well, it's time for supper now, so I'm really afraid that I'll have to close! Have a grand time at your graduation and I'll be seeing you soon. Remember me to all your buddies and the best of luck to all of you! See you soon!

Lots of luck and love
Shirley

Their air cadet's last letter from Pecos to Wilmington is both hopeful and nervous. In thirteen months he made five moves across the country and had taken check flights in a succession of airplanes from the Piper Cub to the two engine Cessna AT-10.

Now only an instrument check remained. Still Lee had misgivings, would he be eliminated or pin on the silver wings?

Sunday evening
March 5, 1944

Dear Dad,

If dust storms and overcasts ever relax their grip on Texas weather and if I can manage to pass the 50 – 3 instrument check during this coming week I will graduate from Flying Training as a Second Lieutenant pilot in the Army Air Forces next Sunday, March 12, 1944, in ceremonies at 10:00 A.M. in the Sub-Depot Operations Hanger.

If ----------------------! Three times since going into active duty with the Air Forces I have had an attack of the jitters about the future: 1. In Santa Ana classification; 2. Just before my first flying check at Thunderbird; 3. During the last ten days of Advanced Flying training. I hope I can make the grade.

If I am lucky I should arrive in Wilmington early Wednesday, March fifteenth. First upon arrival I want to see all the family, eat breakfast at home. Soon I want to arrange for purchase of a complete suntan uniform, a trench coat (delivery is not yet certain here), extra pinks and greens, military socks and a pair of shoes. Thursday and Friday I can rest and visit, maybe go to Carlisle and Williamsport. Saturday we can all go to New York and Sunday return for church! Blue Bombers and a day at home together. I am afraid that by Monday I will have to leave home again for operational transition training. This furlough I think about all the time. I do wish that I could see Julia but I am afraid that is impossible.

This will be the last word until I know yes or no about graduation.

Lee

Graduating with the largest aviation cadet class in history on March 12, 1944, Lee Minker received a pair of silver wings and a commission as a second lieutenant. Colonel Orin J. Bushey, commanding office of Pecos Army Air Field, told the graduating class: "The successful completion of this strenuous course is ample proof that you are fit for the job ahead of you. As fellow officers and pilots in the Army Air Forces, I wish you success in your every venture and many happy landings."

Everyone in the Minker household regretted not being able to attend the ceremony. Ralph Sr. was particularly wistful about missing this milestone in his son's life and Shirley sent her brother a congratulatory telegram. Upon graduation, Lee recalls, the cadets threw their caps in the air and then scattered – at long last a furlough home. (Stevenson 2000)

Silver pilot's wings from graduation.

A classmate from Virginia who had a car offered Lee a ride to the east coast. They planned to drive non-stop, leaving right after the ceremony. An early morning flat tire on a rural Tennessee road caused a delay. Even for two boys in uniform, it was not easy to replace a tire in 1944. The young lieutenants walked into town and were on their way again by five o'clock. (Stevenson, 2000) They drove across the Shenandoah mountains in the early morning of March 15, and onto Washington D. C. where Lee took a crowded train home to Wilmington. We can only imagine the excitement in the Minker household that morning, waiting for Lee's arrival after the long absence.

Edna Minker, Lee Minker, Ralph Minker, Sr. March 20, 1944.
Grandma Jones is leaning out the front window.
Courtesy Historical Society of Delaware

A soldier on leave had to cram a lot into a few days: home cooked meals, sleeping past 5 a.m. in a bed that wasn't a bunk, and time with family. There was never enough time to see all the friends, high school teachers, and family members who called or dropped by the house. Among the pictures taken during that first leave is a photograph of the newly commissioned second lieutenant with his parents while grandmother Jones peeks out the window. And when the furlough was over, Edna's letter echoed the feeling of mothers all over the country, "...this morning you are gone again."

Wednesday, March 22, 1944

Dearest Lee:

I seem to be walking around in circles this morning, not being able to settle down to anything for very long. This time last week we were all excited about your coming home, and this morning you are gone again. I realize it is best for you, as far as training is concerned, not to have frequent or long furloughs; but nevertheless we miss you terribly and are looking forward to the day when this mess will be over and you will be home once more to stay. I hope the days were not too hectic for you,- that you were able to relax some and to enjoy yourself, also. We are very proud of the way you have come along in the air force and hope that after the war you will be able to get some "fun" out of all your training and experience. We'll have to begin now to save up our pennies to buy a plane.

I am sending your bag off on the 1 o'clock trip today.

Well, there isn't much news, of course, but I did want you to know that it was grand to have you home again. Here's hoping that you will soon be allowed to come back. With all my love.

Mother

March 22, 1944

My dear Lee:-

I will be interested to know if you got your reservation West of Chicago. I hope it was O.K., and that you had a reasonably comfortable trip. I wish I could have made it with you. Perhaps we'll do it together some day.

You realize, I know, how much it meant to us to have you home. Thirteen months was an awful stretch of time – and I never thought we could stand it. But we did, and we pulled for you and prayed for you every day. It was a wonderful day for us when you stepped off the train to be with us. We were pretty proud, of course, because you had done so well but we were just happy to have you regardless of the distinction you had achieved.

I don't know whether I congratulated you on receiving a commission. I wish I could have been at the graduation. I was there in spirit. Just about the time you were receiving your wings I stepped out of the pulpit at Westminster, and said to Mr. Warren and Bruce – "I wish I was in Pecos this minute. Lee is graduating." You did a fine job, and I am proud of you – prouder than I can say. I knew you could do it because you were just yourself – and I'm happy to think you realized your goal.

I hope you enjoyed the minutes at home as much as we did. I'll know a little better how to plan a few parties the next time –but I did the best I could. They were really fine basketball games, weren't they? You can think of them for a while. And that family dinner! And Uncle Marion's waistline! Ginger's [the family's German Shepherd] shyness before the camera! Our budding Minker debutantes! The time certainly did fly. I am so glad you didn't have to leave Sunday. The extra days just helped us to round out the visit properly.

We'll be thinking of you as you start your new phase of training. Good luck every minute!

As always --
Dad

Wednesday evening
March 22, 1944

Dear Mother,

I have time to write you a line or two from the Dearborn Station of the Santa Fe, Atchison and Topeka Railroad in Chicago. A three hour wait on my part has just been rewarded with reservations through Clovis, New Mexico, on the train leaving here at 10:05 P.M. tonight. After passing through Kansas City tomorrow I will attempt to transfer my reservation to one of the cars which will be switched off from the regular train at Winatha, Oklahoma, for the run to Roswell New Mexico; otherwise I will have to get up at 3:00 A.M. to switch trains.

I hope you will excuse the bad penmanship but I am using my left knee as a writing table. My new pen writes very well.

Friday night I will write and let you know all about my new situation. I wish that I could have been with you all longer for I had a wonderful furlough "delay en route" but my job can't wait. I will be looking forward to seeing you again.

Love,
Lee

March 26, 1944

Dear Lee:-

Things seem rather dull around here today, compared with last Sunday. I felt it first this morning when I had to sit in church alone, after having had you and Shirley by my side last week. And then when we sat down to dinner four seemed such a small number compared with last Sunday's dinner guests.

Daddy said something about thinking it best to have your savings account made a joint account, in case you needed money for something in a hurry. I deposited $45.00 on Friday. There isn't much news, but I thought you might like to hear from home anyhow. After folks get your new address you will be receiving more letters. Take good care of yourself and remember we are all pulling for you.

With all my love.
Mother

Sunday afternoon
March 26, 1944

Dear Lee: --

It's the loveliest spring day here today and about five of us are out on the back porch in shorts writing letters. I guess you are pretty well settled in your new home now and beginning to work. It was so nice to be home together for a few days but the next time I will see what I can do ahead of time to see about the "date" situation. I had a lovely ride back on the train and it snowed all the way. I was really glad to see dear old Williamsport again and all the girls.

Lee, whatever happened to you after you left me at the station? Mother wrote and said that you came home and were sick all over the place. She said she thought it was the accident but that I probably know more about it! What <u>*accident*</u> *did you ever get into and why involve me? Please explain because my curiosity is killing me!*

We're all going for a walk now, so this is going to be short. Let me hear as soon as you get settled and tell me all the news. Bye now!

All my love -
Shirley

Neither Shirley or Lee recalled what the "accident" during the furlough was about, it remains a family mystery. He left the next day on the train for Chicago, heading back to the west for the introduction to the B-17 at Pecos Army Air Field, Texas.

While Lee was on leave in Wilmington, his soon-to-be comrades in the 447th B.G. flew missions aimed at weakening German air power; hitting aircraft plants at Augsburg, Munich, Brunswick and Munster in Germany, and airfields in Merignac and Chartres, France. While not as devastating as the missions in 1943, loss rates continued to be high. At the end of March 1944, after just three months of combat, the 447th B.G. had lost 32 aircraft and 24 crews. (*447th Bomb Group Comparative Data on Monthly Operations,* March 1944, National Archives)

Chapter Seven

She Sure is a Sweet Ship

March 23, 1944 – July 2, 1944

Dates: March 23, 1944 – July 2, 1944	Location: Roswell Army Air Field Roswell, New Mexico

Progression of Flight Training

Lincoln, NE	Santa Ana, CA	Thunderbird Field, AZ	Pecos, TX	Pecos, TX	Roswell, NM
College Training Attachment	Classification And Pre-flight	Basic Flight Training	Preliminary Flight Training	Advanced Flight School	Transitional
Piper Cub		Stearman	BT-17	Cessna AT-17	B-17

March 23, 1944	Lee arrived at Pecos Army Air Field for transitional training.
April 3, 1944	Lee took his first flight in a B-17, known as the "Flying Fortress."
June 6, 1944	Allied troops landed in Normandy on D-Day.
June 16, 1944	Lee turned 20 years old.
Mid June, 1944	Lee was able to stop in Wilmington for a few days on his way to Tampa, Florida.
June 27, 1944	Lee left Wilmington for Tampa, Florida to begin preparation to go overseas.

The furlough and the family had to be put behind him when Lee once again boarded a train to go across the country, this time to Roswell, New Mexico. At Roswell Army Air Field he would make the considerable jump from the two engine AT-10 aircraft to the four engine B-17. The exhilaration of that first flight leaps off the page of his April 3 letter: "Today I flew a Flying Fortress!" The subsequent flights in the B-17 proved to be more grueling than exhilarating. To pilot the B-17 a student had to master a formidable list of skills: night and formation flying, instrument and solo flying, bomb approach, high altitude and cross country navigation flying.

The WW II B-17 evolved from the original Boeing Model 299 developed in 1935. A number of changes came as the result of early combat experience, which added more armor and guns. The B-17G that rolled out in May 1943 added a chin turret and bristled with firepower: 12 Browning .50 caliber machine guns, a veritable "flying fortress." The final version of the B-17 to enter service, the B-17G became the premier Army Air Corps bomber in the European Theater. This was the plane that would ultimately overwhelm German air defenses.

B-17Gs on the Boeing production line.
The U.S. aircraft industry produced 8,620 B-17Gs in less than two years.

OFFICERS' CLUB
Roswell Army Air Field
Roswell, New Mexico

Monday evening April 3, 1944

Dear Bernice,

Today I flew a Flying Fortress! At 5:30 this morning I went to the flight line to be assigned a transition instructor and to fly the Boeing B-17 for the first time. Lieutenant Jerry Minia of St. Paul and I were assigned to Lieutenant Paul Standage of Phoenix and at 6:00 the three of us were conducting a pre-flight inspection of Anita before going into the blue. Jerry and I alternated at the controls for four hours and 45 minutes of intensive work. I shot seven landings and practiced stalls, climbs, glides and steep and shallow turns. By the end of the period I was really worn out for during the constant maneuvering [sic] every muscle in the body was at work and every pore sweated. For the Fort is a big plane – combat weight 70,000 pounds, wingspan 104 feet, four 1750 horsepower engines, a cruising speed of 250 miles per hour which, above 20,000 feet, figures out to some 350 miles per hour ground speed and which enables it to out climb any fighter at that altitude, most heavily defended bomber with its ten gunners, the most stable bombing platform – big plane or small – in the world, the only plane in the United States Army which is not restricted from flying through thunderstorms. I only hope that I can sweat this transition period through for she sure is a sweet ship even though I damn her for all I am worth when I am holding her straight and level by sheer will power during two and three engine practice.

This past weekend I traveled to Carlsbad, New Mexico, to visit the noted caverns about which you will be receiving ample literature soon. The journey of eighty miles, three hours by Greyhound Bus, was taken with my three roommates – Alfred Murphy and Warren Morris of El Dorado, Kansas, and Robert Todd of Joliet, Illinois. We had a grand time. The caverns were most impressive.

I must give a line or two of credit to the food served here. It is of the finest quality and of any desired quantity. Even ice cream and cake twice a day.

Let me hear from you all.

Love,
Lee

P.S. Please give the enclosed check to Mother.

P.P.S. Get my address right. No mail is coming through.

P.P.S.S. My B-4 bag arrived safe and sound.

P.P.P.S.S. We should get paid this week.

P.P.P.S.S.S. I think that's all.

OFFICERS' CLUB
Roswell Army Air Field
Roswell, New Mexico

Monday evening
April 3, 1944

Dear Bernice,

Today I flew a Flying Fortress! At 5:30 this morning I went to the flight line to be assigned a transition instructor and to fly the Boeing B-17 for the first time. Lieutenant Jerry Minia of St. Paul and I were assigned to Lieutenant Paul Standage of Phoenix and at 6:00 the three of us were conducting a pre-flight inspection of Anita before going into the blue. Jerry and I alternated at the controls for four hours and 45 minutes of intensive work. I shot seven landings and practiced stalls, climbs, glides and steep and shallow turns. By the end of the period I was really worn out for during the constant manuevering every muscle in the body was at work and every pore sweated. For the Fort is a big plane — combat weight 70,000 pounds, wingspan 104 feet, four 1750 horsepower engines, a cruising

Page one of Lee Minker's letter describing his first flight in a B-17. Courtesy Historical Society of Delaware

The sheer physical effort it took to fly the B-17 hounded Lee throughout the spring of 1944. His view rapidly changed from "She sure is a sweet ship" on April 3, to "the damn truck we fly" by April 17. Immersed in classroom work and the demands of flying, Lee still found time to send a corsage to his mother for Easter. Edna wore the flowers on Easter Sunday along with the aviator wings he had given her after graduation from Pecos Field.

Monday, April 10, 1944

Dear Lee:-

Yesterday was a beautiful Easter day with one exception, that you were not with us. Late Saturday afternoon I received a gorgeous corsage of gardenias from you so that yesterday I was very much dressed up indeed, with a new coat decorated on one side with my Wings and the other by the flowers. You don't know how much it meant to me to have you remember me in such a lovely way.

Your bank book is at the house, of course, so I can't tell you now how your account stands. Daddy thinks it would be a good investment to get you some building and loan shares. I think he said by paying $5 a month (5 shares) at the end of 11 years you would have $1,000.

With the terrible strain of flying a fortress it does not seem that you will put on much weight while there.

Did you get your box of candy in time for Easter? Daddy has your shirt and the trousers are supposed to be ready today. If they are I will get them right off to you.

Lots of love to you, and eat plenty of that good food to keep you going under such a strenuous schedule.

Mother

The 1944 campaign for the presidency took place at the height of the war. Even with the demands of his flying schedule, Lee Minker followed the campaign. He shared an intense interest in politics with his dad, commenting on Wendell Wilkie's loss to Thomas Dewey in the Wisconsin primary. Wilkie had run against Roosevelt in 1940, and hoped this was his political comeback. Thomas Dewey, Governor of New York, went on to win the nomination, but lost the election. The country would prove unwilling to change leaders while the war continued.

OFFICERS' CLUB
Roswell Army Air Field
Roswell, New Mexico

Thursday evening
April 17, 1944

Dear Dad,

Tonight the world seems unreal to me for I am tired and lonely. Last week section "J" of which I am a member, was selected for accellerated [sic] B-17 transition training, flying and ground school every day so that it will finish training by May sixth. Since then a third of the group have been eliminated for flying deficiency. The constant pressure, the lack of sleep and the always blowing dust is all that is felt except for the blazing hatred of the damn truck we fly. But I do hope I can make the grade.

I must get some sleep as I must fly at 4:40 tomorrow morning but first I will write down a few thoughts.

The general opinion among my colleagues is that Wilkie will not be missed. Roosevelt should be president again unless something breaks this summer; then Dewey should represent the people.

Just what summer clothing is being shipped from Wilmington?

I have filed my first income tax return and sent in my first quarterly payment of $14.05.

Hal Sites, Pecos groom, is a basic instructor at Merced, California. Grandmother Minker wrote. I will never get my correspondence up to date again.

But don't worry about me, I'll make out alright.

Lee

Friday, April 21, 1944

Dearest Lee:

Your letter, written Monday evening, arrived this morning. It's a wonder to me that anyone ever survives to become a pilot, the grueling pace one has to keep up. You say they are trying to push you thru so you will finish transition training by May 6. Does that mean you will then leave Roswell for Salt Lake City, or have those plans been changed? Is there any chance of your getting home again between transfers? I do hope you get away from all that sand and heat before summer time.

It is pouring rain again today. I'll try to get you some paper the first chance I have to get in town. Get as much rest as you possibly can, for you need it to stand up under the strain; and don't try to answer everyone's letters. They ought to understand that you are a very busy person.

With all my love.
Mother

Edna was concerned about the strenuous schedule, finding it difficult to imagine her slightly built son flying the massive B-17. The strain of flying, the continual checks on progress, and the blowing dust of New Mexico whirled together, leaving Lee tired and lonely. Before he could qualify for assignment, transitional training required 105 hours in the B-17. The student pilots carried no crew while learning how to handle the heavy plane. The course and the number of required hours had been compressed from 125 to 105 hours in response to the pressure for heavy bomber crews. (Cameron 1999)

Within five months Lee would be stationed at Rattlesden Air Field in England with the 447th Bomb Group. A ground disaster struck the group on the morning of April 21, 1944. As the crews walked to the mission briefing that morning, they heard a violent explosion on the runway. While loading bombs made with a new type of explosive, aircraft 42-39864 (709th) on hardstand #16 blew up with the loss of 13 ground and air personnel. (Shields 1996) Ground crews continually faced the hazards of working with explosives and munitions while loading 40 to 60 tons of bombs onto the four squadrons' planes in the early morning hours before a mission.

OFFICERS' CLUB
Roswell Army Air Field
Roswell, New Mexico

Tuesday afternoon
April 25, 1944

Dear Bernice,

I have time to write a word or two between P.T., [physical training] supper, and night flying. Yesterday I passed my B-17 instrument check. Tonight I will be checked out for night solo flying and tomorrow afternoon for day solo flying. I will then have a total of fifty transition flying hours to my credit and the chief flying requirements passed. Finishing phases of this transition flying will be solo instruments, dual and solo formation, dual high altitude, dual bombing and solo cross country. The rumor is strong that we will get a long cross country over Saturday and Sunday. I only wish that Wilmington was within range.

Mother mentions that Grandmother had her 72nd birthday yesterday. I wish I could have been there for the celebration but please give her my best wishes.

Ask Dad about my suntans: are any matching G.I. pair coming? Are any gaberdine [sic] or tropical worsted dress suits coming? I just want to know so that I can plan to purchase what I need here. We get paid next week.

Yours,
Lee

April 25, 1944

Dear Lee: -

The sun is shining once more here at home and it certainly is welcome. Practically all day yesterday and until late last night it rained "cats and dogs". Some of the roads have had to be closed today because they are flooded.

So much talk about "D" day over the radio, in the newspapers, is getting on one's nerves. I hope it is similarly effecting the Germans. Plans are being made for most of the churches to be open for a day of prayer when the invasion really has begun.

Have you seen the picture "Memphis Belle"? It is put out by the war department I believe and is being shown in several of the Wilmington theaters this week. I don't know whether you shall have a chance to see it or not. As perhaps you know, it is the actual pictures taken on a raid of American planes over Germany. You don't have to be told, of course, that I am thinking of you all the time and praying for the end of the war. However, I cannot see much hope of its ending for a long, long time. Take the best care of yourself.

With all my love.
Mother

The loss of bomber crews on an almost daily basis put more and more pressure on the Army Air Corps Training Command for replacement crews. Some raids incurred relatively few causalities, others had devastating results. On the April 29, 1944 mission to Berlin, the 447th B.G. lost 11 of the 29 planes that left Rattlesden that morning. Ten crews went down over Germany, two of which were on their first mission, and one more was lost on the way back to the base. Thirty-eight men were reported killed in action (KIA) on this Berlin raid. (Warfle 1996) Given that pilot training required 400 hours of flight time and took a year or more, the training command could not immediately provide the number of pilots needed by the Eighth Air Force in Europe.

Friday afternoon
April 28, 1944

Dear Lee:--

How's the flyin' business coming along 'way out there? I heard of several people being scalped by big planes out in New Mexico. You couldn't be up to your old tricks, could you Looey?

Gee, it's a beautiful day here! The sky is so clear and blue and I think maybe it might be a nice week-end. Last week-end I went home with Mimi and two other Sophs. She lives in Roaring Spring which is about thirty miles from Altoona. We had a wonderful time because we had been having tests all week and it was beginning to show on all of us. Roaring Spring is a typical small town, it's surrounded by mountains but I guess they wouldn't seem very high after those you've seen out there! I sang the "Lord's Prayer" in church and quite enjoyed doing it!

Honestly Lee, this Air situation is really getting awful. There are only two squadrons left here now and one of them was supposed to have left three weeks ago. They only have a few hours of P.T. and drill and then just sit around. Fred is doing the very same thing out in California. He says they don't have a darn thing to do and they seem to have no plans made for them at all. Girls that write to the other fellows all over the country say that they same thing is true everywhere. I wish they hadn't gotten into such a mess, because think of all the time, money and men they are wasting. Do you know anything about this or isn't it happening in the ranks of the officers? Today the boys here played tennis and baseball all morning and they talk about the tough Army life!

The movie "See Here, Private Hargrove" is here this

week-end. I want to see it because if it is anything like the book it should really be wonderful! Did I tell you that I finally got to see "For Whom the Bell Tolls." It was only here three days and we had to squeeze it in between tests. I think it was every bit as wonderful as they said it was! Ingrid Bergman with that short hair-cut and no make-up looks like a million dollars. She is really a wonderful actress and Gary Cooper did well, too!

Well, let me hear how you are getting along out there, Lee? I know you're busy so don't worry because mother sends me all the news. I hear you're supposed to be through there on May 6. Where to then, huh? Bye now, Looey.

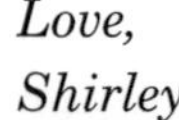

Love,
Shirley

The Girl's Sextet at Dickinson Junior College 1944
Shirley Minker is the last girl on the right.
Courtesy Lycoming College Archives

Which plane would Lieutenant Minker be assigned to fly? The heavy bombers included the B-17, B-24, and B-29. His first choice was the B-17, the demands of the air war in Europe and the Pacific would be the deciding factor. If assigned to the European Theatre, he would most likely fly the B-17; if assigned to the Pacific he would likely fly the longer range B-24 or B-29. Lee reported to his dad that transition training finished ahead of schedule, and that a third of the class had washed out. The Army invested heavily in pilot training, young men shouldered great responsibilities – only the most capable would command a plane and a crew.

OFFICERS' CLUB
Roswell Army Air Field
Roswell, New Mexico

Sunday evening
April 30, 1944

Dear Dad,

I now have sixty hours of flying a B-17 to my credit and have passed my instrument and solo checks. All I have to do now as I complete my transition training is to fill in time requirements for night, formation, instrument solo, bomb approach, high altitude and cross country navigation flying. Shipping orders may be announced at any time during the next thirty days for our transition training will be finished ahead of schedule, it was fast but thorough; a third of our class has been eliminated. As usual, when a shipping date draws near, rumors abound, but as far as I can see it seems as if I will ship to Lincoln Army Air Field, Lincoln, Nebraska, (not Salt Lake City) for assignment to an operational unit for approximately twelve weeks of final training with combat crew and plane before flying to war as: 1. First pilot of a B-17; 2. First pilot of a B-24 (since B-17 production is now B-29 production); 3. Co-pilot of a B-29.

Two things grippe me in considering the future: 1. That I have to fly planes that are a chore to maneuver; [sic] 2.

That I will not participate in the European invasion.

If you have a chance it would be worth your while to see "The Memphis Belle", the Air Forces movie of a bombing mission over Germany. Some of the combat planes shown probably came from Roswell for planes fresh from the factory are sent here for a breaking in period before being assigned to a combat crew. I wish I could show you a Fort and take you for a ride in one. I am sure that you would find it most interesting riding in a 40,000 to 70,000 pound four fan 4,800 horsepower combat bomber. The B-17 was originally designed in 1929, first built in 1935 as an experiment – a four-engine bomber, a bomber that could defend itself. If the Fort were allocated four 2,200 horse engines it would today be the fastest yet for when she gets up to 25,000 feet her ground speed she can register a ground speed of 300 miles per hour. The Fort has a crew of ten, six gun stations, and reserve oxygen systems, 27,000 gallon fuel capacity, eight-ten bomb capacity, wing deicing system, prop anti-icing system, four turbo superchargers, Hamilton Standard three bladed hydromatic adjustable pitch propellers on Wright Cyclone fans, life raft, emergency flares, main and emergency hydraulic brake system, main and alternative vacuum system, six escape hatches, main and emergency electric, in short, everything conceivable to insure a perfect bombing mission against all emergencies.

Tell Mother that I received her cookies and they were fresh and delicious. Also tell her that I would like two links removed from my identification bracelet.

Tomorrow I get paid $268.25. I will pay $35.00 for board, buy a pair of shoes, two towels, a half dozen socks and a gabardine dress summer uniform and work uniforms. After all is taken care of I will send the rest home.

Yours,
Lee

Lee hoped his parents would see the movie *Memphis Belle*, to help them understand the work he would be doing. Produced by the army and directed by Major William Wyler as a training film, the *Memphis Belle* told the story of "...just one mission of just one plane and one crew in one squadron in one group of one wing of one Air Force out of fifteen United States Army Air Forces." The movie gave new B-17 crews a realistic appreciation of what it was like to be in combat, the actual aerial combat footage was shot during several different missions. It took seven months of flying for the *Memphis Belle* and her crew, commanded by Lieutenant Robert K. Morgan, to be the first to survive 25 missions and return safely to the U.S. The crew of the *Memphis Belle* exemplified the courage and fortitude of the men of the Eighth Air Force, which Lee would join in just five months.

May 2, 1944

Dear Lee:-

We scanned every bomber that passed near here over the week-end, hoping vainly, of course, but hoping just the same to sense some how it was you. Perhaps you didn't take your trip after all. Anyhow, you might as well know we were flying too.

The best to you in this strenuous part of your training! You've done a great job – you've taken everything they've given, and you've proved to yourself that you have the thing that life takes. We'll have a great time after this business is over—getting into even great jobs- and doing them the way you will be able to do them.

Goodnight – and God bless you –

Dad

OFFICERS' CLUB
Roswell Army Air Field
Roswell, New Mexico

Sunday noon
May 7, 1944

Dear Mother,

This is a birthday letter to you from your son. I wish that I could be home in Wilmington so that I could personally wish you a happy birthday, but this letter will have to speak for me during my necessary absence. May my mother have the happiest of birthdays and may she enjoy many more in a world of peace and cooperation.

I have now completed the regular transition training but prospects for the future are uncertain. 44-4-B class boys are still waiting for orders so it seems as if our schedule will continue until orders come for shipping, thus we will not get rusty. The cross country scheduled last weekend was cancelled at the last moment by the way.

The last two days have been a sample of what to expect in the line of summer weather in New Mexico. The temperature has been up to 95 F.

While flying yesterday I tuned in the Kentucky Derby on the liason [sic] set radio. Often while flying we listen to the powerful liason [sic] receiver. We can receive all United States regular channel stations and short wave as well. The St. Paul regular station, San Francisco government short wave and radio Tokyo transmit the most popular programs. Tokyo Rose offers the best music and most amusing comments.

Happy Birthday,
Lee

The infamous Tokyo Rose appeared on *The Zero Hour*, broadcast from Japan as part of their psychological propaganda campaign. The program featured popular American music, interspersed with supposedly menacing commentary: *"Hello boneheads… Are you enjoying yourselves while your wives and sweethearts are running around with the 4F's in the States? How do you feel now when all your ships have been sunk by the Japanese Navy? How will you get home? Here's another record to remind you of home."* Soldiers enjoyed the music and laughed at the Japanese attempts to undermine their morale. They named the many Japanese female broadcasters, Tokyo Rose.

May 16, 1944

Dearest Lee:-

It surely was grand to be awakened at 2 in the morning and to hear daddy yell "It's Lee". Shirley had called earlier in the evening – about 11, saying she was broke and needed some money as soon as possible. I do wish you could work a furlough. I am so glad you are able to keep well, however, and I will not worry if you cannot get home.

With all my love.

Mother

The excitement over the occasional phone call from Lee resonated throughout the Minker household. He needed to talk with them as much as the family needed to hear his voice. For millions of families all over the country, letters were the mainstay of communication, but phone calls – no matter what the hour – were always welcome.

OFFICERS' CLUB
Roswell Army Air Field
Roswell, New Mexico

Thursday
May 18, 1944

Dear Dad,

It cheered me up immensely to talk with you and the rest of the family Monday evening. At times the military life gets extremely boring. For instance, this week class 44-4-C carries a full schedule even though regular transition training has been completed. It is a fuller schedule consisting of my fifth first aid course as a member of the Air Forces (again all lecture and no practical application such as in Boy Scout or Red Cross training), dull lectures on various phases of administration (finance, mess, supply, command, operations, operational training, travel, sanitation, VD, conduct in foreign countries, assignment, etc.), physical training and formal retreat. The schedule will be kept full of fillers until we are shipped to another base but it will all be ground material which will be comparatively useless in aerial combat. There are ninety odd B-17's stationed at Roswell but only forty are allowed in the air at a time, regardless of the type of missions to be flown. If one has completed his required 105 hours of transition flying he is not eligible to fly more hours. One fifth of our class has been lucky enough to ship for operational training as first pilots on B-29's. But they are old instructors and B-25 shore patrol pilots with totals of at least one thousand hours of flying time. The rest of us have met the same requirements that they have but we idle away twiddling our thumbs.

However, we were scheduled to complete transition training on June 6, 1944, before the schedule was accelerated. Thus we are not behind the original schedule. Maybe the shift of production from the Boeing B-17 to the Boeing B-29 has caused a temporary lag in B-17 – B-29 training. Maybe we are feeling the results of overestimating the manpower needs for the Air Forces. But then, maybe we are feeling the results of unrestricted and thoughtless strikes against war production, such as the recent foremen's strike which caused the loss of 250 P-51 fighter planes which have needlessly and dangerously prolonged the length of the war and increased immeasurably the problems of postwar resettlement.

Major Haan, Commandant of pilot students, said that he did not expect that class 44-4-C would ship to new jobs before July and that he had been ordered to outline a schedule for us to fill in for two months. So ----------------- !

I see by the Journal that you now have another job – war bond salesman. Congratulations. But after the campaign is over why don't you get away from all the rush for a couple of weeks. You and mother visit New England. Why not spend a weekend in Carlisle or Crisfield? Why don't you reserve an afternoon a week for a round of golf? Is Mother going to Ocean Grove this year?

How is our garden doing now? Has Grandmother Minker started digging yet? How is the farm doing? Don't forget to keep the ground cultivated and moist; keep all dead blooms cut; pull the ticks out of Ginger.

The alarm just sounded for a practice gas alert so I will close this letter and put on my gas mask.

Lee

Monday evening
May 31, 1944

Dear Lee –

I guess you think that I've dropped you off my list of correspondents but here I am again! I finished my finals last Tuesday and from then until Sunday had a grand time! Timmy, Nan, and Chapel left on Friday but Colbos, Walker, and I were still left. The cadets left on Thursday morning so they had a lot of free time too! All I did was eat, sleep and play tennis! The weather wasn't too wonderful but all of us wanted to make our last few days together a big bang!

All of us went down to the station on Thursday morning to say good-bye to the cadets. This is the last squadron and only a few permanent party men are left now to straighten things out! We had gotten to know three boys better than most of the others because we played tennis together. We gave a good-bye party for them, too and it was a great success! I sang at it with a boys quartette! We really hated to see them go on Thursday. We were starting to walk back from the station when the Army truck came along and said they would take us back! I'd never been in one before and what a bumpy ride! It was fun though!

Saturday was class day exercises at school! It wasn't very much, except that they gave out prizes and scholarships. You can imagine my surprise when I heard my name called for one. It was a twenty-five dollar prize for highest in scholarship and deportment in the Freshmen Class! I was so thrilled I didn't know what to do! Then I got another $5.00 prize for the greatest personal contribution to Dickinson or something like that! I felt pretty good about the whole thing!

Ben asked me to come up to Andover for his graduation and Prom! I really think that I should go and I guess mother and dad will let me! I think Ben is going into the Army about July 1st. We saw in the paper last night that Clarence Deaksyne is missing in action. He was with a chemical unit in England. It didn't give many details but if I see anything else I'll let you know. I guess I'll have to stop now and get some work done. I hope you're able to get some flying in. I know you must get the jitters sitting around doing nothing. Write when you can.

As ever,
Shirley

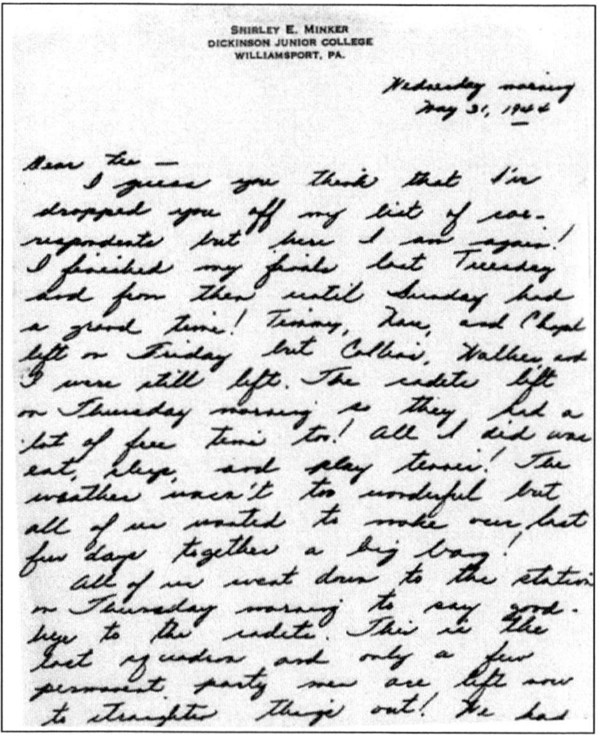

SHIRLEY E. MINKER
DICKINSON JUNIOR COLLEGE
WILLIAMSPORT, PA.

Wednesday morning
May 31, 1944

Dear Lee —
I guess you think that I've dropped you off my list of correspondents but here I am again! I finished my finals last Tuesday and from then until Sunday had a grand time! Jimmy, Kae, and Cheryl left on Friday but Collins, Walker and I were still left. The cadets left on Thursday morning so they had a lot of free time too! All I did was eat, sleep, and play tennis! The weather wasn't too wonderful but all of us wanted to make our last few days together a big bang!
All of us went down to the station on Thursday morning to say good-bye to the cadets. This is the last of cadets and only a few permanent party men are left now to straighten things out! We had

Opening of letter from Shirley at the close of her freshmen year.
Courtesy Historical Society of Delaware

On June 3, 1944 Lee completed specialized four-engine training in the B-17. He regretted that the course of training did not allow him to participate in the coming D-Day Invasion. On June 6, 1944 at 3:33 a.m. Eastern U.S. time, CBS correspondent Edward R. Murrow broadcast General Eisenhower's order of the day:

> *"Soldiers, sailors, and airmen, of the Allied Expeditionary Force. You are about to embark on the great crusade toward which we have striven these many months. The eyes of the world are upon you. The hopes and prayers of liberty loving people everywhere march with you. We will accept nothing less than full victory. Good luck. And let us all beseech the blessing of Almighty God for this great and glorious undertaking."* (Bernstein and Lubertozzi 2003)

Delayed for weeks because of bad weather, Operation Overlord marked the beginning of the liberation of occupied Europe. At 0200 hours on the morning of D-Day, forty-five crews from the 447th B.G began their briefing. Their targets were the invasion beaches and transportation chokepoints in towns immediately surrounding the assault area. The foul weather that produced rough seas for the landings on the beaches of Normandy also brought dense gray clouds that made it difficult for the bombers to see their targets. A number of Eighth Air Force crews were unable to drop their bomb load, others inadvertently hit Allied troops. (Doyle 1996) Throughout June and July, American B-17 bombers flew mission after mission, attacking the German positions in support of the invading ground forces.

The *Wilmington Morning News* printed an "Invasion Extra" on June 6 with two-inch headlines: FRANCE INVADED. The lead paragraph in the paper stated, "Allied headquarters did not specify the location, but left no doubt whatever that the landings were on a gigantic scale." The news reports lacked concrete information however, they were either quite general or deliberately misleading. For example, the front page map showing where the invasion started was not accurate, actual landing positions were not known on the home front for several days. Americans waited eagerly for news, knowing the assault on the beaches would be costly.

June 6, 1944

Dear Lee,

Well, school is finally over. I don't know how, passed everything. We went through the usual boring assembly and scheduling and made the rounds of next year's classes.

Well, today is finally D-Day. We've waited so long and expected so much that when it finally arrives it is anti-climatic. I rather expected shouting and parades but its just another day when we sit with ears glued to the radio hoping for news. I hope, as they say, it's the beginning of the end, but I don't know, we still have the Japs to lick.

I have a horrible case of poison [ivy] all over my face and I look like a zombie because I'm smeared from ear to ear with calamine lotion. I'll simply die if its not cleared up by this week-end 'cause Friday night is Tower Hill's Prom.

Shirley and I filed applications for jobs at All American this summer.

Guess that's all for now, bub.

Lots of Love,
Bernice

The Allies had total air supremacy over Western Europe on D-Day. The Eighth Air Force had continually bombed industrial targets and airfields in France and Germany during the spring of

1944 in preparation for the landing. The German Air Force, without fuel, equipment and pilots was able to launch only 80 planes to oppose the invasion. The initial radio accounts of the invasion reported, "There is no indication that the Germans have put in a counter attack . . . All day allied heavy bombers have been operating in support of the ground troops. They have encountered no fighter opposition." The Allied ground forces faced intense opposition from German troops who were well fortified in defensive positions along the Normandy coast and in the hedgerows of the French countryside. The dense and ancient hedges of Normandy formed a natural barrier between the Germans and the advancing American and British troops. Intense fighting in Normandy throughout the month of June finally secured a sufficient beachhead to bring ashore the men and material needed to sustain the offensive. At home, Americans hoped that D-Day marked the start of a rapid end to the war in Europe, when in fact it would take another 11 months of fighting, at the cost of millions of lives all over Europe.

Thursday, June 8

Dearest Lee:

I am wondering whether you are having time to listen to the radio these days and hearing some of the accounts of the invasion and what reaction it is having on you boys there. I am keeping my fingers crossed for fear these first days are too easy and that some trap is being laid, but I hope my fears are wrong. I suppose it all makes you boys more anxious than ever to "get going".

Our roses are blooming beautifully, the Japanese beetles not having arrived yet. We also have some pretty snapdragons which came up from last year.

We are getting off a box to you, mostly food, to let you know that we are remembering your birthday. It seems so little to send but we don't want to load you down with things which will only be in your way. If there is anything special you need kindly let me know. There isn't any chance of your being able to spend the day at home, is there? I certainly hope you will celebrate your 21st with the family. And now that things overseas are beginning to move we all have hopes that the mess will be cleaned up before too many months go by.

With all my love.

Mother

Sunday, [June 16, 1944]

Dear Lee,

Happy Birthday! How does it feel to be all of 20 years old? Not very different I expect. When I turned 16 I expected to feel old and very grown up but I'm not either and am very disappointed.

Friday night Walt and I went to Tower Hill Prom. We really had a super time. They had the place all prettyed [sic] like a Mardi Gras and it really was very effective. No corsages were allowed but we had flowers for our hair. Afterwards we went to breakfast at one of the girl's houses and saw movies we took on the Junior Senior picnic. They were really good!

By the way, I've been offered a scholarship to Tower Hill [high school]. Don't faint, please. Mr. Guernsey seems to have taken quite a shine to me so he popped up and offered me that. It'll be hard if I change in my senior year but the good effects on my lessons would make up for it. No one knows but the family, yet, but when and if I get and accept it, you'll probably hear me yellin!

Gotta go now as Shirley is calling.

Lots of Love,
Bernice

June 16th

June 16th

Looie Dear

You may be lazy, looie dear,
You may be dead in bed,
You may be sound asleep
With snores emitting from
your head.

You may be crazy, looie dear,
And never learn to spell
Your "i's" are always
mixed "e's" (ease)
'til all your words don't
jell.

You may be all these things
combined
But still we love you plenty.
So greetings to you, looie dea
Today when you are twenty.

Bernice's birthday poem to her brother, Looie was a nickname for Lieutenant.
Courtesy Historical Society of Delaware

Shortly after his 20th birthday, Lee left Roswell Field to begin the last stage of processing before shipping overseas. He managed a short visit to Wilmington while en route to Tampa, Florida. Arriving home only three months after the March furlough, the Minkers were delighted to have a few more days to enjoy as a family. The correspondence does not tell us the specifics of this leave, but we do know that he again said goodbye on June 27 when he took the train to Tampa for preliminary processing The entire family hoped they would see him again before he shipped out.

Thursday evening
June 29, 1944
[Tampa, Florida]

Dear Mother,

Several Roswell transfers are with me in my tent at the Plant Park Fair Ground in the heart of Tampa, Florida, tonight as we write our first letters home since arriving here yesterday. This afternoon we finished preliminary processing (physical, clothing and record checkup) and will now mark time for a couple of weeks while waiting assignment for operational training (probably Florida or Mississippi bases). So that we will not get into mischief however a schedule of lectures, physical training and etcetera will be followed.

My train ride down was uneventful and on time. I hit the hay Tuesday night just as we pulled out of Rocky Mount, North Carolina, and arose for breakfast just as we were nearing Jacksonville. At 3:00 P.M. sharp we arrived at Tampa Station.

As soon as I alighted from the air conditioned Washington College [train] the heat and humidity struck me hard. I have had a clammy feeling ever since I arrived and though it poured rain for three hours this afternoon the sultriness continues. They say that this is the raining season though. Life is gay in Tampa and growing things make it a welcome change from the southwestern desert country. Last night it did cool off slightly and no mosquitoes bothered me so I slept very well.

Last night several of us gathered around a portable radio to listen to the speech of Thomas E. Dewey as he accepted the Republican Presidential nomination. The general opinion is that Dewey is spotless and would make a great peacetime president, but his experience?

I certainly enjoyed my unexpected visit home although I didn't seem to be able to do everything I wished. I should have seen more of Jeff, Aunt Flossie and Aunt Grace as well as cleaned up the garden. I'll take care of those details next time.

Please don't send anything to me until I tell you to do so. When I settle down at an operational training base I will want my cap rain cover, low cut shoes, News Journal, etc. I received my parachute bag by Railway Express yesterday. I purchased a dog tag chain at the P.X. today by the way. Don't forget to give Julia a pair of the small pilot wings for her birthday July 8, 1944. Do you think that the two young cherubs [his sisters] would like a pair? I wish that you would send my camera in the next shipment too. I will try to get a picture taken soon. Please try to keep all that I send home separate and neat. (Shirley can file and make a scrapbook.) I weighed in at 146 pounds at a height of 5 feet 9 inches today.

Love to you all,

Lee

July 2, 1944

My dear Lee:-

Your letter, the first from you since you left last Tuesday, came this morning before I left for church. It is needless to say that we had been anxiously awaiting its arrival – and that all of us had to read it individually. You see how you rate. I'm glad you made the trip from here on time, and that you will have a few days of conditioning before you have to go strenuously.

I think it is wonderful the way you have been able to adapt yourself to the varied climates you have been in during the past year and a half. It shows you are in good shape.

How great it was to have you home! The days flew—and yet we didn't rush. We just lived together – all of us – again, and tried to make up for such a long separation. Everybody was so glad to see you – and every place I've gone people have spoken of how fine you looked and fine it was to see you. I stopped at Boykins for a Coca Cola on the way home from church today—and Jack asked how you were. I told him he ought to know after the way you did away with that fried chicken the night we were there.

The Bond Drive is on in earnest now – and I think we'll be "over the top" by the middle of the week. A great many people wait until the last minute no matter how hard you work to get them in line earlier. Well, the best to you, kid.

Sincerely,
Dad

As Lee began the last steps of the journey to England, the Battle for Normandy was reaching its climax. By July 2, 1944 the Allies had landed a total of 900,000 men and 177,000 vehicles and supplies to carry out the offensive against Germany. As the news of heavy losses in Normandy reached the U.S., the Minkers realized that their son was getting closer to entering combat. Yet, their letters spoke of pride in him and the necessity to end the war. Lee stayed in the tent barracks in Tampa only a week, then shipped to Gulfport, Mississippi to meet his crew and lead them through final operational training. The uncertainty over making the grade to pilot and the days of training were over, only breaking in the crew and final shipping orders remained before overseas duty.

Chapter Eight

I Hope I Can Make a Good Leader

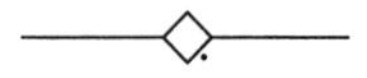

July 9, 1944 – September 29, 1944

Dates: July 9, 1944 – September 29, 1944	**Locations: Gulfport, Mississippi** **Hunter Field, Savannah, Georgia**

July 1944	Specialists are assigned to the Minker crew for operational training.
August 1944	The crew practiced long distance and operational flying.
August 25, 1944	Paris liberated by Allied and French troops.
October 4, 1944	Lee and his crew departed for England from Hunter Field, Savannah, Georgia.

Gulfport, Mississippi – a hot, sultry, and mosquito ridden staging area for the Army Air Force – where Lee and the members of his crew would come together for the first time. He had ten weeks in the clammy southern climate to weld boys from Minnesota, Pennsylvania, South Carolina, Georgia, Arizona, and New Mexico into a crew whose lives would depend on each other. Gulfport served two purposes: shaping the crew into a fighting team and advanced operational training. Flying concentrated on high altitude and formation missions, Lee was checked out for landing, day and night flying, and also went to engineering ground school.

July 9, 1944

Dear Dad,
Greetings from Gulfport, Mississippi!!!

Friday afternoon of last week 56 B-17 heavy bombardment combat crews, complete except for bombardiers and navigators, shipped aboard a special troop train of the Atlantic Coast Lines. The following afternoon the group disembarked at Gulfport Army Air Field, Gulfport, Mississippi, where they will be given final combat crew training in Flying Fortresses.

I am first pilot and plane commander of combat crew

number 156 of the third flying section of the 43rd training wing of the third army air force. As such it is my job to whip a combat crew of great precision into being in ten weeks of operational training in this replacement training unit for the Eighth Army Air Force. My crew: Arthur D. Rohl, 2nd Lieutenant, co-pilot; James E. Shannon, corporal, aerial engineer; Max G. Shepherd, private first class, assistant radio operator; Donald W. Miller, private first class assistant aerial engineer. These men, plus a navigator and a bombardier to arrive later, have had prior training in their own particular fields. The work here consists of perfecting their work and becoming a positive unit of a combat crew team. (Don't misunderstand, all are gunners but all have some particular other job.)

I hope that I can make a good leader. Now is when it counts.

So far I have not had a chance to learn everything about Gulfport Field and vicinity but here is a varied assortment of data. It is hot and mucky here and now. We sleep under mosquito nets at night. The coast is over run with navy men. Gambling and liquor are taboo by law in this state but along the coast both flourish in the open and the state collects ten percent of taxes on it. Pralines, a pecan and brown sugar, rum, butter mixture (very sweet) are a very tasty native specialty. The venereal rate is higher here then in any other state of the union; also illiteracy and the proportion of blacks to whites. The memory of Jefferson Davis still lingers on.

The Air Field is comparatively new. The base is large, well equipped and well administered – the best yet! Eighty percent of our instructors have seen service in either England or China. From here we will go to final staging, units at either Hunter Field, Savannah, Georgia, or Langley Field, Virginia. Sixty percent will fly across to combat. There will be no more furloughs before combat and no overnight cross countries. All crew members will be at least the rank of corporal before leaving here; 25 percent of the first pilots will become first lieutenants before leaving here. The schedule ahead seems to be hard (more intensive and complete) than any yet experienced. The food is really like home, wonderfully prepared and all you can eat.

That should give you a general idea of my present setup. Let me know if there is anything you would like to know further.

Please send all my clothing (WINTER) as soon as possible as it must all be checked before leaving here. (shoes, greens, pinks, blouse, caps, dress hats, coat). I could use a dozen pair of socks, Julia's picture, my camera, one more towel. I have made arrangements for the U.S. Army Finance Department to send home fifty dollars of each monthly pay starting in August. I will probably send more with which you do as you think best. Please arrange to send the News Journal to me again.

How are the Blue Rocks doing? Is Granny Minker home yet? Has Ginger had a family? Are you ready to begin your long freshening up vacation after the bond drive is over?

As always,
Lee

Lee expressed his concern about his role when he wrote his dad, "I hope that I can make a good leader. Now is when it counts." The Army Air Force pilot's manual made clear what was expected of a commander.

> *Your assignment to the B-17 airplane means that you are no longer just a pilot. You are now an airplane commander, charged with all the duties and responsibilities of a command post. You are now flying a 10-man weapon. It is your airplane, and your crew. You are*

responsible for the safety and efficiency of the crew at all times – not just when you are flying and fighting, but for the full 24 hours of every day while you are in command.

On July 11, 1944 the Eighth Air Force launched a thousand plane raid against Munich in the continuing effort to bomb the German Army's lines of communication and supply to their troops in Normandy. This raid and other raids deep into Germany were aided by long-range escort fighters like the P-47 and P-51 Mustang. One by one, Germany's cities were being reduced to rubble.

Thursday noon
July 13, 1944

Dear Mother,

At last I am back to work! Wednesday morning I began the old grind again by rising at 3:00 A.M. for the early morning flying period. By noon I had worked off quite a bit of rust and had started to re-learn basic flying fundamentals.

My flying work here will consist of high altitude and/or formation missions. But to start with I must be checked out in landings, day and night flying (we will have very little night work), instruments and formation. My crew co-pilot, engineer and radio operator must also be checked out and then special gunnery, bombing and navigation missions will be scheduled before combining all in simulated tactical operations.

My first flight instructor, Lieutenant Dickey, was tops but the instructors continually change crews so that the students can get several slants on flying. The B-17Gs that we fly here are almost new, 300 hours of flying time, and are kept up very well.

This afternoon I will spend an hour in the high altitude chamber and then begin engineering ground school. At 3:00 A.M. Friday morning, and Sunday too, I will report to the flight line. So you see that there is work ahead.

I haven't heard from you since Plant Park [Florida]. Did my first letter from here get through to you? Don't forget to ship my "stuff" as soon as possible (pinks, greens, blouse, coat, caps, rain cover, writing paper, swim suit, (2) towels, (6) handkerchiefs (3) tee shirts, low cut shoes, Journal Every-Evening.)

Write and let me know how you all are and what you are all doing.

Love,
Lee

July 13 [1944]
Thursday

Dear Lee,

Just a note to keep you posted! That sure was a super letter from Mississippi! Just please don't do too much of that or you'll develop writers' cramp and not be able to fly!

Yes, Ginger had her pups, on Monday, 14 wriggling black, squealing, infants. Only three have survived. The doctor said there was too much acid in her milk. It all happened so suddenly I can't realize it. I hope at least these three live.

Granny Minker left Monday and is home now. She was quite upset, though when she left; because Carolyn [a cousin] announced her engagement to a boy she's been going with a long time, which is a Catholic. Carolyn isn't going to change, but Granny seems to think she's done a capital sin and will be punished in hell. The boy, man really, is awfully nice, 27, and has a lot of sense. Carolyn's twenty and old enough to make up her own mind, I should say, though Granny said she ought to wait 'till she was thirty! My God! If I'm not at least engaged at twenty, I'll give up!

We certainly have been busy, working and with Brandywiners 3 nights a week! I wish you could come to see it, though in its present state it seems a little hopeless.

Lots of Love,
Bernice

Friday night
July 14, 1944

Dear Lee –

This is the first time this week that I've been able to sit down and write to anyone. My friends are all going to think that I'm a member of the Lost Generation, but really I've been awfully busy.

I like my job very much. The people in the office are all as crazy as I am, do you know I feel right at home. Since the Dupont Building is air-conditioned, it's wonderful to work there in the summer. I haven't been hot yet! The work is very interesting and I really do work. From the time I get in there until I leave at five; I'm going all the time. Every other job I've had has always had some spare time to it, but this is one steady stream. The only thing I can find to kick about is that I have to get up so early, but it happens in the best of families.

I guess you know all about Ginger and the bad luck we had with the pups. Two of them are still alive and I'm pretty sure they'll remain all right. They are both so fat – and all they do is eat and sleep and make funny noises. They really are very cute! Though I would have liked fourteen, I guess it would have been a lot of work for both Ginger and mother. We'll try to get some pictures of them to send to you. Here are some of the ones we took when you were home. None of them turned out particularly well because they were too far away. We'll learn by the trial and error method, I guess. Does seem a shame to waste film though, because it is too scarce.

Lee, the very afternoon that you left I bumped into an old friend of yours downtown. I was walking down Market Street after work and I ran right into Greg White. He's in the Navy and said he was going to school down in South Carolina now for his officers rating. He looks the same as ever and said he wished he had known that you were home.

The "wolves" were home in full for over the 4th. Taylor had an eight-day leave. He is soon leaving for overseas duty (Formosa, he thinks!) Gabby was home for one night and then for the week-end. He is due to be shipped out soon, too. Harry Conley was home and Bill Baird also. Almost like the good old days!

Well, I guess I've told you all my news for now. Write and tell me more about your crew (especially your co-pilot! Sounds good to me!) Take care of yourself and be good. Pups and Ginger send a wet, slobbery kiss and so do I. Bye now!

Always,
Your loving sister –
Shirley

Saturday morning
July 15, 1944

Dearest Lee:-

It was wonderful to hear your voice last night. What a pity that daddy was not at home either time!

I know this is the opportunity for which you have been working and planning so long and I also know that you are ready for it. I would not hold you back if I could. I am proud of you. I know you will be conscious of a Presence and Strength other than your own in these coming days and whatever comes you will be able to meet. You are always in my mind and on my heart and so I can hardly say that I shall be thinking of you more. We shall keep sending you letters even though we may not be able to hear from you for sometime after this week, and one of these days you will be getting a real "shower" of mail.

It was nice having Julia [Lee's girlfriend] with us for a while last night. While waiting for the second call to come thru she, Shirley, May and I tried to do some bridge playing. None of the girls know much about it, and I don't know a whole lot but we had some fun out of it, nevertheless.

I am mailing you the overseas cap today, so it ought to reach you before you leave Gulfport. We haven't been able to get any pictures of the pup "Pilot" lately because we can't get any films. These pictures were taken when the puppies were about a month old. Naturally Pilot has changed a lot since then. We'll send you pictures from time to time, whenever we can locate film.

With all my love,
Mother

By mid-July of 1944 the Allies were fighting a desperate battle in France to break out from the Normandy Beach head. The Eighth Air Force launched a tremendous air bombardment to pierce the German lines on July 25. A few days later the Allies succeeded in breaking out from the limited confines of Normandy and gaining access to the interior of France. In early August when the Allies moved across Normandy, Brittany, and Flanders toward the borders of Germany, it seemed as if the war would soon be coming to an end. Later events proved this to be an optimistic assumption as the Allies ran short of food and fuel, and men and equipment wore out. The German Army was still a formidable fighting force that would demonstrate its defensive power in battles in Belgium and Holland. The tide of the war had changed in favor of the Allies, yet it was difficult to foresee the end of hostilities in Europe. The Eighth Air Force bomb groups all over East Anglia continued to need replacements for the losses suffered in the first year of combat.

Saturday, July 22.

Dearest Lee:-

We read with interest the description of your first solo flight with your entire crew. Congratulations on coming thru in such fine shape.

I suppose you have heard the rumors of the crack-up in Germany. Whether it is propaganda or not I suppose we will not know for a few days at least. As one commentator said last night, when Germany begins to fold up she will fold up fast; but I guess we are all keeping our fingers crossed, for it seems too good to be true that the end in Germany is near. And things don't look any too good for the Japs. Maybe you'll be home for Christmas after all.

Ginger's two pups seem to be thriving, - in fact they are as fat as butterballs. We are anxiously waiting for them to open their eyes, and that should happen any day now. She guards them jealously. I don't know yet whether we will sell them or not. I think the girls would like to keep one, but I think it best not to.

I have a boy out picking blackberries for me today, and I hope to get time to make some jelly this afternoon. We had pie last week.

Did your box of clothing arrive O.K? I sent the cap and camera a day or two later by parcel post, so don't worry it if has not come yet. You may have noticed that I left moth flakes in the pockets of your winter clothes and I would leave them in if I were you. I don't know what you have to keep your clothes in but this warm, mucky weather they should be protected against moths.

Best of luck and all my love.

Mother

The rumored "crackup in Germany," referred to an unsuccessful attempt on July 20, 1944 to assassinate Hitler. Several German Generals, fed up with the mounting losses and Hitler's inept meddling, plotted to assassinate Hitler. Count von Stauffenberg, a senior aide, planted a bomb at Hitler's afternoon staff briefing. Hitler escaped relatively unscathed when a heavy oak leg in the conference table blunted the force of the bomb; three generals and the stenographer were killed. Count von Stauffenberg and other army officers implicated in the plot were immediately executed. The failure to assassinate Hitler ensured that the war would go on for another nine months; an average of 25,000 people died each day until the war ended in early May, 1945. Germany did not, as Edna hoped, fold up quickly.

Friday noon July 28, 1944

Dear Dad,

This week we are flying from 2:00 P.M. till 10:00 P.M., the night shift. A new group of crews started training this week on the 3:00 A.M. till 11:00 A.M. shift but next week I am afraid we will be following that early morning shift. Last week we flew from 10:00 A.M. till 6:00 P.M. and I think that is the best.

Operational training is proceeding smoothly with the accent on long flights of low and high altitude formation. During the low altitude flights P-40's [fighters] make simulated attacks and the gunners keep them in their sights while their accuracy is recorded by built in cameras; during high altitude flights B-26 tow cloth targets across our path or parallel to it while our gunners shoot with live ammunition.

How did the War Bond drive end out? Isn't it time you were taking a week's vacation? Why didn't the Governor mention post war development for Ferris School in his address to the Republican state convention?

Lee

Saturday morning –And it is HOT
8/5/44

My dear Lee:-

You are certainly putting in a schedule. I hate to think you have to do it at all – but this isn't the time to discuss that. You're in it, and you're doing your best, and I'm as proud of you as any father could be. You've proved to your own satisfaction what you can take and what you can do – a wonderful set of discoveries for a person under twenty-one years of age. I hate to think you have this stepped up schedule in the heat. However you know how to keep yourself in shape, and you'll stand up under it alright.

You have probably seen that our 5th War Loan Drive was successful. It was a very hard pull. Some people do wonderfully – and some are plain slackers. However, this has always been so everywhere where freedom of personal choice is maintained. We don't want to slug people into cooperating but one feels like it at times.

Well, take good care of yourself, kid, and know I'm with you every minute.

Dad

Friday evening
August 7, 1944

Dear Mother,

Today has been one of those hot sultry days old timers refer to as dog days. We have had several thunder showers but the heat cooks on.

This is definitely not good flying weather for the moisture and heat combine to form great billowing cumuliform clouds — thunderheads with terrific ice, hail, rain and convective current conditions. A prime rule of flying is to stay away from these clouds, quite a problem when they are everywhere and at all altitudes and you are trying to make a bombing run, fly cross country or lead a twelve ship formation.

How are Ginger's pups now; just beginning to get into

mischief? How is the garden, is Bernice weeding it carefully daily? How do Shirley and Bernice like their jobs? What will the girls do with all their spare time after Brandywiners finish? I notice that Mr. Frank gave their show a rave notice.

Did you receive my money order for $200.00 yet?

I find that I am getting far behind in my correspondence and I expect that I will fall even further behind in the future. I wish that you would explain to old friends why I do not write as often as I should.

Love,
Lee

Monday afternoon
August 7, 1944

Dear Lee:

It's raining outside now and as I cannot go out and do the shopping that I planned to do, well, I thought that I would write to you. We've really had some hot weather lately and with Brandywiners going full blast, it has seemed worse than usual.

We have given our first three performances of the operetta and they have all been very successful. We have been sold out for all three and all three for this week are sold out too. I guess that you have seen all the pictures and write-ups in the paper, haven't you? I have barely been able to make myself get up and go to work each morning because I don't usually get into bed before two. I can sleep any where or any time at this date.

You should see the puppies at this date. Yesterday we

had them out on the front porch almost all day and of course had to follow them around with a mop too. They are getting very playful and can't resist playing with anything that they can get hold of.

Mother said that you wanted a new wallet with room for snapshots in it. Bernice will get you one if you want us to because we didn't get you very much for your birthday. Would [you] like a copy of Bob Hope's new book? It's supposed to be very good and I'm going to get one for Fred. I don't imagine that you have too much time to read, but this is something you can pick up and it would not bother you if you had to read it on the go. Say so, and your wish shall be granted.

I wish that you would try and get mother to go away on a vacation. I think that she is going to be sick if she doesn't get a few weeks rest. I don't think that daddy realizes what a strain she is under and she has been working for over a year now without a break. See if you can't persuade her to do something. I would like her to go away with me if I go anywhere at the end of the summer. I will have to stop now and go back to work. Bye for now.

Lots of love,
Shirley

Wednesday evening
August 16, 1944

Dear Bernice,

From the tone of the reviews in the Journal-Every-Evening the Brandywiners performance of the Vagabond King was excellent. It must have been a grand experience for you and Shirley to take part.

But life must seem commonplace now with only work at Crosby's, AWVS work, gardening and the puppies to keep you occupied – plus a movie or dance with Walt every now and then.

I want to thank mother for the beautiful wallet she sent me. It is exactly what I wanted. Maybe you can send me some pictures to put in it. (As yet I have not been able to get any film for my camera here.). I wish you would send copies of my old pictures too for my present copies are getting dirty.

The war is certainly moving in our favor in France. Maybe victory will come sooner than expected. We have been primed for combat in the European Theatre of Operations but we may be slated for some other theatre in some bigger plane if there is no need for us there.

Training continues as usual with routine missions. The crew is shaping up well.

Friday is this week's day off but as we will finish flying Thursday noon and as we are not scheduled for flying until late Saturday we actually have two days off. So I think that Art and I, and most of flights "L" and "K" will visit New Orleans.

It is 8:30 P.M. I must rise at 3:00 A.M.

Love,
Lee

August 21, 1944

Dearest Lee:-

Your letter to Bernice came this morning. As we did not

hear from you all last week we were getting a little anxious. Did you get to New Orleans and how did you like it? How far away is it from Gulfport?

Things are surely moving now in Europe, aren't they? I haven't heard the radio since this morning but would not be surprised if Paris is already occupied by allied troops. Did you mean by a bigger ship that you might be shifted to a B-29? Aren't they using B-17's in the Pacific area?

Love from all of us.
Mother

Families on the home front stayed close by their radios during the summer of 1944 waiting for news of the liberation of Paris. By mid-August, the Allies were moving rapidly across France towards Paris and the German Army was in full retreat. After four years of German occupation, Parisians were delirious with joy on August 25, 1944 when Allied troops under Eisenhower and the free French under Charles De Gaulle rolled into Paris.

In Gulfport, training got more realistic as P-40s made simulated attacks, and gunners used live ammunition on the targets towed by B-26s. Each new crew was required to train a minimum of 150 flying hours. By August 25, 1944 Lee's crew had logged their hours and was impatiently waiting for orders.

Friday afternoon
August 25, 1944

Dear Mother,

Please excuse me for not writing more often but please don't worry when I do not write. I am in fine shape even though the Air Forces leave me little spare time to let you know.

Tonight I am to fly from 2000 to 0300 on a night celestial navigation mission to Evansville, Indiana and return. That means no sleep until at least 0500 Saturday morning which means that Saturday will not be much of a day off. Then we fly at 0300 Sunday morning.

While in B-17 operational training each crew is required to log a minimum of 150 to a maximum of 195 flying hours. At present our crew has flown a total of 117 hours and is high for the section. The last couple weeks of training coming up will see the section cramming to complete the schedule.

Nobody here knows what the future will hold but certain facts stand out. (1) B-17's are now fighting only in Europe (2) B-17 production is down to almost nothing except for some replacements (3) the war in Europe should end this winter (4) armed might must be shifted to the Pacific and Chinese areas after the fall of Germany (5) veterans will return to the States after the fall of Germany (6) an occupational AAF of 15,000 planes is to be based in Europe. We here are curiously waiting for orders. We feel that we have trained enough; we wish to help win this war.

Thank you for sending the family picture taken at the Iceland in New York. It came out very well. I would like to keep it if I may.

Enclosed you will find the receipts of two $100.00 money orders which you can trace, if you have not received them already. A $50.00 allotment check will come to you the first of next month and I will again send you a $100.00 money order.

Love,
Lee

P.S. I saw Dragon Seed last night. It was very good.

Wednesday noon
September 6, 1944

Dear Mother,

By the time you receive this letter you and the girls will probably be chocolate brown from the rays of the seashore sun; Shirley's nose will be beginning to peel. I hope you have favorable weather during your vacation. I know the rest and relaxation of a week at Rehobeth will do you all good before the start of winter activities. I wish that Dad would take a break too for he is in a rut. Do you realize that three years ago this September I entered Dickinson College and that last year at this time I was just beginning Primary Flight Training at Thunderbird Field, Phoenix, Arizona? It seems much longer. These years have been a great experience – I have learned new subjects in school and how to fly high in the sky, I have seen new places, met new people and observed different ways of living. As yet I don't know what changes will result or have resulted in me. I hope that I can make you proud of me!

Operational training still progresses uneventfully but it is scheduled to end September 22, 1944. As yet I do not know what the future will bring but the glorious victories of the Allied Armies will command us.

I went to the dentist this morning – he took out all my old fillings and put in new ones. ??? I then had my teeth cleaned.

I have another money order for $100.00 but will not send it until you return home. You should get a check from the government for $50.00 class E allotment (payroll savings plan). I will take care of my quarterly income tax payment.

I didn't have time to see real New Orleans. What I saw

was crowded and ill kept. Four of us stayed up to listen to the All Stars football game a week ago.

I am planning to have my picture taken and that of my crew soon. I am going to write Dad and Julia now.

Love,
Lee

Monday morning

My dear Lee:-

Well, it looks as if you're going to see the world before you're twenty-one. You've covered a good portion of this country already. When you get through this next chapter you will be qualified to be introduced as a cosmopolite. That two dollar word will make many an introducer clear his throat before proceeding.

You've done a grand job in every way, and I'm as proud of you as any father could be. The same steady, clear-cut attitude you have shown to date will be your greatest asset now. As I have said to you – you've first got to be yourself, and usually respect and position follow.

All goes well here—so don't worry about any of us. Mother is fine since her vacation – the girls are alright – and I never felt better in my life.

We'll be with you every minute of every day and night – pulling for you. The best to you!

Dad

Thursday night
September 14, 1944

Dear Louie,

I hope that you haven't been caught in the terrible storm that we had here for the last three days. We really did have a wonderful time at the shore and I think that now we shall all be ready to go back to school and work feeling better. Most of the regular crowd had left and it was rather empty, but we all decided that we liked Rehobeth better in September than earlier in the season.

I guess that you will be leaving Gulfport the same day that I leave for school. I had the dates all mixed up, and thought that I had to leave tomorrow, but I have another week now. That was a big relief, as mother and I didn't know how we would ever get ready on time. We have been trying to get my (your) trunk packed, but don't seem to have accomplished too much. By the way, I'm confiscating another piece of your clothing – your reversible coat. I needed a new raincoat, and wanted a boy's coat, but they are very expensive this year. So---mother and I decided. I hope that it's okay with you, but you probably won't be able to fit into it when you come home. I'm still wearing that corduroy jacket of yours, and it's really grand. What would girls ever do without being able to borrow their brother's clothes? Oh well ---

I guess that it won't be too long before Fred is sent over. He seems to think that they are headed for a POE [port of embarkation] before too long. I guess that all my boy friends are going to leave me at once. Do you think that you will be going over right after you leave there, but I guess you are still up in the air about all your plans.

Let me know your plans and your new address as soon

as you can, please. If there is the slightest chance that you will get home, well you know what to do. Be good now and give me love to all the fellows in your crew.

Your moron sister,
Shirley

Monday evening
September 17, 1944

Dear Mother,

It was good to talk to you Friday evening even though it was long distance. I am sorry that so much confusion occurred in calling you but I had intended to put a call through to you and another through to Julia about seven Wilmington time so that I could beat the evening rush and get some sleep before flying at three in the morning.

Present plans call for me to ship out of Gulfport for Hunter Field, Savannah, Georgia, on September 23, 1944, for final staging and post of embarkation. It should be less than a week after that before I am flying overseas to combat. Seventeen crews are leaving here on the twenty third, including ten of the eleven pilot volunteers of the 3rd Air Force from Roswell Army Air Field. Of course we don't know where exactly we will go from Savannah and from the time we leave Gulfport until we reach our destination we will be under secret orders so there may be a period of a couple of weeks during which you will not hear from me and during which I will have no permanent address. But I will write just as soon as I can – Please don't worry about me.

Enclosed is a money order for $100.00 for my account.

I think that I have been saving rather well recently but I will not send any money home this month for I must purchase some new equipment (G.I. shoes, raincoat, O.D. suit, white gloves, leggings, etc.) for overseas and keep a bit on hand for any emergency. I think that I will increase my allotment checks as the quickest, easiest, cheapest and most dependable way to send money home from overseas. I wish that you would send me a statement every once in a while of how I stand financially, savings account, bonds, etc.

Sometime this week I will ship home a package – letters, flying manuals, bathing trunks, etc. I wish that you would file the letters and manuals in my already overstuffed room. I will try to buy occasional [sic] souvenirs to send you from overseas but please don't expect me to remember Christmas on the dot.

Don't forget to write me on V-Mail— a couple of sheets at a time. Clippings are probably against the rules so you will have to write news of others in service, Wilmington, Blue Bombers, sports, marriages, etc. I won't be allowed to write in much detail but I would like to give you a rough idea of where I will be – the first letter of the first paragraph of my first three letters will be the first letter of the country in which I am based; first letter of closing sentence will stand for North, South, East or West; the rest you will have to puzzle out.

I wish that you would keep in contact with Julia. I think that she is tops, and someday maybe I will ask her to be my wife.

More later.

Love,
Lee

P.S. Send any 620 film you can get.

Tuesday [September 19, 1944]

Dear Lee,

Well, here I is, I don't know how whole in spirit but whole in body at least. As for mind . . . You see I've been taking tests for the last two days from nine o'clock 'til about two in the afternoon. Yesterday the whole time was spent in English, in five different parts. One was a literary acquaintance test and really a pip. Today I had spelling, French and a psychological exam in which you filled in little boxes and did crazy things like writing down the first word that popped in my head at the mention of another word. My course includes French II, English, History and Chemistry, plus electives like music, art, etc.

Tomorrow school opens officially and I'm anxious to see how I'm going to like it. Most of the teachers seem pretty nice but I'm not sure about the kids yet.

Pilot [the new puppy] is getting absolutely enormous, Lee, and it seems he'll be able to hold his own as he bats Ginger right back when she starts to bully him. Ginger is back in her childhood again and beats the puppy to chewing on the shoe.

By the way, son, you will certainly not find me getting a private school complex. There's nothing I detest more. Most books always picture the little sister as a brat, so I imagine I fit in swell. But in that case you fit in, too, as the big brother usually hands out advice to the bratty sister. I'll try to heed it.

Bud Tisdale expects to get home for about fourteen days at the beginning of October. Taylor Hollingsworth, Hy Simmons, and Babe Rydings were all home on leaves recently. When I was over at A.I. [duPont High School] they were all over talking to Miss Webster. She always asks for you.

Friday night I'll be over at school attending a new comers party given by Mr. and Mrs. Guernsey. Fly over and flap your wings so I can give you the "hi" sign.

Lots of love,
Luck,
Bernice

Breezy and brash in her letters, Bernice quietly observed the toll that Lee's absence was taking on her mother. With both Lee and Shirley away, she was the only child at home in 1944. Sometime during that year Bernice captured her feelings about her mom in a charming poem. There is no reference to the poem in the correspondence, the original became a part of Lee's post-war scrapbook.

The Soldier's Mom

1944..Bernice Minker

She hasn't changed a bit
Since she kissed him and said "Goodbye"
You couldn't know to see her face
How much she longs to cry.

She goes about her household chores
With that same sunny smile
You'd never know how much she longs
To sit with him awhile.

But every now and then she'll go
Into his attic room
And dust each corner carefully
With mop and cloth and broom

Then turning to his picture,
She'll whisper soft "Hello"

You wouldn't guess to look at her...
But she's my mom...I know.

Courtesy Historical Society of Delaware

Minker crew in Gulfport, Mississippi shortly before leaving for combat tour in England.

Front Row L-R: Lt. Lee Minker - pilot, Lt. John Rosiala - Bombadier, F/O Wes Pitts -Navigator, Lt. H.D. Rohl – Co-pilot. (Rohl became ill and was replaced by Gordon Dodge.)
Back Row L-R: Cpl. Max Shepherd - Ball Turret Gunner, Cpl. Olaf Larsen – Radio Operator, Cpl. Harold O. McKay – Armorer, Sgt. James Shannon – Engineer and Top Turret Gunner, Cpl. D. W. Miller – Waist Gunner, Cpl. Joe Trambley – Tail Gunner.
Courtesy Historical Society of Delaware

Friday evening
September 29, 1944

Dear Dad,

There is an unexpected and unexplainable delay in my schedule. For two days I have just stood by. If I had known that this situation would arise I could have arranged to see you and the family while here.

Saturday, September twenty third, twenty one B-17 combat aircrews cleared Gulfport AAF. Mississippi, prior to a Sunday shipment to final staging at Hunter Field, Savannah, Georgia from operation training. Sunday noon, three hours late, the twenty one shipped from Gulfport in wooden wicker seat coaches of the Louisville and Nashville Railroad. Late Monday the group, tired, stiff, hot, sooty, arrived at Hunter Field, unpacked, cleaned up and settled down. Tuesday and Wednesday we broke into two shipping orders, were briefed, processed and drew flying and overseas equipment. Since then we have done nothing.

The delay makes me fret; I don't want my aircrew to become stale or to have to sweat out the future.

But my chief concern is an unparalleled disaster which hit me and my crew while clearing Gulfport Field – co-pilot Lieutenant [sic] Arthur D. Rohl was stricken seriously ill and Flight Officer Gordon B. Dodge (25, Duluth, Minnesota married with a girl of two) was assigned as replacement. Dodge has a good record and so should work into our crew team but loosing [sic] Rohl was like losing my right arm.

Hunter Field is a large field devoted to sending all types of aircrews to embarkation. The turnover in men and equipment is remarkable.

Savannah seems to be a very nice southern town of about eighty thousand population. Tonight the crew is to dine in town and then see the Savannah High School – Glyn Academy football game.

From now on, I must take constant precautions as an officer in the United States Army Air Forces to safeguard any information affecting the security of the nation for I will be in or near combat with our enemies.

Don't worry about me.

Yours,
Lee

P.S. If I happen to fly north for embarkation at Bangor, Maine, I will make a point to buzz home.

Monday [October 2, 1944]

Dear Lee,

It certainly was surprising to hear from you this morning. Sure is tough about your co-pilot, but your new one will probably be o-kay after you're used to him.

There must be men at college, or something, 'cause we've only received two hurried letters from Shirley.

Listen, bub, how about some Xmas suggestions? We don't want to ship you a mess of junk you can't use or don't want. Need a watchband, sweater, razor blades, soap, walett [sic] shaving cream, hot water bottle, silk nighties or a make-up kit? Then tell me what you do want immediately! Catch! Since we-uns have to send 'em as soon as we get yer new address.

Mom is popping around trying to be in everything as usual. She had a War Fund Meeting yesterday and a Girl Scout shindig this afternoon. What a woman!

School is o-kay, but hard! I've never seen such English and French has me absolutely floored. I'm Ok in Chemistry and History which helps a little. It's all very new and strange, and different from A. I. [duPont High School]

Our dog, Pilot (we can no longer say pup) is getting huge. He and Ginger fill the living room. It certainly must be an odd picture to see two mammoth dogs overflowing the floor and the family just managing to squeeze in the doorway.

Well, Lee. That's all for now.

Lots of Love,
Luck,
Bernice

P.S. Don't forget about buzzin' home.

Nearly three years after the bombing of Pearl Harbor and after 18 months of grueling training, Second Lieutenant Ralph "Lee" Minker and his crew were now ready to join the bomb groups fighting Nazi Germany. On short notice, second lieutenant Gordon C. Dodge replaced the ailing Don Rohl as co-pilot. Each crew member left behind a family and friends as had the thousands before them who joined the great air armada in England that became known as "The Mighty Eighth." They left Hunter Field, Savannah, Georgia on Wednesday, October 4, 1944, ferrying a B-17 across to England. Lee alerted the family that the flight path north would take him over Wilmington, Delaware. He promised to buzz the Ferris Industrial School and their house on his way to Bangor, Maine; the first segment of the long overseas trip. He would then fly to Greenland, finally landing in Wales before proceeding to Suffolk, England. The weather over the mid-Atlantic coast on October 4th was overcast with limited visibility, threatening his descent out of the clouds to below 5,000 feet.

October 7, 1944

Dearest Lee,

Well, dear, you certainly gave us a thrill of a lifetime

last Wednesday. I shall never forget it as long as I live. Thinking you would arrive about 10 daddy had all the staff and boys assemble on the athletic field at 9:45. There we waited until about 11 and then decided that the visibility was so bad we could not see you. Daddy called the duPont airport and they checked on the weather and reported that planes were clearing Savannah for Bangor but if you were flying a B-17 you would have to stay at about 7,000 feet on account of the ceiling and of course could not be seen. Daddy had just gotten back from in town and was standing in his office with Aunt Margaret looking out the door when he saw your plane headed straight for him. Aunt Margaret called me at the house and Bernice, grandmother and I rushed out. Bernice had not been well and happened to be home from school. Even Ginger and Pilot followed us out on the field. Could you see them?

You almost gave me heart failure when I saw you coming down so low. If only Shirley could have seen you, too. Needless to say my heart went with you as you dipped over the house and flew away. By this time I suppose you have reached your destination, although this has been a terrible week for flying and maybe you were held up. This morning, however, the sun is shining brightly and it ought to be a good day for football.

All my love,
Mother

October 7, 1944

Dear Lee,

It certainly was wonderful to see you in your plane

Wednesday. We had waited from 9:45 until 11:00 on the athletic field for you. School had been dismissed and all the boys and staff were there. Of course, we were awfully down-in the dumps when you didn't show up. What a super surprise, though, when you did come! I'm certainly glad I was home sick or I wouldn't have seen you. Shirley was very disappointed, as you can imagine. The dogs were both there, though, and as excited as the rest of us.

Love and Luck
Bernice

Williamsport, PA
October 8, 1944

Dear Looie,

I just finished talking to mother and Bernice on the phone and they gave me your address, so here I am. I certainly am sorry that I missed seeing you the other day when you flew over home and gave everyone such an enormous thrill. I know what you must have felt as you left your old co-pilot back there sick but I guess the new one is working out alright isn't he?

We've really been awfully busy since I came up to school. I am going home next week-end since I have a music lesson coming up. Do be good and don't stab all those girl's hearts with your silver wings. Have fun and drop me a line when can –

Always and all ways,
Shirley

10/8/44

Dear Lee:-

This is a new experience – fitting into this space. But I'll get used to it.

What a thrill you gave us Wed. I hope you could tell how all of us on the ground were enjoying ourselves. The plane seemed to be all you called it. We followed as far as we could – and then went right with you in spirit. Here's hoping all has gone well on the long hop – and that you won't be too long away.

Political broadcasts are being stepped up – and from now on there should be fireworks. Dewey seems to be edging ahead. The pres. voice is old—and is not going over so well. He's in an awful spot—and probably in no humor for a campaign. I don't think I would be.

The best to you, kid. You've learned to make the most of every situation – and you'll make the most of this one.

Dad

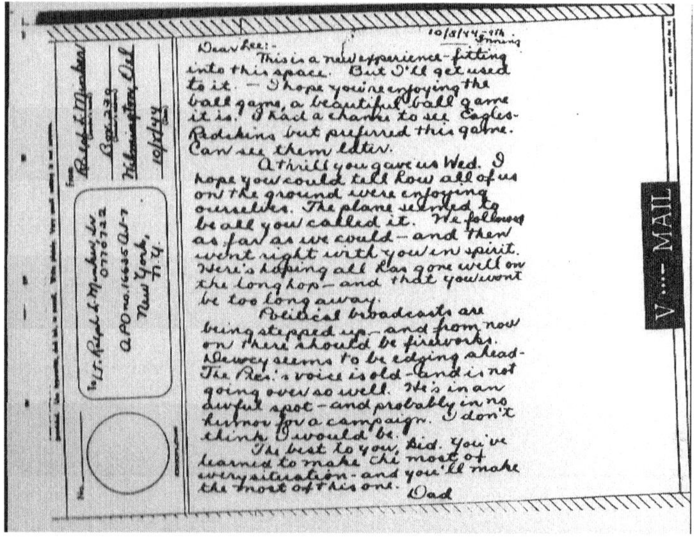
10/8/44 – 9th Inning
Dear Lee:-
This is a new experience – fitting into this space. But I'll get used to it. – I hope you're enjoying the ball game, a beautiful ball game it is! I had a chance to see Eagles-Redskins but preferred this game. Can see them later.
A thrill you gave us Wed. I hope you could tell how all of us on the ground were enjoying ourselves. The plane seemed to be all you called it. We followed as far as we could – and then went right with you in spirit. Here's hoping all has gone well on the long hop – and that you won't be too long away.
Political broadcasts are being stepped up – and from now on there should be fireworks. Dewey seems to be edging ahead – The Pres.'s voice is old – and is not going over so well. He's in an awful spot – and probably in no humor for a campaign. I don't think I would be.
The best to you, kid. You've learned to make the most of every situation – and you'll make the most of this one.
Dad

First V-Mail letter from Dad, October 8, 1944
Courtesy Historical Society of Delaware

Short for Victory Mail, V-Mail was a valuable tool for the military as the size of the overseas force grew to millions. Specially designed letter sheets were microfilmed to a quarter of the original size, shipped overseas and then enlarged at their destination before being delivered to military personnel. Writers had to fit their news into a small space on tissue-thin paper. V-Mail letters could be difficult to read, however, the process saved millions of tons of space for equipment on supply ships plying the Atlantic and Pacific oceans.

When Lee was classified a pilot in 1943, the army wrote his father that, "[he will have] … the best [training] our Country can give to fit him for his future duties and responsibilities as a member of the Army Air Forces." That training was now complete, departure for England was imminent, and soon thereafter – combat with the Eighth Army Air Force. The entire family faced an uncertain future, the slow voyage of overseas mail would be their only connection to each other.

Chapter Nine

Blue Hen Chick

October 13, 1944 to December 31, 1944

Dates: October 13, 1944 to December 31, 1944	Location: Rattlesden, England

October 13, 1944	The Minker crew arrived in Rattlesden Air Force Base, England.
October 18, 1944	Lee wrote his first letter home.
October 25, 1944	Lee Minker flew his first mission, as co-pilot on a mission to Hamburg.
Late October	Aircraft B-17G # 43-38719 was assigned to the Minker crew.
November 2, 1944	Lee flew his second mission as co-pilot, to Merseburg.
November 7, 1944	Franklin Roosevelt won a 4th term as president.
November 9, 1944	First mission for the crew in the *Blue Hen Chick.*
December 16, 1944	The Germans launched a new offensive in the Ardennes Forest, Belgium.
December 24, 1944	Eighth AAF launched a maximum effort mission.

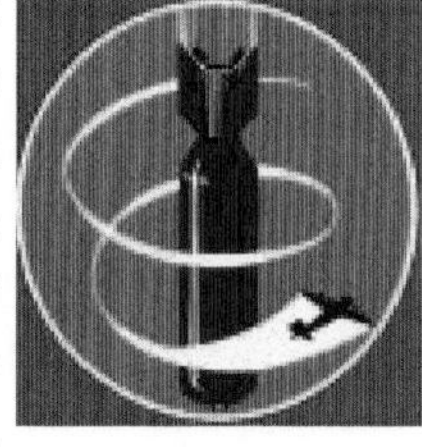

Second Lieutenant Ralph L. Minker and his crew arrived at Rattlesden Air Base, home of the 447th Bomb Group on October 13, 1944. Rattlesden AFB designated as Station #126, some 60-odd miles north of London, was one of 19 airbases that abruptly appeared in the county of Suffolk in 1942. Carved out of several farms with concrete laid in their fields, the base had three runways and hardstands for 55 aircraft. Before the arrival of the "Yanks", Rattlesden was a small village surrounded by hamlets of working farms and homesteads totaling a population of about 500. At the *Brewers Arms* where "The welcome was as warm as the beer" American airmen mingled with the locals who came to the pub for a pint and to play cribbage. An everpresent smoky haze from the wood burning fireplace, mixed with cigarette and cigar smoke clung to the wooden rafters in the low ceiled pub. The *Brewers Arms* was a haven, where airmen seeking a brief refuge from life at the base and harrowing days in the air, precariously perched their pints of "half and half" on an old upright piano and engaged in a friendly game of darts. Getting back to barracks was difficult in the complete darkness of the English night; all of the houses had black-out curtains and the country lanes had no lighting or signposts, a precaution taken in case of a landing by the Jerries. (Grant 2005)

Wednesday evening October 18, 1944

Dear Mother,
Greetings from Merry England!

A couple of weeks ago I left Hunter Field, Savannah, Georgia, with my B-17 combat aircrew en route over the North Atlantic Air Route of the U.S. A. A. F. Air Transport Command for combat service against Nazi Germany. We ferried a B-17 across which was loaded to the bursting point with our equipment, spare parts and mail for men in the ETO (European Theatre of Operations). It was an uneventful and very fatiguing trip but also most interesting; our great European air supply route, the ocean, ice cap, ice bergs, glaciers, fjords, northern lights, etc.

And now I am in England! First impressions are always based upon sketchy knowledge but as you are probably wondering what the world is like and I must find material for this letter here follow my first impressions of England (from the safety of an U.S. Army Air Field.)

The country is wet and cold and green, wonderfully tidy, but so small and old. The people seem much like Delaware folk with an accent. But the English monetary system is a relic of medieval torture (to be continued).

It has been said that the airplane caused the world to become smaller but I say that it has widened world horizons. By air one can travel great distances to heretofore isolated outposts in a minimum of time. As a result great are the problems to be faced as new regions and resources are developed and new peoples seek a better place in the sun side by side with established regions, resources, and peoples.

From now on I will try to keep up a fairly constant correspondence with you all back home. But sometimes a priority job will cause a break. Please don't worry – I am in fine shape. I think of you all often.

Love,
Lee

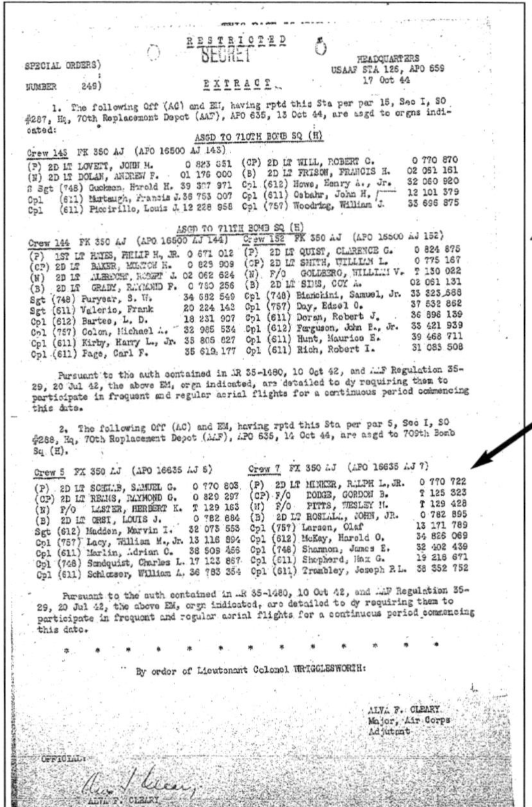

RESTRICTED
SECRET

SPECIAL ORDERS)
:
NUMBER 249)

HEADQUARTERS
USAAF STA 126, APO 659
17 Oct 44

EXTRACT

1. The following Off (AC) and EM, having rptd this Sta per par 15, Sec I, SO #287, Hq, 70th Replacement Depot (AAF), APO 635, 13 Oct 44, are asgd to orgns indicated:

ASGD TO 710TH BOMB SQ (H)

Crew 143 FK 350 AJ (APO 16500 AJ 143)
(P) 2D LT LOVETT, JOHN M. 0 823 651 (CP) 2D LT WILL, ROBERT C. 0 770 870
(N) 2D LT DOLAN, ANDREW F. 01 176 000 (B) 2D LT FRISON, FRANCIS H. 02 061 161
S Sgt (748) Guckeon, Harold H. 39 387 971 Cpl (612) Howe, Henry A., Jr. 32 060 920
Cpl (611) Murtaugh, Francis J. 38 753 007 Cpl (611) Osbahr, John H. 12 101 379
Cpl (611) Piccirillo, Louis J. 12 228 958 Cpl (757) Woodring, William J. 33 696 875

ASGD TO 711TH BOMB SQ (H)

Crew 144 FK 350 AJ (APO 16500 AJ 144) Crew 152 FK 350 AJ (APO 16500 AJ 152)
(P) 1ST LT HAYES, PHILIP H., JR. 0 671 012 (P) 2D LT QUIST, CLARENCE G. 0 824 875
(CP) 2D LT BAKER, MORTON H. 0 829 909 (CP) 2D LT SMITH, WILLIAM L. 0 775 167
(N) 2D LT ALBRECHT, ROBERT J. 02 062 624 (N) F/O GOLDBERG, WILLIAM V. T 130 022
(B) 2D LT GRADY, RAYMOND F. 0 780 256 (B) 2D LT SIMS, COY A. 02 061 131
Sgt (748) Puryear, S. W. 34 682 549 Cpl (748) Bianchini, Samuel, Jr. 33 323 688
Sgt (611) Valerio, Frank 20 224 142 Cpl (757) Day, Edsel O. 37 532 862
Cpl (612) Bartee, L. D. 18 231 907 Cpl (611) Doran, Robert J. 36 896 139
Cpl (757) Colon, Michael A. 32 985 534 Cpl (612) Ferguson, John P., Jr. 33 421 939
Cpl (611) Kirby, Harry L., Jr. 35 805 827 Cpl (611) Hunt, Maurice E. 39 468 711
Cpl (611) Page, Carl F. 35 619 177 Cpl (611) Rich, Robert I. 31 083 508

Pursuant to the auth contained in AR 35-1480, 10 Oct 42, and AAF Regulation 35-29, 20 Jul 42, the above EM, orgn indicated, are detailed to dy requiring them to participate in frequent and regular aerial flights for a continuous period commencing this date.

2. The following Off (AC) and EM, having rptd this Sta per par 5, Sec I, SO #288, Hq, 70th Replacement Depot (AAF), APO 635, 14 Oct 44, are asgd to 709th Bomb Sq (H).

Crew 5 FX 350 AJ (APO 16635 AJ 5) Crew 7 FX 350 AJ (APO 16635 AJ 7)
(P) 2D LT SCHWAB, SAMUEL G. 0 770 803 (P) 2D LT MINKER, RALPH L., JR. 0 770 722
(CP) 2D LT REAMS, RAYMOND G. 0 829 297 (CP) F/O DODGE, GORDON B. T 125 323
(N) F/O LASTER, HERBERT K. T 129 163 (N) F/O PITTS, WESLEY M. T 129 428
(B) 2D LT ORSI, LOUIS J. 0 782 884 (B) 2D LT ROSLAK, JOHN, JR. 0 782 895
Sgt (612) Madden, Marvin I. 32 073 553 Cpl (757) Larsen, Olaf 13 171 789
Cpl (757) Lacy, William M., Jr. 13 116 894 Cpl (612) McKay, Harold O. 34 826 069
Cpl (611) Marlin, Adrian C. 38 509 456 Cpl (748) Shannon, James E. 32 402 439
Cpl (748) Sandquist, Charles L. 17 123 867 Cpl (611) Shepherd, Max G. 19 218 671
Cpl (611) Schlosser, William A. 36 783 354 Cpl (611) Trombley, Joseph R.L. 38 352 752

Pursuant to the auth contained in AR 35-1480, 10 Oct 42, and AAF Regulation 35-29, 20 Jul 42, the above EM, orgn indicated, are detailed to dy requiring them to participate in frequent and regular aerial flights for a continuous period commencing this date.

* * * * * * * * * * * * *

By order of Lieutenant Colonel WRIGGLESWORTH:

ALVA F. CLEARY
Major, Air Corps
Adjutant

OFFICIAL:

ALVA F. CLEARY

Order showing arrival of the Minker Crew at Rattlesden on October 13, 1944. Official Unit History, 447th Bombardment Group Maxwell Air Force Base, U.S. Air Force Historical Research Agency

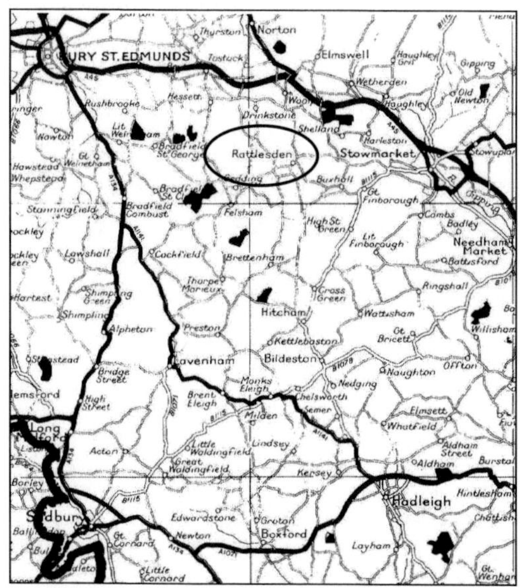

Detail map of Essex showing location of Rattlesden, north of London and southeast of Bury St. Edmonds. MAP COURTESY G.I.BARNETT. UK. GRANT. DV.

On Monday, October 16 Edna Minker opened the morning paper to stark headlines: "WHOLE WEST FRONT ERUPTS INTO HEAVY ACTION." Whatever fear embraced her that morning was warranted; the Eighth Air Force was flying daily missions in support of the Army's break through of the Siegfried line at Aachen along the Rhine River. In September the air war strategy called for "vastly heavier attacks" on marshalling yards, bridges, and train movements. This strategy would continue throughout the fall. Lee took four days to acclimate himself to the air base and the town before he wrote home. In his first letter from England, he described the air base and the country that he now called home. He appealed to his mother as he had in training, "Please don't worry about me." It's doubtful Lee's assurances had any affect on his mother.

The silver wings of the departing B-17 on October 4, 1944

were the last they knew of Lee until October 17th when a telegram announced his safe arrival in England. Life on the home front was full of war-related activity. The *Morning News* of October 19 reported that Mrs. Ralph L. Minker's suburban division raised $1,128.09 for the United War Fund, a charity that met the increasing burdens of families with loved ones serving in the military. That same morning Edna wrote an upbeat letter to her son and with characteristic modesty, she did not mention her fund raising efforts. Shipping packages overseas was another problem. Due to the heavy volume at Christmas time, the deadline for shipping to service men was October 17, which resulted in long lines at the Wilmington Post Office.

When Lee arrived at Rattlesden, the 447th B.G. had lost 71 crews with 731 personnel killed or missing in action. He was one of the many replacement pilots which brought the group back to full strength in the fall of 1944. This slim, blond young man with the intense blue eyes had yet to shave or cast a vote in an election. Initially the Squadron Commander, Lieutenant Colonel Robert G. David, was reluctant to let Lee fly, thinking him too young. Replacement pilots had to be combat-seasoned by flying co-pilot on several missions. After the two break-in missions, Colonel David decided the "Minker crew will be ok." (Stub Warfle, operations staff officer in 1944.)

Thursday, Oct. 19, 1944

Dearest Lee:-

We received your cable on Tuesday, - Oct. 17. Of course we did not know the date or from which base it was sent, but it was good to know you are well and safe. Now we shall await your first letter. We called Julia and told her, of course.

We are having delightful weather now and I hope the days wherever you are are just as beautiful. Is your new co-pilot working out alright and do you get a replacement for the gunner you said you lost? Great gains are seemingly being made against the Japs in the Pacific.

We tried to get some pictures of the pup on Sunday. If they are any good I'll send them to you; but the way she wiggles I am not too hopeful.

Bernice is anxious to know if you have named your plane and if so what do you call "her"? Well I must stop now. I am experimenting with this airmail letter to see if it gets thru better than the V-mail. Let me know.

With all my love.

Mother

Saturday evening October 21, 1944

Dear Mother,

I have just returned from radio ground school and in the hour remaining before 2100 lights out I must write several letters.

During the past several days I have been almost totally occupied with a concentrated ground school introduction to the U.S.A. Eighth Air Force, the ETO (European Theatre of Operations) and air combat against Nazi Germany. (oxygen, frost bite, air-sea rescue, radio, engineering of operation, code, aircraft recognition, tactics, ditching, bail out, gunnery, prisoner of war, escape, weather, security, briefing, interrogation, intelligence, first aid, health and hygiene, combat flight.)

My entire B-17 crew is to be checked out on the ground

before flying. But soon I will start flying again! I will fly with a skeleton crew (pilot, co-pilot, engineer, radio operator) on practice missions during which I will be given flying checks (transition, night, formation, emergency). As veteran aircrews graduate from combat upon completion of thirty five missions I will replace them. But practice missions will be scheduled during my entire tour of duty and on an off day I may be scheduled to slow time a plane (break in new engines.)

Love,
Lee

Lee attended his first combat briefing at 0630 on the morning of October 26. He flew as co-pilot with Lieutenant Joseph Wessling on a break-in mission to Hannover. Four members of the Minker crew were also on the mission: navigator William Pitts, flight engineer James Shannon, ball turret gunner Max Shepherd, and waist gunner Harold McKay.

Sunday evening October 29, 1944

Dear Mother,

I am now operational – that is, my crew and I have been checked and found ready for the air war against the axis. But training will continue on days that no bombing mission is scheduled as part of the constant effort to gain complete mastery of the air for the United Nations.

You all back home are probably wondering just how the airbase of the 447th Bomb Group of the Eighth U.S.A.A.F compares with a typical airbase in the United States. The most striking difference is that here in England there is no fenced off plot of ground reserved for the military – planes, personnel, equipment and buildings are scattered for protection against possible enemy attack. I have to skirt a turnip field to go to the mess hall and a small English pub stands by field headquarters. Barracks are also different – Low long Niessen huts with bricked up ends. But the remaining features of this base are no different than at any continental U.S. base. The situation might be summed up as adequate. Little lacks such as fresh eggs, ample lighting or sidewalks cause most peeves.

As yet I have had no time to go on pass but from now on I should be getting a couple of days a month. Of course I will make a point of visiting London and if given enough time I will see Edinburgh. I would also like to see Cambridge and Ipswich.

Love,
Lee

Monday evening October 30, 1944

Dear Mother,

This afternoon mail reached me from the States for the first time since I took up residence in England. It was great to hear from you and the family, from Julia and other friends again. To read the delivery of mail forwarded from Gulfport A.A.F. or sent to either my temporary or permanent A.P.O. number was a most enjoyable two hour job.

Because of winter and resulting bad weather mail delivery between the U.S.A. and the E.T.O. will be erratic and delayed. But nevertheless it will be the high spot of my days. In the afternoon's delivery the latest letters were two V-mail written October fifteenth one from you and one from Dad; I received several airmail letters written October eleventh. A V-mail letter from Bernice came general delivery because she did not fill in the required data in the inside of the envelope; Grandmother Minker wrote her V-mail script too small to be legible; I do not know whether V-mail may be typed. How is my mail to you coming through?

From now on maybe mail will come more steadily. V-mail or airmail are almost equally good, but you can write more in airmail. I wish that every now and then you would send clippings on people I know, sports, college, Wilmington, etc. Some city papers have special battle editions sponsored by local interests and there is a Newsweek battle issue and a New York Times reprint of the News of the Week – Maybe it could be arranged for me to get some such publication. But other than that there is nothing I need – that is, except for 620 film, any and all you can send and new and old pictures from and of home.

Love,
Lee

P.S. Of course I am looking forward to the Christmas box of goodies.

Officer's quarters were in a Quonset hut – far removed from the comforts of life in the States. A small coal-fired stove supplied the heat; the sound of rain was frequently heard drumming on the tin roof. He wrote often about familiar pleasures – fresh eggs, baseball, mom's applesauce cookies— a way to establish a link with home in the strange world of 5:00 a.m. flight briefings and nine hour missions at 25,000 feet into Nazi Germany.

Operations Headquarters, Quonset hut similar to those used for barracks. Courtesy Historical Society of Delaware

His name was posted on the board to fly on November 2 1944, the briefing began at 0530. This second break-in mission was to one of the most dangerous targets in Germany, the heavily defended Merseburg synthetic oil plant. The plant converted coal into oil which the *Luftwaffe* desperately needed. Merseburg had been bombed repeatedly, only to be quickly rebuilt by the Germans using slave labor. Lee flew co-pilot with Lieutenant Hatfield in A/C #43-37795 *Dixie Marie*, along with the other members of the *Blue Hen Chick* crew. The group encountered heavy flak over the target losing one aircraft to a mid-air collision. In another loss, the formation leader, Major Allen, took a hit over the target and the plane exploded; several planes went down on the way home from damage inflicted by flak. Seven aircraft and four crews did not make it back to Rattlesden that night. Lee's letter the next evening to his mother did not give any indication of the harrowing mission to Merseburg, or what he might have felt about the losses and the now empty beds in the silent barracks.

Friday evening November 3, 1944

Dear Mother,

As yet I have not received any letters indicating that you have received any letters from me since I went abroad.

But maybe that is because of slow mail delivery of soldier "Free" mail. How are you all at home? What is doing? How is your district drive of the United War Fund progressing? When does Dad begin organizing the next War Bond Drive? How is everything at the Ferris School? What is the local sports and political news? How is Shirley doing as a high and mighty college sophomore; Bernice as a learned senior in high school? How is Ginger and son Pilot? Has the garden been winterized? How are all our friends? What is what in entertainment?

Life here is routine – practice or actual bombing missions every day. It is mighty hard work but it will be worth it if as a result the world will learn to live in peace and work for freedom, justice, security and equality for all.

Love,
Lee

Flying Fortress #43-38719 A [Able] was assigned to the Minker crew in late October. The aircraft arrived in Rattlesden on September 28, 1944, flying eight missions with various crews. Lee named the B-17 *Blue Hen Chick* in honor of the mascot of the state of Delaware. Blue Hens were celebrated fighting chickens of the First Delaware Regiment in the American Revolution. The Delaware General Assembly made the "Blue Hen Chicken" the official state bird of Delaware in 1939. Their first mission as a crew on November 9 was not in the *Blue Hen Chick*, rather a seasoned aircraft named *Li'l Eight Ball.* The primary target, transportation sites on the French-German border was cloud covered; so they hit the secondary target, the marshalling yards at Saarbrucken, with 1000 lb GP (General Purpose) bombs.

Sunday evening November 5, 1944

Dear Mother,

Last week B-17 G 719 was assigned to crew forty one of the 709th Squadron of the 447th Bomb Group of the Eighth U.S.A.A.F. – my crew. The ship had been built and checked at a Boeing aircraft factory in the mid west United States and then flown to a staging camp where it was assigned to a combat air crew to be flown across the ocean for combat in the E.T.O. At a base somewhere in England the plane was rechecked and modified for combat and then flown to the airfield of the 447th bomb Group for assignment to an operational combat air crew – mine. After final checks it is now ready for action against the enemy. It's name? Blue Hen Chick.

Today has been a typical November football day – cool, windy and grey. Last evening, and every Saturday, at 1900 EST (English Summer Time), I listened to a football broadcast from the States – Navy – Notre Dame.

The small English papers furnish further news and pictures but much of their content is foreign to our world and their comments are on inter-party squabbles or calls for British imperialism. Despite all claims movies are six months old. Or older. As yet I know nothing of England except of this air base I call home.

Love,
Lee

P.S. Last letter received from you 10-19-44 mailed.

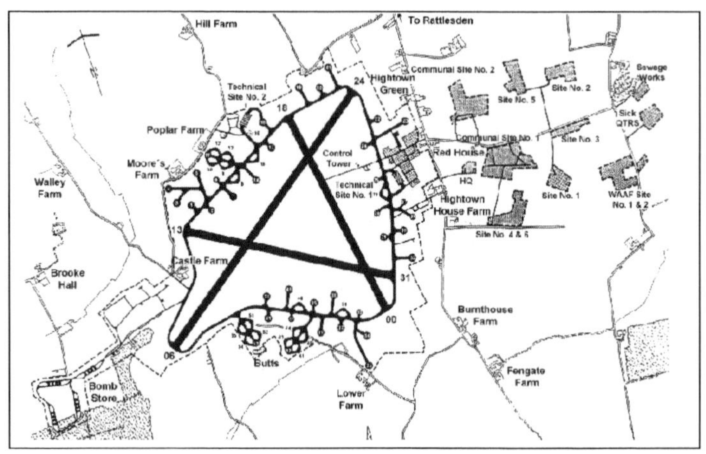

"This air base I now call home."
Map of Rattlesden Army Air Force Base, Station 126.
Courtesy www.447bg.com

Lee Minker in the pilot's seat of the Blue Hen Chick
Courtesy Historical Society of Delaware

On November 7, 1944 President Roosevelt won a fourth term in office, defeating Thomas Dewey with 53.5 % of the popular vote, sweeping the Electoral College 532 to 99. Dewey referred to Roosevelt as "that tired old man," while Roosevelt urged the nation not to "change horses in mid-stream." The Army Air Force took little notice of the presidential election, the war continued with crews taking to the skies every day. Edna shared her own fears about the election results in her letter of November 9.

Wednesday evening November 8, 1944

Dear Mother,

The results of the 1944 U.S. presidential election have been radioed to the U.S. troops in the E.T.O. [European Theatre of Operations] throughout the day. They have caused interest, no excitement and general approval.

Servicemen wish the war to end and for peace to prevail in the world. And Franklin D. Roosevelt seems to be the best qualified and most determined leader to achieve that.

And now that the campaign is over maybe Congress and the president can concentrate on more efficient domestic administration and postwar planning.

Somehow a presidential election seems to be in some other world of the dim distant past with the folks we love and Saturday football games and real fresh eggs.

A horrible reminder of our present exile is the English monetary system which is the system used in the U.K. by U.S. troops. [He then gives a detailed description of English monetary system.] If you ever tour the Isles or the empire you can use this letter as a monetary guide.

The best to you all.

Love,

Lee

After two missions with an experienced pilot, a new crew was considered ready to fly with their first pilot. On November 9, 1944 the crew of the *Blue Hen Chick* took off for their first mission together, to transportation centers on the French-German border. Crews were identified by the name of the first pilot, the group of nine became the Minker crew.

The descriptions of each mission throughout Chapters 9, 10, and 11 are drawn from the *History of the 447th Bomb Group* by Doyle Shields, the mission operations records housed at the National Archives, the lists posted on the 447th B.G. website, and the log maintained by Flight Engineer James Shannon. The flight engineer had responsibility for all the mechanical systems on the plane, he stood behind the cockpit watching the gauges, listened as the crew reported in, and advised the pilot on the plane's systems. Shannon maintained the log for each mission, and then reported problems to the ground crew that kept the *Blue Hen* flying. The last thing a pilot and his crew wanted to do was "stand down."

Mission # 3 #42-107215 *Li'l Eight Ball* **Thurs Nov 9 1944**
First Mission for Minker Crew

Target – Marshalling Yards, Saarbrucken
Briefing at 0330 hours
Take off began at 0520
Target was cloud covered, bombed secondary target at Saarbrucken and Koblenz.
Landing began at 1311
Log: Mission lasted 8.00 hours. Flak was moderate – our ship hit in the waist. Had to feather propeller on #1 engine after leaving the target.

Thursday, November 9, 1944

Dearest Lee:-

I expect you knew the result of the election almost as soon as we did here, for I read [in] the papers that the English papers gave it full, front-page news. The latest reports that Roosevelt carried 38 states. I guess none of us thought that Dewey really would be elected, but I did think he would gather in more votes that he did. I hope and pray that Roosevelt's health will be such that he can carry on for the full term, for I tremble to think of Truman at the head of the nation.

In Tuesday night's paper there was a short item which said that 3 Delaware men recently completed an orientation course at an Air Service Command station in England. They were a 2nd lieut. by the name of Adkins from Holly Oak., Corp Robert Hocker, S. Bancroft Parkway, and Lieut. Ralph L. Minker, Jr. So far nothing has come thru from you except a letter which Uncle Marion had written you and an order of Sunday service from the base at Manchester, N.H. We gather, if the newspaper article is correct, that you are now a 1st. lieut. Is that correct?

Have you seen anyone you knew or anyone from Wilmington over there? I expect we shall be receiving several letters at one time, - at least I hope so.

We are all fine. Daddy is in the midst of preparations for the next War Bond drive which begins next week.

With all my love,
Mother

For weeks after the first cable from Lee the family lived with unremitting anxiety. Delays in the mail from overseas were routine, especially when there was a move and change in assignment. Life continued quietly at the Ferris Industrial School and the Minker household until November 11 when the first letter from England, written on October 18, arrived. The entire family erupted in joy and relief. For family members and the servicemen, mail and morale were one and the same.

November 12, 1944

Dear Lee,

Well, yesterday we received your first letter and what a thrill! I was at work, but mother called and I felt like screaching [sic] at the top of my lungs. What makes your mail take so long? How's the food? Please request some stuff in your letters so we can send you things.

The house is certainly upset today. People keep calling for Daddy, doorbells ring, planes buzz. The 6th War Loan is coming up and Pop's head up to heels in that.

Say, what do the figures before the number up in the left hand side of your letters mean? Do you censor your own mail? How are the English women?

Please try to answer <u>some</u> of these questions.

Lots of Love Luck
Bernice

For the thousands of airmen stationed in England, leave in London offered a break from the tedium and tension of the war. The officer's club at Grosvenor House and the Red Cross were a welcome oasis providing a warm bath, decent food, and entertainment. Like most of his fellow airmen, Lieutenant Minker had not been in Europe prior to the war. London, while "drab and battle scarred," offered a taste of cosmopolitan life to American airmen with theatres, restaurants, and sites seen only in schoolbooks. After a train ride from Stowemarket, Lee visited London, enjoying the sites and time away from the roar of engines and flak over Germany. At times Lee's letters have the eerie quality of a young man on holiday rather than at war. Yet reminders of the war are everywhere in London – from the bombed out buildings to the sparse food.

Tuesday evening November 14, 1944

Dear Shirley,

I recently visited London. London, England – the center from which Anglo-Saxon culture and civilization have spread throughout the world, second largest city on earth, great financial, commercial and manufacturing center, nerve center of the United Nation's victory drive in the west.

After an early morning train ride from a town near my present airbase I arrived at a great London station, caught a ride in one ancient looking cab and engaged a room in the Regent Palace Hotel in Piccadilly [sic] Circus, heart of the entertainment district. After a spare wartime English lunch I went to the well stocked Central Officers Clothing Post Exchange to purchase needed clothing, returning to the hotel for tea. I ate dinner at the best restaurant in England – American Officers Mess at the Grovesner House. In the evening I did the town.

Next day, after breakfast in bed and a warm tub bath,

I took an American Red Cross limousine tour of the town: Piccadilly [sic] Circus, Trafalgar Square and Admiral Nelson's statue, Tower of London, London Bridge, Tower Bridge, east side slum and warehouse district, Fleet Street newspaper area, the Temple law and court center, Old Curiosity Shop, Buckingham Palace, Hyde Park, Baker Street, number 10 Downing Street, houses of Parliament, British Museum, U.S. embassy. I went through the massive awe inspiring war damaged St. Pauls Cathedral, which is kept like a museum, and Westminster Abbey and Cathedral. Seeing the top movie An American Romance completed my first visit to London.

London today is not catering to tourists, she is drab and battle scarred. If you will read William L. White's report in Reader's Digest of the great fire night of the 1942 London blitz and multiply that by five years of war (rockets still cause frequent tragedy) you will have an idea of this great city today.

Must close now.

Love,
Lee

In mid-November the Supreme Command launched an all-out effort to breach the last vestiges of the Siegfried Line (the defensive line along the border of Germany and France) facing the American Army. This breakthrough focused on territory between Aachen and Duren where Lee flew a mission on Nov 16. Four B-17's were lost that day; poor visibility on the English coast forced the 447th to land most of their bombers in Western England.

Mission # 4 #43 38719 *Blue Hen Chick* Thurs Nov 16 1944
First mission for the Minker crew in the *Blue Hen Chick*.

Target – Transportation targets, Duren
Briefing at 0500
Take off began at 0727
Bombed through the clouds. On return to base, majority were advised to land in West of England due to bad weather over Rattlesden.
Landing began at 1443
Log: Mission lasted 6.00 hours. Flak was light- Ship hit in wing. #1 & 2 Propellers nicked by Flak. We had bomb release trouble. Carried Propaganda leaflets. Did not land at our own field – had bad weather. Stayed two days at a field called Welford Park.

November 20, 1944

Dearest Lee:-

Last night we received the second letter from you, the one written on November 5, which contained the receipt for $300. If you don't watch out you will soon be a millionaire! Daddy and I were over to Cavanagh's to a tea when the letter came, so Bernice called me and read it over the telephone.

We had a little bit of snow this morning, but now it is pouring down rain. I do hope all the bad weather gets over before the weekend. I suppose Bernice wrote of our plans for Thanksgiving.

We were interested in your name for your ship. Of course no one but you could be responsible for it. Do the members of your crew know anything about the significance of the Blue Hen? If I can find a write-up I'll send it along. I hope you will be able to keep the chick under control at all times and that she will safely gather all the crew under her wings as she flies about. Our very best to you all.

With all my love.
Mother

Wednesday evening November 22, 1944

Dear Dad,

Today the first round trip mail from me in the U.K. of the E.T.O. to you at home in Delaware, U.S.A, and back to me at my B-17 bomber base came through – thirty eight days after joining the 709th Squadron of the 447th Bomb Group of the 4th Bombardment Wing of the Eighth U.S.A.A.F. Now that the route has been pioneered may be communication will be faster. But at present the Christmas rush is causing delays in mail delivery. Needless to say, however, I look forward to your letters more than anything else in the day. I wish to take advantage of this letter to wish you a happy birthday, tardily.

I am sad to hear of the death in action of Wally Wroten. I hope that it will not be in vain.

From now on winter weather is going to keep English based bombers grounded very often. But that will not mean a relaxation of our schedule. Practice missions and ground school will keep us busy. Probably as our ground troops advance we will hit almost as many tactical targets as strategical.

Everything is going fine with me and my crew. So please don't worry about us.

As ever –
Lee

November proved to be a difficult month for the 447th. "Operations were considerably hampered by the extremely large numbers of new crews in training. However, by the end of the month, the situation had clarified itself and the group was again on its feet with a full strength group available for almost every mission." (447th operations report, November 1944) The fresh crews were needed for attacks on German marshalling yards and fuel supplies. The Minker crew flew three missions in a row on Nov. 25, 26, and 27, each in a different plane. Saturday, November 25 their mission was to the oil refinery at Merseburg which had over 1000 German flak guns. The 447th had already paid a heavy price at Merseburg on November 2, 1944 with the loss of seven B-17's. On November 30, on another mission to Merseburg, the Eighth A.A.F. lost 29 B-17s.

Mission #5 A/C #43-38230 *Wolf Wagon* Sat Nov 25 1944

Target – Leuna synthetic oil plant, Merseburg
Briefing at 0500
Foul weather assembly procedure over the field. Target was cloud covered, easily identified by dense black smoke from the plant. Lt. Norman K. Wiggin (710th) flying *Shack Happy* took a direct hit and exploded mid-air.
Landing began at 1602
Log: Mission lasted 8.10 Hrs. flak was moderate. This was a good mission. Had little trouble. Jerries hit other groups with fighters as we had our biggest fighter support.

Mission #6 *Blue Hen Chick* Sun Nov 26 1944

Target – Railway at Hamm oil & Refinery at Misbury
Briefing at 0600
Take off began at 0730
Bad weather assembly over the field. Encountered some flak over the target.
Landing began at 1602
Log: Mission lasted 6:15 Hours. Flak was light and rocket bombs were in area. Hit by flak in waist and tail. After we left target had a gas leak. Plane full of gas fumes. Saw bomber go down in flames.

Mission #7 A/C 42-97296 *Royal Flush* Mon Nov 27 1944

Target – Rail yards at Bingen
Briefing at 0600
Take off began at 0850
Bad weather assembly over the field, all of Europe cloud covered. Uneventful bombing run. Strategic mission that drew Luftwaffe fighters which were hit by force of 460 P-47 fighters. Luftwaffe lost 98 fighters in the air and 4 on the ground.
Landing began at 1433
Log: Mission lasted 4:40 hours. Our third Mission in a row. We were all tired. They had heavy guns at target. Air was so rough made flying formation hard. Had bomb rack trouble.

Dec 1, 1944

Dear Lee:-

Mother has told you already how much it meant to us to hear from you. The letters came like an old-fashioned "Northeaster"– concentrated within forty-eight hours. We could now stand another "Northeaster." We are hoping our letters are getting to you. We can take it here if you are getting the news.

I just came back from John Davis, the barber down the road. He sends his regards. I think he could have clippered my hair all off if I hadn't promised to include this greeting of his. He is doing our hair cutting at the school now, by the way. Every Friday he has a habit of imbibing a bit—and it seems I am usually getting around to a haircut on Fridays.

The Sixth War Loan Drive is taking plenty of time and work. Some people lack the spirit altogether. But most of them are having their pay deducted regularly and so do not feel like responding to these special appeals. We'll get across however. I am in about three meetings a night – and the grind is really on.

I've rambled along at a great rate. Love to you, kid, and the very best every minute of every day and night.

As always,

Dad

The mission on December 4 was a "maximum effort" – every plane that could fly, every crewman who could get into flight gear went into the air. Merseburg was the most difficult and dangerous target in Germany. The location of synthetic oil plants that produced aviation fuel for the *Luftwaffe*, it was repeatedly bombed by the Eighth AAF. The Germans used slave labor to quickly repair and rebuild their plants and railways. With German fuel supplies critically short, formidable defenses were placed around Merseburg, a lifeline for the *Luftwaffe*. Over the target the *Blue Hen Chick* developed a runaway propeller, a hazardous condition where the propeller speed outstrips that of the engine. It required "feathering" the engine to maintain propeller pitch, a maneuver that was practiced in the skies over New Mexico.

Mission #8 ***Blue Hen Chick*** **Mon Dec 4 1944**

Target – Marshalling yards, Mainz
Briefing 0730
Take off began at 0930
Dropped 500 lb.GP [General Purpose] bombs to destroy rail lines, incendiary bombs to destroy cargo. Target was cloud covered, used PFF, clouds prevented observing results.
Landing began at 1619
Log: Mission lasted 7.20 hours. We were hit by flak in waist. A piece of flak casting made a big dent in leading edge of left wing. Late getting back to field – strong head wind.

Mission #9 ***Blue Hen Chick*** **Wed Dec 6 1944**

Target –Leuna Synthetic Oil Plant at Merseburg and rail yard at Bielefeld
Briefing at 0500
Take off began at 0815
Bad weather assembly. Flak over the target. Lt. H.R. DeMallie (708th) and his crew, on the first mission, hit by flak, went down over Germany.
Landing at 1523
Log: Mission lasted 7.20 hours. This is the target that scares most of the crews as it has a 40 mile stretch of flak and over 400 flak guns. Had a leak in prop governor and a runaway propeller over the target.

December 7, 1944

Dearest Lee:-

This is the third anniversary of Pearl Harbor and also Shirley's birthday. I guess we all remember that tragic day 3 years ago, and the end does not seem to be anywhere in sight. The Draft Boards are having to dip into the married men's and father's groups in order to get their quota for this month. And always in the back of one's mind seems to be the question "Will we win the peace?"

Perhaps you have learned from the English papers of the difference in American and British opinion concerning the interference's in the government of Italy, Greece, etc. And we don't feel sure about Russia's future course in Europe. And so it goes.

Love from every one of us.

Mother

As the pilot, Lee was in charge of reading and censoring letters of his crew. His letters mention little about missions or

Germany. Writing just two days after the mission to Merseburg, his letter is brief sharing no sign of the stress from the bombing run and flak over the oil refinery. Instead he tried to allay his mother's anxieties with reports of crew and plane and assurances he had given ever since training – "I'm fine – don't worry about me." As the family spent yet another Christmas separated by the war and now an ocean, they shared their Christmas preparations in letters full of longing to be together. Everyone reports to Lee on the holiday activities hoping to send Christmas cheer.

Friday evening
December 8, 1944

Dear Mother,

Even if my letters take a month to reach you I hope you understand that I am thinking of you always. Over here one looses [sic] count of the days; the past home life often seems far from present army life. Because of exasperating slowness of mail delivery the last letter received from you was written November ninth. So if at times you do not hear from me for several days please do not worry.

There really is not much news from here. I am fine; my air crew is fine; Blue Hen Chick is fine. Time is spent in combat flying, practice flying, test hops, ground training, visits to London and self maintenance. But – it is not dull and routine. Enclosed you will find a receipt for $130.00 which I am sending through the base finance office.

Let me hear from you.

Love,
Lee

Mission #10 ***Blue Hen Chick*** **Mon Dec 11 1944**

Target – Rail yards at Frankfurt and Giessen
Briefing 0530
Take off began at 08016
Bombed Koblenz as the last resort target. The usual flak, uneventful return.
Landing began at 1454
Log: Mission lasted 7.20 hours. This was the largest force of Heavy Bombers ever dispatched in daylight on a single mission. Flak was light. We hit the secondary target.

Mission #11 ***Blue Hen Chick*** **Tues Dec 12 1944**

Target – Rail yards at Darmstadt
Briefing at 0530
Take off began at 0818
Fighter escort of P-47s and P-51s. Bomb run was visual, Germans use smoke pots to confuse target area. Results rated poor.
Landing began at 1551
Log: Mission lasted 7.50 hours. This was a bad one for me. Flak hit top turret by right gun. Had to put new Dome on turret. Visibility was very poor. Had a tough time landing.

December 13, 1944

Dearest Lee:-

I had a few minutes in town yesterday after a meeting so I went looking for Julia's Christmas present from you. I had talked to her mother and she said Julia would like to have a pin for her coat lapel. I think you will be pleased with what I found. It is a gold chick with a blue stone eye. It fits in so nicely with the name of your plane that I think Julia will be pleased with it, too. It cost $6.00 and $1.20 tax.

Last night's paper carried an article about Wallie Wroten [family friend] who won a Silver Star for gallantry in France. The citation reads "During a daylight attack by his company against a strong enemy hill position, Sergeant Wroten, an automatic fireman, noticed a seriously wounded comrade lying on dangerously open terrain between his position and the enemy. On his own initiative and with utter disregard for his personal safety Sergeant Wroten left his foxhole and crept across the open terrain in clear sight of the enemy under direct enemy machine-gun, rifle and mortar fire to the side of his badly wounded comrade, and dragged him a distance of approximately 100 yards to safety." Wallie was later killed in action.

Thursday night of this week the boys here are putting on the first performance of their new play – "When Johnny Comes Marching Home Again." Next Thursday we will have our Christmas dinner, followed by another performance. To this the Governor, Mayor James and about 20 others have been invited.

Love from all of us.

Mother

The largest battle in the Western European campaign began on December 16, 1944 in the Ardennes Forest of Belgium. Over a million men (600,000 American, 500,000 German) fought doggedly through the snowy mountainous region of the Ardennes Forest. Air support from the Eighth A.A.F. helped to cut the flow of German supplies to their troops in the Battle of the Bulge.

Bad weather kept the Eighth grounded in England for a week and when the skies cleared on Christmas Eve, the *Blue Hen* flew the first of 13 missions during the Germans' last major offensive. The majority of these bombing missions were to synthetic oil plants and marshalling yards where troops and materials gathered. Lee's family tried not to let the news of the Battle of the Bulge dampen their Christmas season. Attending church services and shopping for gifts was interspersed with reading about the Eighth Air Force attacks over the western front in terrible weather as the war dragged on into the fourth Christmas.

Between missions, Lee once again explored battle-scarred London, amusing his parents with notes on British food and prices after his latest pass. The Officer's Club at Grosvenor House Hotel hosted dances for the airmen on leave in London. Princess Elizabeth, then eighteen years old, occasionally came to dance with the American boys. The royal family elected to stay in London throughout the war. One evening Lee was selected as one of her partners and "danced my 12 steps" with the young princess.

Tuesday evening
December 19, 1944

Dear Mother,

I returned from pass last evening only to find the airbase fog bound. I sincerely hope that the weather clears up soon so that we can help the ground troops break the German counter offensive in France.

I visited London again on this last pass. This time I assumed the role of a gourmand and sampled wartime meals of London restaurants. The Grosvenor House American Officers Mess serves the best balanced meals, the best prepared and the breakfast. (26, two and six fifty American pennies). There is also a good bar and a nice reading room. The dining room of the Regent Palace Hotel offers poor sparse vegetable dinners for six shillings amidst elegant atmosphere. Lyons Corner House, a six story Horn and Hardart, offers much the same although better prepared and cafeteria style. Drivers [restaurant] serves very good seafood meals: oysters on the half shell, lobster, trout. In the small Pompeian Restaurant one can get a fine spaghetti dinner and small but excellent steak. At Prices [restaurant] on the Strand for a ten shilling note you get all the chicken you can eat. (No remarks).

But with your meals in London today you can get no milk and very poor coffee. Tea or beer are served, some wine and water, if you ask for it. Tea at four is just another meal with everyone stuffing himself full of pastry (hardly any sweetening), toast and tea.

Between bites I managed to see the changing of the guard at Buckingham Palace (no fancy dress during war.) and a fair revue: "Happy and Glorious." A new pass policy has been instituted in this Bomb Group now. Every twenty four days we get a two day pass and a two day stand down for training.

I have received an impressive lot of Christmas packages. The last, except for one very good fruitcake, remains unopened until Christmas. This will be my second Christmas as an Air Force soldier and, I hope my last. But the enemy is strong and he may force our fight to continue past other Christmases. I sort of feel that I should stay in action here with the 8th, at least until Germany is defeated. But I will come home and then we will have a real Christmas together.

Merry Christmas to you and all the family.

Love,
Lee

December 21, 1944

Dearest Lee:

My mind seems to be very much in a whirl so I suppose I should not try to write you, but there doesn't seem to be much chance to let up for a few days and I guess you will excuse any lack of unity, coherence or emphasis.

This is the evening we have our Christmas dinner here at the school, with guests; then the play, then the Christmas parties in the cottages. I have been busy all morning trying to get things in shape for the dinner,-arrangement of guests, etc. and going over toys to be sent to Ball and Dunbar [cottages at the Ferris School]. Now I must go home to lunch, press Bernice's gown for this evening and then come back to the office.

Did I tell you that daddy was giving us a trip to the Metropolitan as his Christmas gift to us? We had planned to go up during the Christmas holidays, but the tickets arrived last week and are for this Friday, December 22, and they can't be exchanged; so we shall leave tomorrow for New York. It is a terribly hectic time for either daddy or me and we won't be able to do all we planned, but we are all delighted with the prospect of our first trip to the Met. We shall hear Rigoletto with Lawrence Tibbet. How I wish you could be with us! But when you come home on your furlough we can arrange something of the sort. As we are going to the evening performance we shall stay overnight and return sometime on Saturday. We'll write and tell you all about it after it is over. The only thing worrying us at present is the weather. Ordinarily I am delighted to see snow for Christmas, but we are hoping it will hold off until we get back. The roads are bad in some places now, from ice; and the radio predicts snow in N.Y. for tomorrow. It will only make the driving for daddy so much harder.

I do hope you will not be going out on a mission on Christmas day. This German offensive looks bad, although I guess we don't know too much about it, for there is a news blackout.

Needless to say our hearts go out to you at this Christmas season as at no other time.

With all our love,
Mother

The news of the brutal and bloody battle in the Ardennes Forest unfolded throughout the last weeks of December, dampening the Christmas spirit on the home front with reports of heavy casualties and terrible weather. An editorial in the *Wilmington Morning News* on Friday December 22 titled "Anxious Hours" expressed everyone's feelings on the home front: "Not since the early days of the war have Americans had to face a situation as grave as the one that confronts us on the battlefields of Western Europe. Worry tears at all our hearts as the American lines reel backwards before a tremendous German drive. Half-forgotten fears revive as the enemy rolls on and it remains uncertain when and where our troops will be able to halt him." The Minkers knew that their son was part of the air war over German lines that dismal December and that the casualties mounted to the tens of thousands. The tension and worry during Christmas of 1944 was unrelenting both at home and in England.

December 23, 1944 9:30 p.m.

My dear Lee: -

Mother, the girls, and I returned from New York City about four hours ago. We went up yesterday to hear the opera, Rigoletto, with Laurence Tibbit singing the lead. I'll let them describe it to you if they wish. It ought to be something they will always remember.

We're thinking of you a great deal these days. The papers give us the usual articles on the European theatre. There's a new seriousness settling over everyone – and it will mean some real knuckling down to business, I think. Here's hoping our offensive can get going again – and the whole thing ended up. Maybe we can all do a better job toward making it forever unnecessary to sacrifice so much that is precious and irreplaceable in another war.

We are well. We're with you every minute – God bless you.

As ever,
Dad

Mission # 12 ***Blue Hen Chick*** **Sun Dec 24 1944**

Target – Airfield at Babenhausen
"This was the mission to end all missions. The groups were instructed to put up everything that would fly." First clear day since the beginning of the Battle of the Bulge on Dec. 16.
Log: Mission lasted 7.00 hours. This was biggest single mission. Hell [to] try to stop German counter-Attack. [Saw] ship in our formation go down in flames. Hit in right wing by flak. Had to crank up bomb bay doors. German Fighters in the area.

On Christmas Eve the weather in England finally cleared. The Eighth AAF launched an all out attack on German airfields and communication centers and the Third Air Division [Lee's group] lost eight B-17s that day. After each mission intelligence officers interviewed the crew and then wrote up the mission interrogation report. Lee's report for the Babenhausen mission notes three planes observed in distress.

FRIENDLY AIRCRAFT LOST OR IN DISTRESS: (Group and A/C Number - Condition where down - chutes seen - any unusual occurances of interest - altitude.

(1) 447th 13:03 Time {5018 0535 Position 20500' Alt PFF Major Bar...
No Chutes Seen

(2) Group Ahead - 13:11 Time {5015 6551 21200' Alt
No Chutes seen disintegrated?

(3) Group Ahead - 14:05 {5039 0908 disintegrated? 21600 Alt

flak hit left wing ... , went into spin ; disintegrated

OBSERVATIONS OF CREWS: Baloons - Battle Evidence {5022 0520
Red & Purple Flack Burst

(1) B-17 Left wing on fire - Spinning down - ship broke up & on fire - ...

(2) B-17 Seen going down in distance
No Chuttes

(3) Ship - Thought B-17 down at one o'clock
Possibly ... chutes

Minker crew Mission Interrogation Form for December 24, 1944.
447th B.G. mission records, National Archives

The crew of the *Blue Hen Chick* saw carnage in the sky on Christmas Eve, they were among the fortunate ones who returned to a quiet Christmas Day and three days off. At home, millions of families tried to celebrate Christmas while loved ones were in the midst of battle. Edna Minker's poignant Christmas night letter echoes the feelings of every mother with a child in the service.

Christmas night, 1944

Dearest Lee,

Your cablegram came this morning before we had breakfast. It certainly changed the whole day for us. The last letter received was written November 29 and naturally we were anxious to have some word. Thanks so much. It was the best of our Christmas gifts. We do hope your boxes all arrived top side up in time for you to have some semblance of Christmas. Of course our thoughts have been continually with you beginning last night when the tree was trimmed and the stockings hung. Fred arrived about 6 p.m. and left on the 12:45. Bernice said he was as particular as you about the arrangement of the lights, balls, etc. on the tree. Luckily our bulbs were all in good shape for there are none to be bought this year. Our tree is very pretty, though smaller than we usually have.

Uncle Roger and his family were out this morning bringing grandmother who is staying overnight. We didn't have dinner until about 3:30 for I roasted my turkey at home today and it was late when I got it in the oven. We expect Julia over for breakfast tomorrow morning. It seemed to be the only time she could fit it in before going back. She and May both look fine. We had a wonderful treat Friday night when daddy took us to the Met to hear Rigoletto with Lawrence Tibbett and Josephine Antoine in the leads. It was something none of us will ever forget.

Now dinner is over and the house quiet and in some order. Shirley has run up to May's, Bernice and Walter are over at his house, daddy resting, grandmother looking at cards.

And now, dear, another Christmas is almost over. I wish I could think the day had been for you just a little bit like ours, - with friends and loved ones, warmth and a nice dinner; but always there has been in the back of our minds the thought that you had to go out on a mission regardless of the fact that it was Christmas.

I hope the Christmases we have spent together have been pleasant memories which have helped you through the day. Today grandmother Minker said she hoped that some Christmas just once more she could have all of her children and grandchildren with her for dinner. That may not be possible – at least not at her house – but maybe we can all celebrate together sooner than we think.

It will perhaps be a new year when this reaches you. May it be a year we shall always remember as the one when hostilities ceased and men worked as hard to make a lasting peace as they had to wage a terrible war!

With all my love,
Mother

I hope the Christmases we have spent together have been pleasant memories which have helped you through the day. Today grandmother Minker said she hoped that some Christmas just once more she could have all of her children + grand-children with her for dinner. That may not be possible – at least not at her house – but maybe we can all celebrate together sooner than we think.
It will perhaps be a new year when this reaches you. May it be a year we shall always remember as the one when hostilities ceased and men worked as hard to make a lasting peace as they had to wage a terrible war!
With all my love,
Mother

Christmas night 1944.

Dearest Lee,
Your cablegram came this morning before we had breakfast. It certainly changed the whole day for us. The last letter received was written November 29 and naturally we were anxious to have some word. Thanks so much. It was the best of our Christmas gifts. We do hope your boxes all arrived top side up in time for you to have some semblance of Christmas. Of course our thoughts have been continually with you, beginning last night when the tree was trimmed and the stockings hung. Fred arrived about 6 p.m. and left on the 12:45. Bernice said he was as particular as you about the arrangement of the lights, balls, etc. on the tree. Luckily our balls were all in good shape for there are none to be

Pages 1 and 4 of Edna Minker's Christmas letter.
This is one of only two handwritten letters, her other letters were typed.
Courtesy Historical Society of Delaware

His mother's hope that Lee would have some "semblance of Christmas" was realized a few days later when a heavy frost in Rattlesden covered everything with a light dusting of white.

Lee's barracks at Rattlesden did not go without a Christmas tree; he told Bernice about the unique decorations scavenged from the base. On December 27 the 447th hosted a party for 600 orphans who were given candy, fed ice cream and cake, and entertained by a USO show. The Red Cross staff reported, "It is hard to determine who had the most enjoyable time, the Post personnel or the children." – Administration Report, Jan 1 1945.

Mission #13 ***Blue Hen Chick*** **Thur Dec 28 1944**

Target – Rail yards & bridges between Saarbrucken & Cologne
Briefing at 0600
Take off began at 0830
Bad weather assembly, bombing altitude 26,000 feet.
Landing at 1514
Log: Mission lasted 6:45 hours. This mission we all were sweating out as it's the jinx. [Mission #13] Flak was light. Had Bomb Release trouble, also bomb doors wouldn't operate.

Mission # 14 ***Blue Hen Chick*** **Sat Dec 30 1944**

Target – Marshalling yards at Mannheim
Briefing at 0530
Take off began at 0822
Target was cloud covered, ran into turbulence over the target. Two planes from the 708th crashed together, Lt. W.Leverett and Lt. B. Bates spiraled down into the clouds.
Landing at 1623
Log: Mission lasted 7:45 hours. We were Chaff Ships. Lead the whole 3rd Division over the target. We were sweating out Fighters and flak. Flak was moderate.

When writing home, Lee did not mention the horror of the December 30 mission, when two planes from the 708th collided over the target: #42 97400, *Fuddy Duddy*, flown by Lieutenant Wylie Leverett, and #42 97473, flown by Lieutenant Bruce Bates, were seen spiraling down into the clouds. The Missing AirCraft Report (MACR) states: "#473 lost altitude and #400 gained altitude at same time. Reason for this is unknown, but believed prop wash responsible...No chutes observed from either plane." Two crews (18 men), who took off with the *Blue Hen Chick* that morning did not return.

Sunday evening
December 31, 1944

Dear Bernice,

Whenever there is a rush of bombing missions letters home are neglected. Please be patient, I think of you all always.

I am fine but the Blue Hen Chick is out for an engine change and a new rudder.

December twenty seventh I received fifteen letters. I am saving all the letters I receive and I wish you would hang on to those I send home.

This is a new way to spend New Year's eve. For the Christmas Holidays the sixteen occupants of Barracks Eleven secured, raised and decorated a lovely five foot fir Christmas tree. Tonight we will take it down. The letters will be completed and sleep will come early.

Ribbons from Christmas boxes, cotton from the infirmary, candy canes from a home package and chaff tinsel, snow and balls decorated the tree. (Chaff is a tinsel like paper thrown out of planes over enemy country to cause radar jamming.)

Let me hear how you are and what you are doing.

Love
Lee

447th Bomb Group
Monthly Operations Reports

November 1944	Missions 168 - 180	Month	Total
	Missions	*13*	*180*
	Sorties	*342*	*4778*
	Aircraft Lost	*12*	*106*
	Crews Lost	*8*	*84*
	Personnel Killed	*1*	*49*
	Missing	*73*	*789*
	Wounded & injured	*6*	*101*

December 1944	Missions 181 - 191	Month	Total
	Missions	*11*	*191*
	Sorties	*446*	*5224*
	Aircraft Lost	*4*	*110*
	Crews Lost	*4*	*88*
	Personnel Killed	*1*	*50*
	Personnel Missing	*37*	*826*
	Wounded & injured	*2*	*103*

Operational in England for only a year, the losses for the 447th Bomb Group were mounting. The monthly statistical record reports the totals: 876 personnel KIA [Killed in Action] or MIA [Missing in Action]. Nearly 900 families of the 447th B.G. had received the dreaded telegram from the War Department: "The Secretary of War desires me to express his deep regret that your son . . ."

The 447th was but one of 48 bomb groups in the Eighth Air Force. In 1944 alone, the bomb groups of the Eighth Air Force lost 2400 bombers and 55,000 airmen. The losses would continue into 1945.

Chapter Ten

The Lucky Bastards' Club

January 1, 1945 – February 27, 1945

Dates: Jan 1 1945 – Feb 27 1945	**Location: Rattlesden AFB Suffolk England**

January 1 1945	The *Luftwaffe* launched their last major attack, bombing supply columns and airfields of Eisenhower's army.
January 1 1945	Lee received a promotion to First Lieutenant.
January 25 1945	The Ardennes offensive ended with 81,000 American casualties.
February 26 1945	The crew of the *Blue Hen Chick* flew their 35th mission, completing the required tour of duty.

On January 1, 1945 the *Luftwaffe* launched an attack on the supply columns and airfields of Eisenhower's army as the Battle of the Bulge raged in the deep snow of the Ardennes forest. The flying forts of the Eighth Air Force were in daily combat providing tactical support. The 447th B. G. hit key industrial and transportation targets in an effort to choke German supply lines.

For the Minkers, the lack of public information and letters from Lee during the Battle of the Bulge made this the most worrisome time of the war. They had received the news of Lee's promotion to First Lieutenant, the official order was dated January 1,1945. The Christmas celebration at Rattlesden was quickly forgotten; there was no holiday in the skies over Germany and Belgium. January 1 dawned chilly and cloud covered, the usual weather for an English winter. The mission to Dolberg began with the customary briefing, this cold morning however, mishap and death waited on the runway: in an effort to avoid something on the ground, two planes crashed at take off. The crew of Lieutenant Bleighley's plane, A/C # 42-31100, survived the crash, that of Lieutenant Sills, A/C 42-102567 K *Sarah Gray*, did not.

Mission # 15 A/C #107215 *L'il Eight Ball* Mon Jan 1 1945

Target – Oil plant, Dolberg
Briefing at 0500
Take-off began at 0726
Two planes crashed on the runway during take off. The first crew escaped, the second crash killed the entire crew of Lt. Sills flying A/C 42-102567 K Sarah Gray. The bomb run was uneventful but results were poor.
Landing began at 1554
Blue Hen out for repairs.
Log: Mission lasted 6:30 hours. Two ships blew up on take off. No flak at target. On way back was hit by flak from Hanover- very heavy.

Hanover after a raid
Courtesy Historical Society of Delaware

Monday Jan. 1, 1945

Dear Lee,

This is the first letter I've written in 1945. Feel honored.

Last night I celebrated the New Year at a party. The kids were mostly soldiers and sailors from last year's class. We really had loads of fun, ending the evening, excuse me, morning by cooking hamburgers, guzzling cokes and munching potatoe chips.

My last letter was written on Christmas Eve. I certainly hope you got your Christmas packages o-kay. Were any of the eggs good? We kept one home but were unable to eat it. It didn't seem as if we were sending you much, but I hope you liked everything.

Santa Claus really treated me well. Besides the trip to New York I received lots of nice things, including mittens, scarf, writing paper, jewelry, pitchers. Santa left an IOU for a new coat which has been taken care of. I bought a black fitted reefer with silver buttons and red embroidery. By the way you bought me a real neat black hat with a white feather in it to go with it.

Today it's pouring rain just like Christmas Day here. Are you allowed to say anything about the weather in your letters? Does it ever snow?

Say why don't you request something in your letters? We could send you eats an' stuff.

Well, Happy New Year.

Lots of love
Luck,
Bernice

P.S. Would it by o-kay to write on V-mail? They're urging more of it's use.

The boys of the *Blue Hen Chick*, like most crews, came from all over the country: Minnesota, South Carolina, Arizona, Pennsylvania and Georgia. Without the war, they never would have crossed paths, yet forged a life-long bond in the midst of war. Except for radioman Olaf Larsen, they were all in their early twenties. At age 28 Olaf was considered "The Old Man" of the crew. Larsen and Gordon Dodge, co-pilot, were the only married men in the group. Lee relied on Olaf to offer a prayer with the crew before each mission. In early January 1945 Lee asked his mother to write to the family of each of the crew members and enclose a copy of the article about the history of the Blue Hen. In turn, he had sent each of the families a Christmas card from England. The leadership of the pilot shaped the band of men who every day relied on each other to complete their mission.

"The Best Damn Crew Ever"
Front row L-R : Joe Trambley (T.G), Max Shepherd (BT), Olaf Larsen (R.O), Jim Shannon (E), Harold McKay (A). Back row L-R: Gordon Dodge (CP), Wes Pitts (N), John Rosiala (B), Ralph Minker (P).
As recorded on the back of the photo by Lee Minker.
Courtesy Historical Society of Delaware

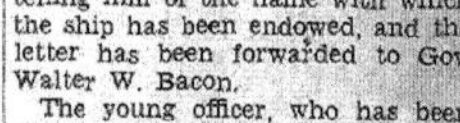

Delaware Pilot Flying B-17 'Blue Hen Chick' Over Europe

The "Blue Hen Chick" is flying high and wide over Europe—bristling with 50 mm. guns and laying blockbusters on Nazi installations.

She's a B-17 piloted by a Delaware man proud of his ship that's carrying on the fighting traditions of his native state.

The young pilot who named his Fortress after the famous Blue Hen's Chicks of the War of Independence is Lieut. Ralph L. Minker, Jr., 20, son of the Rev. and Mrs. Ralph L. Minker. His father is superintendent of the Ferris School for Boys.

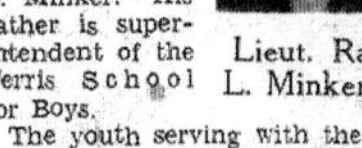

Lieut. Ralph L. Minker, Jr.

The youth serving with the 447th Bomb Group of the Third Bombardment Division of the Eighth Air Force, based in England.

Lieutenant Minker wrote home telling him of the name with which the ship has been endowed, and the letter has been forwarded to Gov. Walter W. Bacon.

The young officer, who has been overseas about two months, said the ship was built and checked at a Boeing Aircraft factory in the Mid-West, then flown to a staging camp where she was assigned to a combat crew to be flown across the ocean for combat in the E. T. O.

The Blue Hen's Chickens, that nickname proudly accepted by all Delawareans, was originaly given to Col. John Haslet's First Delaware Regiment in the American Revolution which reported for duty in January 1776. Although often referred to as the Fighting Delaware's Haslet's regiment early won the sobriquet of "The Blue Hen's Chickens."

The name originated from the men of Capt. Jonathan Caldwell's company who took with them game chickens celebrated for their fighting qualities, of the brood of the Kent County Blue Hen.

The regiment fought at Long Island, White Plains, Trenton and Princeton. In the latter battle, Colonel Haslet was killed while leading the advance.

Article from the Wilmington Paper that
Lee told his mother to send to the families of the crew.
Courtesy Historical Society of Delaware

Mission # 16 A/C # 38524 *Blonde Bomber II* Wed Jan 3 1945

Target – Marshalling Yards, Koblenz
Briefing at 0500
Take off began at 0721 hours
Instrument take off due to intense fog. Attacked marshalling yards, rail junctions, and communication centers.
Landing began at 1401 hours
Blue Hen out for repairs
Log: No notes – Shannon probably did not fly this mission with Minker crew.

Mission # 17 A/C # 44-6016 *TNT Jeanie* Fri Jan 5 1945

Target – Communications Center, Waxweiler
Briefing at 0530
Take off began at 0801
Target was close to the ground battle area. Encountered a lot of flak. Two planes landed in Belgium due to battle damage.
Landing began at 1551
Blue Hen out for repairs
Log: First of four missions in a row. Mission lasted 7:15 hours. Shepherd passed out over the target. Oxygen mask froze. McKay is in hospital. Weather bad on take-off.

Mission #18 *Blue Hen Chick* Sat Jan 6 1945

Target – Marshalling Yards, Worms
Briefing at 0500
Take off began at 0741
Ground was cloud covered with occasional breaks. Released bombs through the clouds, trip home was uneventful.
Landing began at 1450
Log: Mission lasted 7:40 hours. Had a different waist gunner. He passed out over the target. Flak was moderate. McKay still in Hospital.

The family had no way of knowing the intensity of the flying schedule. When Ralph Sr. described the Sixth War Loan Drive in his letter of January 6, 1945, Lee was out on his fourth mission in six days. A vigorous leader, Ralph Minker Sr. proved to be a highly effective fundraiser. An activist by nature, he embraced the bond drives with a highly personal commitment.

January 6, 1945

My dear Lee:-

Life is settling down a bit after a rather strenuous December – the Sixth War Loan Drive and Christmas. We got by far the best cooperation to date on the War Bond Drive. The response during the last two weeks of the Drive was just wonderful. My big day was a "four speech" tour of the Dravo plant. You know the plant, I think – building P.T. Boats in big quantities. They would assemble the workers of one section. I'd get upon a table on some scaffolding and open up on them with everything I had. The response was fine – they bought $600,000 worth of bonds during the drive.

Christmas was made into something like Christmas by your cablegram. That really made the day. Everything fell into its proper place – the giggling girls, the two grandmothers and unsurpassable mother. I hope you had your drumstick – Walter and I ate the one here (Turkeys were pretty high by the way – sixty cents per pound, i.e. seven cents over the ceiling price.) Julia came over and had breakfast with us on Tuesday. Julia looked fine and seems to be getting a great deal out of the school. Shirley is continuing her good work. In another five months she will have completed her course. It hasn't seemed very long ago that she was first starting. Bernice is in everything at Tower Hill – and you don't have to worry about her. She has a pretty level head on her shoulders. We're keeping the home fires burning. Be assured of that.

Everyone was so delighted with your Christmas letter. Congratulations on the promotion – and good flying, Lieutenant!

I saw a preview of "Combat America" the Clark Gable

description of the 8th Air Force. You can imagine what it meant to me. We're planning a War Bond Night at the Playhouse featuring the film. I'll take mother and Bernice.

I was interested in your word about the survey being taken of Air Force personnel looking forward to postwar plans. You know some parts of the picture – and I know you'll make the best decisions possible. I do think you are wise in showing an active interest. They are probably anxious to feel that many of the fellows like the life so well they want to stay in it. I also think you are wise in not tying yourself up too tightly. Feeling is at fever pitch now – a war is on. Unless I miss my guess terribly – the world is going to be fed up with war for a long time after this is over. You know I'd say "God bless you," if you felt this was what you wanted to do. I am simply giving you a slant from my own background. You don't have to worry about security, income, etc. Those things will take care of themselves because "you know how to pitch and to keep pitching." The Law School doors will be open to you if you care to enter them as an interim training. My own thought is that there is no better preparation for any field, humanics, legal, business or political. All that you are doing now plus all that you will do will gear into your total life program in a way you can't foresee.

How I've enjoyed chatting along this way with you! Maybe it won't be too long until we're face to face talking things over. Here's to it.

The best to you always and everywhere!

As always
Dad –

On the ground, the Battle of the Bulge intensified as Allied troops slogged through the snow and mud of Belgium in the coldest winter on record. The Eighth Air Force undertook a campaign of precision bombing to destroy vital industrial installations, fuel plants and the columns of supplies needed to support the Germany army. Lieutenant Minker's mission list for the first two weeks in January tells the story of attacks on the German supply lines. The targets came from a list of bombing priorities set by the Allied High Command in London. Both a primary and a secondary target were selected for each mission, because weather determined where the bomb load could actually be dropped.

Flying eight-and nine-hour missions every other day took their toll on all of the crews. The Minker crew, like many others, seldom returned without incident: flak damage, runaway propellers, bad weather, near mid-air collisions and German fighters. The *Blue Hen Chick's* flight home from the marshalling yards in Frankfurt on January 8 was especially harrowing. The squadron encountered heavy flak on the approach to the Dessau oil plant; they had to bank sharply after bomb release to escape the flak. The crew of the *Blue Hen Chick* was on oxygen for five-and-a-half hours as they flew out of Germany, over the channel and home to Rattlesden.

The family kept up their regular correspondence despite the overwhelming silence from England. When Lee was awarded the Air Medal for "meritorious achievement while participating in aerial flight," the Minkers read about it in the morning paper.

Mission #19 ***Blue Hen Chick*** **Sun Jan 7 1945**

Target – Marshalling Yards and bridges, Cologne
Briefing at 0500
Take off began at 0740
Bombed the secondary target with no losses. Encountered heavy flak probably due to proximity to the ground battle area.
Landing began at 1435
Log: Mission lasted 7:15 hours. Morton flew waist with us. McKay still in hospital. Flak was moderate. Had a Runaway propeller. Flying was rough as there were heavy contrails. Visibility poor on landing.

Mission #20 ***Blue Hen Chick*** **Mon Jan 8 1945**

Target – Marshalling Yards, Frankfurt
Briefing at 0400
Take off began at 0632
Cloud cover on approach to the target. Lt. Weeks (710th squadron) flying #43-37938, *Little Rock Blonde*, "Seen to explode from a direct hit."
Landing began at 1445
Log: Mission Lasted 8.35 hours. Had another waist gunner. McKay still in hospital. This was coldest Day 58 Centigrade Below Zero. Lead pilot [in the group] Passed out. We had no Evasive action through heavy flak. Ship in our group went down. [Lt. Robert Weeks] We had flak holes in our right wing. On oxygen for five and a half hours. Fourth mission in a row. All of us tired. Heavy flak at the target.

Tuesday, January 9, 1945

Dearest Lee:

It's a good thing we have the newspapers so we can keep tabs on what you are doing. Your picture is in the Morning News and a brief item saying that you have been awarded the Air Medal for outstanding performance in a bombing mission over Europe. It makes my heart swell with pride, but on the other hand I wish your fine talents could be used in building up instead of destroying; and I hope the day is not too far distant when that will be true.

Don't be too modest to tell us about your air medal. Does it mean that you have completed a certain number of missions, or does it have some other meaning?

Our best to you, dear, and all our love.

Mother

Mission #21 ***Blue Hen Chick*** **Wed Jan 10 1945**

Target – Marshalling Yards, Karlsruhe
Briefing 0530
Take off began at 0812 hours
The day was foggy and dismal with freezing rain. The base closed in, seven crews were diverted to other bases.
Landing began at 1515
Log: Mission Lasted 7.20 hours. This was a hard one, right after take off air speed dropped to zero. Vapor Trails were very heavy. Only flew with 4 ships from our squadron over the target. Had to feather #3 propeller. Hit by flak in #1 engine, had to feather #3. Visibility for landing was poor. Temp was 55 below at 28,000 ft.

January 13, 1945

Dear Looie:

I'm not sure just how much I can write to you tonight. It's close to midnight, and I'm so sleepy I can hardly see. It's probably Sunday morning already over there in England. I've been so busy all week that I have only the week-end to catch up on my sleep.

The mail came through very well this week. I got your letter of New Year's Eve on the 10th. I'm glad you got a tree for Christmas. It sounds as if you really used your ingenuity to trim the tree. These Air Corps fellows are pretty good, aren't they?

Tonight in the movies we saw the first pictures of the Norden bomb-sight. Do you know why they suddenly released such a closely guarded secret? They had lots of pictures of crews over in England getting their planes ready for raids and showed pictures inside the planes during a raid. It was very interesting. I wonder if you could have been in any of the pictures, but they were probably taken before you even went over.

Hope your "Chick" is back in operation again. We'll have to call her the "Ruptured Duck" if you don't watch out. Alright now, put that gun away.

Well, I'm at the end again. Not very much new going on here. Say hello to all the crew for me. I sure would like to have them all out for dinner when you're on one of those week-end leaves. Bye, good luck, and take care of yourself.

Lots of love,

Shirley

After getting Shirley off for her last semester at Dickinson Junior College, Edna wrote to Lee about filing his income tax. She managed his financial affairs throughout the war. The pay for a pilot with the rank of first lieutenant was $166.00 a month in 1945. Each month Lee sent home a portion of his pay for savings through the Army Financial Affairs Office.

Despite the ongoing battle in Europe, the end of the war was in sight. While still concerned about their son's survival, mother and dad both wrote of post-war plans and what the war has done to his generation. Lee was too busy flying to think much about the future. The mission of January 14 marked a return to strategic bombing of oil plants rather than tactical support of ground troops. The crew of the *Blue Hen Chick* bombed the oil refinery at Magdeburg, Germany.

Mission # 22 ***Blue Hen Chick*** **Sun Jan 14 1945**

Target – Oil Refinery, Magdeburg
Briefing at 0630
Take off began at 0749
Carried 500 lb bombs, one plane carried leaflets. P-51's destroyed 90 enemy fighters in the air. Made visual attack on the oil refinery. Lead ship severely damaged. The Germans lost a total of 189 fighters.
Landing began at 1540
Log: Mission Lasted 6:20 hours. We went past Berlin. There were enemy fighters in the area. Saw dog fights and ships going down in flames. Flak was moderate. Top turret inter-phone system out. Had a monitor with us. Jerries followed us back to the coast. Larsen on a propaganda program. New record for knocking down fighters.

Mission #23 ***Blue Hen Chick*** **Mon Jan 15 1945**

Target – Messerschmitt aircraft plant, Augsburg
Briefing at 0515
Take off began at 0741
The target was cloud covered, instead bombed marshalling yards returning home with no losses.
Landing began at 1610
Log: Mission lasted 8.15 Hours. We went past Munich, Enemy fighters in the area. Flak was heavy. Piece [of] flak hit Navigator in back of his neck. Had to feather #3 propeller. Had a different radio operator.

Mission #24	**A/C 42-32080**	**Tues Jan 16 1945**

Target – Oil Plant, Dessau
Briefing at 0450
Take off began at 0713
Bad weather assembly over the field, climbed to bombing altitude of 26,000 feet over the Dutch coast. Assigned target cloud covered, bombed secondary target at Dessau. Had to land at 8 different bases as Rattlesden was fogged in.
Log: Mission lasted 9:45. This was our longest mission. Weather poor at take off. Flak was light. Had to land at another field. Visibility zero at ours. Had to hand crank up bomb bay doors.

January 15, 1945

Dearest Lee:

I don't know what you want to do about filing a 1944 income tax return. If you don't want to bother with it now you don't have to, you know. "If you are in the armed forces and, on the filing date, are on sea duty or outside the continental U.S., you may postpone filing your return until the 15th day of the 4th month after you come back to the U.S." I am enclosing the form and you do what you want about it. If I had the figures I would fill it out for you. I have paid the last installment on your 1943 tax, $14.03. I have a duplicate of this form, so if you just want to send me the amount to be filled in, Income-contributions or deductions of any kind – I'll fill out the form.

There was a very interesting article in yesterday's N.Y. Times concerning the "lost generation" of youth – young people now at work who will be squeezed out of jobs by returning veterans, too young for the glory of having been in the war and passed over when jobs are given returning veterans. Mayor LaGuardia warned against training youth for jobs that would be more than adequately filled by returning servicemen. It seems to me it certainly will require a lot of consecrated people, people with vision and brains (like you), to work out all the multiple problems which are confronting us now and will increase after the war. It will require such fine young men as you to help bring order out of this chaos.

According to reports we are now making some headway in Germany. We hear of large number of American fliers and the number of planes they are bringing down. Are you having good flying weather or are you flying in spite of the weather?

Now don't let this tax return worry or bother you. If you don't have time for it just forget it.

With all my love,

Mother

Pilots fresh from training gained combat experience quickly. After barely three months in England, Lee Minker had flown 25 missions – the number it took to complete a tour of duty in 1943 — many of them during the Battle of the Bulge. The flying schedule was brutal; the crew of the *Blue Hen Chick* flew ten missions in the first sixteen days of January. The continual flying took its toll on the men and the plane. Ground crew chief Carlos Cardova and his crew frequently had to stay up all night to get the *Chick* back in the air.

Mission #25 ***Blue Hen Chick*** **Sat Jan 20 1945**

Target – Marshalling yards, Heilbonn
Briefing at 0430
Take off began at 0704
Bad weather assembly over England, flak was light, had to release bombs through the clouds. Heavy headwinds on the way home.
Landing began at 1506
Log: Deputy squadron leader for 1st time. Mission lasted 6:55 hours. We were element lead for the first time. Weather so bad we lost our squadron. Had to fly through clouds with no visibility. Flew through another formation. Pilots and co-pilots windows frozen. Temperature was 67 centigrade below. Coldest its ever been.

Mission #26 ***Blue Hen Chick*** **Sun Jan 21 1945**

Target – Highway and rail bridges, Mannheim
Briefing at 0500
Take off began at 0744
Carried 58 tons of 500 lb G.P. bombs and incendiary bombs. Two planes carried leaflets. One crew had to bail out over France. Released bombs through the clouds.
Landing began at 1519
Log: Mission lasted 7:20 hours. Mission almost the same as yesterday. Lost lead and low squadrons. Visibility very poor. Ball Turret oxygen froze. Last two days weather very bad.

The January 20 mission to Heilbron gave Lee his first experience flying deputy lead. The next day he flew deputy lead in the high squadron as the group bombed industrial targets in the city of Mannheim. Upon return to Rattlesden, he did the required pilot's de-briefing, reporting no enemy fighter opposition. After a day that began at 4:00 a.m. and included a seven and a half hour mission, Lee went to his quarters and wrote to Shirley. Mindful of the family's anxieties, he offered an apology for neglecting his correspondence, even though he had flown almost daily missions for two weeks.

Sunday evening January 21, 1945

Dear Shirley,

I have been neglecting my correspondence of late but will now attempt to reform.

Since the rush of the German Christmas counter offensive against us I have been flying at a great rate in an attempt to bomb out rear supply depots and to draw the Luftwaffe from tactical action. A year ago such concentrated effort in winter bad weather would have been useless but development of master path finder equipment now makes bombing through clouds a routine matter. Here's hoping our efforts will help bring this war to an early close.

When does second semester begin? How is your voice training progressing? Bernice wrote me of the wonderful time you had at the performance of "Rigoletto" at the Metropolitan Opera. I wish that you would take more time during typing classes for writing your letters—your penmanship! How is Fred and what is he doing? What news do you have of the old gang? After a hard day's work the sack has overwhelming charms so I will close for now.

Study hard!

Love,
Lee

By January 25, 1945 the Battle of the Bulge in the Ardennes Forest had come to a costly close. The failure of the offensive cost the Germans 100,000 casualties: killed, wounded or captured, an irreplaceable loss after so many years at war. The loss of over 800 tanks and 1000 planes further stretched German resources. Precision bombing of aircraft plants and fuel targets by the Eighth Air Force throughout January had crippled the

Luftwaffe. In a bit of understatement, after flying 12 missions deep into Germany in 21 days, Lee told his dad that he had not written because of "working rather hard this month." Now Lee's letters contained general information about targets and flying missions in bad weather. Perhaps censorship had become less important as the battle wound down.

Wednesday evening
January 24, 1945

Dear Dad,

I have been working rather hard this month and as a result I have sadly neglected my correspondence.

Since the rush of the German Christmas counter offensive against us I have been bombing rear supply and repair depots, transportation centers and Luftwaffe bases. We have been flying in unimaginable extremes of weather and bombing by means of master pathfinder equipment which makes possible bombing through clouds. Here's hoping our efforts and those of our ground troops will join with the Russian winter drive in bringing a quick end to the German phase of this war.

The sobering effect of the German counter offense should put the United States in the right attitude for settling post war problems after prosecuting with full vigor the defeat of Germany and Japan. It seems to me that Senator Vandenburg [Michigan Senator who spoke about the international leadership role of the U.S.] has found a good formula for a postwar foreign policy: full presidential freedom of action concerning Germany and Japan, but reserving the Senate's right of review of other problems and right of censure of all. We must maintain a large Navy and Air Force and an Army large enough to form a fighting and training nucleus if total mobilization is necessary. We must have outlying bases. We must uphold world wide freedom of trade, press, speech and religion. We must realize our responsibilities in the world.

As Henry Wallace says, we must strive for a full employment of manpower in private industry but excessive slack must be provided for by the national government. The problem is so large that it must have national direction but it must be more decisive than in the past. (shift unemployed from crowded areas to frontiers; work to eat). Backward areas must be developed. Business must be regulated.

Discharge and assimilation of servicemen must be handled carefully. Men with dependents should be discharged first but there should be no difference between married and single men. Age and combat experience should count. Those who have had schooling interrupted should be allowed to continue on a semi-duty status.

Today – typical army waste – the 447th Bombardment Group "Stood down" while Major General Partridge, C. O. of the 4th Combat Wing, Third Division, U.S. 8th Army Air Force, inspected the base and personnel.

Will write soon again.

Yours,
Lee

On January 27, 1945 First Lieutenant Minker attended a party at the officer's club to celebrate the 447th Bomb Group's 200th mission, flown on January 13, 1945. Their first mission was flown on December 24, 1943. The loss-rate of aircraft and crews was improving, yet each mission was perilous. The fall of

Germany was imminent with the advance of Russian troops on Germany's eastern front and of the Allied forces on the western front. Hoping for the cessation of hostilities in early 1945, families on the home front absorbed every piece of available battle information. Hitler preferred continued destruction in the face of certain defeat.

Mission #26 ***Blue Hen Chick*** **Monday Jan 29 1945**

Target – Henschel aircraft plant, Kessel.
Briefing at 0530
Take off began at 0744
Due to haze bombed the marshalling yards as secondary target.
Landing began at 1439
Log: Mission lasted 7:00 hours. Snow on runway for take off. Element lead in Lead Squadron. This was a good mission. Flak was light. Two ships cracked up on landing.

Bombing results of a German airfield
Courtesy Historical Society of Delaware

January 29, 1945.

Dearest Lee:

Things are looking brighter in the European situation with the Russians advancing so rapidly; so maybe it won't be too many months before Germany collapses, although I imagine that as the armies get closer and closer to Berlin the fighting will become fiercer and fiercer.

We think of you always, dear, as you very well know I am sure.

Love,
Mother

Tuesday evening
January 30, 1945

Dear Mother,

A spell of "poor" weather is at present hampering operations of the United States 8th Air Force. I hope that it will not be too long before we can be back again hitting key strategic centers and helping the troops on the western and eastern fronts though. Not that I am eager to face our enemy, but to achieve victory we must batter them until they call quits and decide to live under liberty and democracy.

The other day in London I had a great treat: I saw Alfred Lunt and Lyn Fontane in the comedy "Love in Idleness." It was indeed a pleasure to watch and listen as Lunt and Fontane lived their parts so freshly, naturally, totally. I have also seen the entertaining shows "Blythe

Spirit" (U.S.O., Noel Coward's comedy), "Uncle Harry" (a psychological mystery) and the good movie "Constant Nymph" (Charles Boyer, Joan Fontane) recently.

General Notes:

Pay day is February first and, I will then send some money home through the base finance office. Another regular monthly allotment and war bond will also be sent. An occasional box of goodies would hit the spot but I have no great wants.

Say Hello to everybody for me.

Love,

Lee

Mission #27 ***Blue Hen Chick*** **Thurs Feb 1 1945**

Target – Railway bridge over the east side of the Rhine River at Wesel.
Briefing at 0845
Take off began at 1108
The 9th Army and the British Army XXX were approaching the Rhine near Wesel.
Landing began at 1630
Log: Mission lasted 4:50 hours. Help support Ground troops. During taxiing tail wheel tire blew out. No Flak at target—Some Rockets. Flew with a different group.

At home Americans faced restrictions on travel, the coal shortage and an embargo "on all kinds of freight." Knowing how important fuel and other supplies were to the troops, the Minkers dealt with rationing as merely an inconvenience. Clearly victory over Germany was going to come at a terrible price. In February, 1945 Edna Minker received letters from families of his crew who wrote about Lee's skills and leadership; their comments were a source of enormous pride to the family.

Bombing results bridge over the Rhine River
Courtesy Historical Society of Delaware

February 1, 1945.

Dearest Lee:

I have just finished reading a very fine letter from Mrs. Pitts, mother of your navigator. I hope some of these days we shall be able to have Wesley in our home along with your other crew members,- if not all at one time at least one or two at a time.

I reached Wilmington about 7 o'clock last night and needless to say have been quite busy catching up loose ends today. There was much to do both at the house and in the office. The first night I was gone Clarence, the houseboy, who lost his shoes when trying to get away a few weeks ago, walked off again. The police caught him, however, soon after he left. He is now in Detention and I shall not take him back again. All of this, course, made it hard for Grandmother Minker.

Love,
Mother

Bernice's high spirits and busy days as a senior in high school are evidenced in her letters. She reported on dreaded senior exams, the family's winter activities and a fund-raising show for a "recreation hall on the base." She referred to New Castle Army Air Base, just south of Wilmington, the home of the Women Air Force Service Pilots (WASP) who ferried planes from factory to point of embarkation. To her amazement the show featured Gypsy Rose Lee, one of the most famous strippers of the time, doing her *entire* show.

February 3, 1945

Dear Lee,

Boy, does it feel good to relax! All last week I had midyear examinations at school, so was practically dead by the time the weekend arrived. We get blue-books, the same as college exams, which are pretty stiff. I passed all of mine, but not with ninety's. Most of my marks were seventies which satisfied me. History and French were my best subjects.

Last week Mother went to Atlantic City for an executive meeting of some sort. I was here alone with the two Grannies, one of which, Jones, is laid up for a while with the grip. We lived on fried egg sandwiches and spaghetti, so all were relieved when mother arrived home. I'm still eating her salt water taffy.

One of the reasons why I didn't get much studying done for my tests was that Shirley arrived home last week accompanied by two of her dorm-mates, Timme and Collie. We did the town, seeing Winged Victory and Meet Me in St. Louis, both of which you shouldn't miss.

Mother wrote letters to all of your crew and has so far

received three answers. They were all very nice letters and your crew sounds super. They have all mentioned receiving Christmas notes from you.

Joke: Why is a crow?

Answer: Caws

Last week the Junior Chamber of Commerce presented an all-star show in the armory to build a recreation hall for the noncoms at the Air Base. Some of the stars featured were Jessica Dragonette, Jane Whithers, Joe Louis, and Gypsy Rose Lee who presented her compleeeeeeete act. Wow! It was a pretty good show and the net results have paid for one half of the hall.

Well, pardner, Keep 'em flyin'.

Lots of Love,
Bernice

Monday, February 5, 1945

Dearest Lee:-

The way things look now it might easily be that by the time this letter reaches you Berlin will have been entered and the European phase of the war at an end. With the terrific air bombardment which the city is evidently getting and the approach of the Russian Army I don't see how the Germans can hold out much longer. And today we are heartened by the news that our armies are in Manila. The end can come none too soon for any of us. I expect you have had almost your required number of missions already and we are hoping you will be coming home for a rest this spring to say the least.

I have had two more nice letters, one from Mrs. Dodge

and another from Mrs. Trembly. We were delighted to hear from them. They all speak very highly of you and are looking forward to the day when they can meet and learn to know you.

Daddy is busy with committee meetings getting ready for the next War Bond Drive. He has three such meetings today,-12:15, 2:30, 3:15. Yesterday he spoke at Friends Meeting House at 11 a.m. and in the afternoon saw the Bombers lose another game. Next week he is scheduled to attend the annual meeting of the Superintendents' Conference in N.Y. which will at least give him a change. You may know that the government is calling off all meetings of 50 or more people unless special permission is obtained. This is meant to save railroad facilities for troops and necessary war materials, and to prevent hotel congestion. On account of the coal shortage and the severe weather we have been having there is an embargo at the present on all kinds of freight except coal and war materials.

Of course I do not need to tell you that our hearts and thought and prayers are with you more than ever as we hear of the offensive against Germany, in which you no doubt are taking part. I know it has been a terrific experience for you.

Love.
Mother

The day after Edna wrote this letter, Lee flew a long and difficult mission to a German oil refinery. When bad weather made it impossible to bomb the primary target, the group changed course for the secondary target – the marshalling yards at Chemnitz. The *Blue Hen Chick* was hit by flak after the bomb run. With less than full control of the plane when landing, Lee hit one of the trees at the end of the runway.

Mission # 29 ***Blue Hen Chick*** **Tuesday Feb 6 1945**

Target – Oil refinery at Bohlen, south of Leipzig.
Briefing at 0430
Take off began at 0700
Weather was unsuitable for bombing at Bohlen. Changed course to go the secondary target, marshalling yards at Demnitz. Return home uneventful.
Landing began at 1611
Log: Mission lasted 9:10 hours. Visibility was poor all day. Almost had mid air collision. Flew over Dunkirk Hit by Flak. Hit a tree just before landing. Put a hole in left wing.

Now in her last semester of a two-year program, Shirley continued to tease her brother about his success in the Army Air Force. She reported on the presence of film star Gene Kelly who was making a training film for the Navy. It would have been one of many such films made with the support of Hollywood stars and directors. The Office of War Information (OWI), formed in 1942 , "coordinated its efforts with the film history to record and photograph the national's war-time activities." (Dirks 1996-2005) The excitement of a movie star aside, Shirley's letters show the ever present shadow of the war as she wrote of boys either killed or missing in action, or home on leave. Shirley's life at college was a sharp contrast to Lee's flying nine-hour missions over German targets.

Friday Morning
February 9, 1945

Dearest Looie:

Again you are lucky! Yes, I guess that I have time in class to write, and you can't complain that my typewriting is illegible. Or can you?

I had a letter from you this week and I think that the date was sometime in the latter part of January. I don't have it here because I sent it on home to mother. She probably heard, but sometimes here mail doesn't come through as fast as mine. Mother wrote to me and said that it was in the paper that you had been awarded an Oak Leaf Cluster. I don't think that you will be able to walk home, let alone to fly, with all of your medals and decorations. She has also heard from mothers of fellows in your crew, and I think that she is just tickled pink every time that she does. It's good to know that there is such good feeling between all of you fellows.

This morning I had three letters from Fred. Yes, he's finally landed in France. He said that there was an awful lot of mud, but he doesn't complain. He also said that all the parts of France that he had seen had been unnecessarily ruined and almost [all] of the countryside was in ruins. It doesn't seem at all real to us here at home, just what war can do to a country. I guess that you have to see it to fully realize it's meaning.

A group of movie people are here this week and for a month or so, I believe, to make some Navy movies. Gene Kelly is among them, and all the girls in town are going crazy trying to see him and get his autograph. I haven't seen him yet, but maybe I will yet. The rumor is going around that Frankie [Sinatra] is going to come in a few weeks, but I don't think that I will believe that until I see it with my own eyes. I would like to see him in person again.

Love,
Shirley

For a regular mission, the bomb groups launched three squadrons, providing a rotating rest period for one squadron. When the 709th squadron "stood down" in early February, Lee hitchhiked to Cambridge where he explored one of the oldest universities in the world. When he returned, the letter to his mother vividly describes the scene in the officer's barracks as well as his travels to the university town.

Monday evening
February 12, 1945

Dear Mother,

It is cold outside; the wind is whistling and rain is pattering on the long barracks's roof. I am setting on the end of my bed by a bright warm coke and wood fire writing letters, listening to AFN [American Forces Network] "On the Record" and participating in a general bull session.

On my last pass I visited Cambridge and had a grand time. It is a clean, fresh, middle-sized college town in marked contrast to large, drab, brawling London. I went through the great Cambridge University and rested. Traveling to and from I hitch hiked. There is very little civilian road traffic but a constant stream of army vehicles. (British and American).

This past week a deluge of mail has come through. I certainly look forward to your letters. Good shows seen recently are Saratoga Trunk (Ingrid Bergmen and Gary Cooper) and Rhapsody in Blue. I am looking forward to seeing Winged Victory and Thirty Seconds Over Tokyo.

Figures for compiling my income tax this year. $166.00 – monthly pay from 1-1-45 ($150.00 prior) _ base pay is *flight pay, $6.50 – for monthly insurance, 10% base pay is overseas pay, $ 18.75 for monthly war bond, get my social security number (mail me a copy) check which year filed for (last year's – this).*

Several of the crew have mentioned your letters to their homes. They are a fine bunch to fly with.

Love,
Lee

The newspapers carried several accounts of the meeting in the Crimea with Churchill, Roosevelt and Stalin. During the first week of February, 1945 the three Allied leaders planned the final attack on Germany and discussed the post-war boundaries of Europe at the Crimea Conference. Edna commented in her Valentine's Day letter, "… it really gives us some hope about the world after the war is over." The news reports, however, did not reflect the deep division among the Allies over the future of post-war Europe. These differences were the first signs of what was to become the Cold War. The Allied leaders talked while the losses for the Eighth continued as they bombed Germany into submission.

Mission #30 ***Blue Hen Chick*** **Wed Feb 14 1945**

Target – Highway bridge across the Rhine River at Wesel.
Briefing at 0455
Only the 447th was able to bomb the primary target. Results were rated as good.
Landing began at 1400
Log: Mission lasted 6:30. Had to feather #3 Engine. Made a second run on the target. No flak first time. Heavy flak the second. Target visual.

Mission #31 ***Blue Hen Chick*** **Fri Feb 16 1945**

Target – Railroad bridge, Wesel
Briefing at 0900
Take off began at 1129
Coastal areas of Holland still held by small pockets of Germans. Made visual attack on bridge over the Rhine River at Wesel. Uneventful return with no losses.
Landing began at 1830
Log: Mission lasted 5:20. Bombardier [John Rosiala] hit in the right arm by flack. Ship had several small flack holes. Bad weather at our own base. Landed in France near Criel. [north of Paris] Had a bloody nose just before target.

Friday, February 16, 1945.

Dear Lee:-

We were so glad to get your letter of January 24th this morning. Although it was written to daddy I opened it for I couldn't wait until he returns from N.Y. this evening. In the same mail I received a lovely letter from Mrs. Larsen.

I think I did not tell you about Leland Inscho [son of friends] being missing, for I know how much you thought of him and I did not want to upset you unduly. We were so glad to read in last night's paper that he is a prisoner. One always has a reasonable hope that a prisoner of war will one day be released, and from what we hear the men in the German prison camps are not too badly treated. Of course the picture of him is terrible.

We are glad to hear the news of the bombing of Tokio [sic] by 1500 navy planes and hope this is only the beginning of what we may expect as the end of the European war draws to a close.

Today is the World Day of Prayer for women of all denominations all over the world. The Wilmington churches are having the service at Trinity Episcopal church and I am planning to go this afternoon. More than in any other year our prayers will be for you separated from us and for a just and lasting peace.

Love.
Mother

The missions were getting longer; flights deep into Germany and back took over eight hours. The longest lasted 9:45: a long time to be inside of a B-17 which is treacherous, cramped and cold at 25,000 feet. When the full bomb load could not be released on February 20, the bombardier walked on a narrow metal beam to the bomb bay to replace the pins for the flight home and the landing with munitions in the belly of the plane.

Mission #32 ***Blue Hen Chick*** **Tues Feb 20 1945**

Target – Marshalling yards at Nurnburg
Briefing at 0600
Take off began at 0844
Bombed railway and locomotive repair shops at Nurnburg, 95 miles north of Munich.
Landing began at 1702
Log: Mission lasted 8:00 hours. Visibility very poor. Almost had mid-air collision. Flak was heavy and accurate. Had bomb rack trouble. Couldn't release all our bombs.

Mission #33 ***Blue Hen Chick*** **Sunday Feb 25 1945**

Target – Railline at Neuberg
Briefing at 0500
Take off began at 0844
Bombing altitude 22,100 feet. Visual run on the target without encountering much flak.
Landing began at 1702
Log: Mission lasted 8:20 hours. Had to feather #3 engine. Came back by ourselves. Flight was light. Had a blow out in our left tire when we landed.

Mission # 34 **Monday Feb 26 1945**

Target – Railway stations in Berlin
Take off began at 0831
Trip to the target uneventful. Used Pathfinder equipment to make the bomb run. Passed north of the city. No losses.
Landing began at 1708
Log: Mission lasted 8:30. Navigator finished up on this one. Flak was moderate. Ran out of gas on #2 & #3 engines.

On Tuesday, February 27 the crew of the *Blue Hen Chick* took off on the mission they had been waiting for, their 35th – which meant a ticket home. Colonel Wrigglesworth started the briefing at 0600 hours. The black curtain was pulled back to reveal the target – a Communication Center in Leipzig. The nervous chatter at take-off in the *Blue Hen Chick* that morning was heightened by the knowledge that a safe return would complete the tour of duty. They had defied the odds and survived – now they had to go to Germany and back – just one more time. They encountered moderate flak, dropped their bombs over the target, and had an uneventful flight back to Rattlesden.

With the completion of his 35th mission, First Lieutenant Lee Minker qualified as a member of the "Lucky Bastards' Club." This award was given to an elite group of pilots and their crews: "... who achieved the remarkable record of sallying forth and returning no less than 35 times, for braving the hazards of Hun flak...." He was four months shy of his 21st birthday, the youngest pilot of the 447th BG to become a Lucky Bastard.

Mission #35	***Blue Hen Chick***	**Tues Feb 27 1945**

Target – Communication Center at Leipzig.
Briefing at 0700
Take off began at 0939
Route to the target was uneventful, the trip home was without problems.
Landing began at 1743
Log: Mission lasted 8:20 hours. Had a good mission. Flak was moderate. Pilot, Radio Operator, Ball Turret Gunner, Tail Gunner and myself finished up last mission.

On this 27th day of Feb. nineteen hundred and forty five, the fickle finger of fate finds it expedient to trace on the roll of

the
LUCKY BASTARDS' CLUB
THE NAME OF
Ralph L. Minker
pilot on the Flying Fortress Blue Hen Chick

for having this day ~~achieved the remarkable record of~~ sallying forth and returning no less than 35 times, for having braved the hazards of Hun flak, for bringing to Hitler and his cronies tons of bombs, for bending the Luftwaffe's back; all through the courtesy of the Eighth A.A.F. who sponsors these programs in the interest of liberty loving people everywhere.

447

COMMANDING OFFICER
SQUADRON C.O.
AIR EXECUTIVE
SQUADRON OPNS. O.

The Lucky Bastards' Club certificate signed by: William J. Wrigglesworth, commanding officer; William S. Boyd, Air Executive; Lieutenant Colonel Robert G. David (signature was supposed to be in the Squadron C.O. block); and Ernest H. Skinner, the Squadron Operations Officer.
Courtesy Historical Society of Delaware

447th Bomb Group
Monthly Operations Reports

January 1945	Missions 192- 206	Month	Total
	Missions	*14*	*206*
	Sorties	*474*	*5698*
	Aircraft Lost	*11*	*121*
	Crews Lost	*2*	*90*
	Personnel Killed	*11*	*61*
	Missing	*9*	*835*
	Wounded & injured	*5*	*108*

February 1945	Missions 207- 221	Month	Total
	Missions	*15*	*221*
	Sorties	*553*	*6251*
	Aircraft Lost	*2*	*123*
	Crews Lost	*2*	*92*
	Personnel Killed	*0*	*61*
	Missing	*19*	*854*
	Wounded & injured	*3*	*111*

Chapter Eleven

Final Victory is Almost Here

March 2, 1945 - May 1, 1945

Dates: March 2 , 1945 to May 1, 1945	Location: Rattlesden AFB Suffolk England

March 2, 1945	The new pilot and crew flew their first mission in the *Blue Hen Chick.*
March 6, 1945	Lee wrote his parents that he had signed on for a second tour of duty.
March 7, 1945	Allied forces breach the final German defense line in the West when they cross the bridge over the Rhine River at Remagen.
April 1, 1945	Lt. Minker was designated PFF (Path Finder Force) Lead Crew.
April 12,1945	President Roosevelt died, vice president Harry Truman became president.
April 21, 1945	Lee flew the last mission of the 447th to the airfield at Inglostadt, Germany.
April 25, 1945	The Eighth Air Force flew their last mission of WWII to Pilsen, Czechoslovakia.
April 29, 1945	Royal Air Force began flights to Holland with food drops called Operation Manna.
May 1, 1945	U.S. AAF began flights to Holland with food drops called Operation Chowhound.
May 1, 1945	General "Hap" Arnold, Commander of the Eighth Air Force sent a memo to all the troops congratulating them on Victory in Europe and outlining plans for the struggle with Japan.

After "returning from Hun Flak" 35 times, Lieutenant Minker's required tour of duty was over, he was entitled to return home. Lee wrote his parents that he had signed on for a second tour "to finish up the job" (Stevenson 2000) – a decision that stunned his parents who were fully expecting to see him in March. Several members of the Minker crew left Rattlesden for the U.S.: James Shannon, crew chief; Olaf Larsen, radio man; Joe Trambley, tail gunner; and Wes Pitts, navigator. Gordon Dodge, John Rosiala, Harold McKay and Max Shepherd each had a few more missions to fly to complete the magical thirty-five.

A new crew took over the *Blue Hen Chick* in early March 1945. The Mustaleski crew arrived at Rattlesden in December of 1944, they flew 14 of their 30 missions in the *Blue Hen Chick.* The photograph shows the Mustaleski crew after their April 4, 1945 mission to Kiel, Germany.

Rear, L to R: Thomas M. Mustaleski, pilot; James B. Grewe, co-pilot; George E. Szewczyk, togglier; Armando Ciocci, waist gunner; Alex T. Staples, radio operator; John H. Kirkwood, navigator. Front, L to R: Pfc Ullrich (This man was sent along, on this mission, to monitor German (Luftwaffe) radio traffic); Paul L. Farley, top turret gunner; Clarence F. Walker, tail gunner; Carlos Cardova, crew chief for 42-97976; William H. Grove, ball turret gunner. Courtesy of John and Rob Kirkwood

---

March 2, 1945
Dearest Lee:

Daddy's German and mine have grown rather stale, so were unable to read the leaflets which you enclosed. However, Bernice took one to school and we learned that they are propaganda evidently dropped by our planes behind the German lines.

You remember the Hollingsworth farm, don't you, where the Dermans now live? It is being recommended as the site to build the proposed Veteran's Hospital in Delaware. A large assembly plant for General Motors is to be built somewhere in Elsmere after the war. So you see we are going to be a busy place in this neighborhood.

Love to you, dear, and take care of yourself.

Mother

Both the Allies and the Axis powers made use of various forms of propaganda throughout the war. Millions of leaflets were dropped over Germany from the bellies of B-17s and B-24s. The bright red leaflet with bold black letters that Lee sent home warned German civilians that the end of the war was near.

IM WESTEN:

Der Westwall durchbrochen!
Über 1 000 000 Gefangene
seit der Invasion!
Anglo-Amerikanische Luftoffensive
vom Rhein bis zur Ostfront!

IM OSTEN:

Ostpreussen, Wartheland und
Schlesien überrannt!
Die „Ruhr des Ostens" verloren!
Rote Armee tief in
Brandenburg, Sachsen und Pommern!

Phamplet that Lee sent home to his parents.
Courtesy Historical Society of Delaware

IN THE WEST
The west wall has been broken!

More than 1,000,000 prisoners have been taken since the invasion!
Anglo-American air offensive extends from the Rhine to the Eastern Front!

IN THE EAST:
East Prussia, Posen (Poland),and Schlesia have been overrun!
The "Ruhr" of the East has been lost!
The Red Army is deep in Brandenburg, Saxony, and Pomerania!

Translation of German Propaganda Leaflet by Harry Butowsky

Sunday evening
March 5, 1945

Dear Dad,

After another long period of neglect I am again attempting to answer letters that have piled up. Most important news from here today, as I see it, is that my combat aircrew of the Flying Fortress "Blue Hen Chick" has completed its combat duty of 35 missions against Nazi Germany. But I have decided not to return to the United States for three or four more months. Don't worry – I will be home to celebrate the fourth of July with you.

At present I am enjoying a seven day rest leave before taking up new work in group operations. Do my letters seem extremely short? I often find it hard to know what to write you and hard to concentrate.

John Rosiala was wounded by flak a few missions ago but he is now up and around again – he had been a fine bombardier. Johnny and ball turret Max Shepherd are staying with the group for a few months more. Armorer-Waist Gunner Harold McKay has a couple more missions to fly.

The very best to you all.

Lee

On March 7, 1945 the U.S First Army crossed the Rhine River at Remagen into Germany. The Rhine served as Germany's last defensive barrier on the Western front. The hard-fought battle across the Ludendorf Bridge, halfway between Cologne and Koblenz, signaled the final days of destruction of the Third Reich. That same day the Mustaleski crew, flying the *Blue Hen Chick*, bombed the marshalling yards at Frankfort. Lee was on leave, hitchhiking through the English countryside. He did not find it difficult to get a lift along the way, the English drivers happily picked up a Yank flier. Back in Wilmington, Edna struggled with feelings of pride mixed with dismay that her son would not home in March.

March 10, 1945

Dearest Lee:

Your letter written March 5th came this morning – better time than anything before. I know you think you are doing the right thing and I admire you for it; but after receiving your cable last Friday – March 2, we were sure that you must be on your way home. We have not written you this week because you said to hold all mail. Will you have a new crew now, with the exception of Johnny Rosiala and Max Shepherd? If so let us know who they are.

I suppose your decision to stay was based on the fact that you believe the war in Europe will soon be brought to a close, at least as far as attacks from the air are concerned. It is terrible that Hitler has seemingly decided to allow Germany to be blasted from one end to another.

Love to you, dear, and God bless you.

Mother

Edna Minker was quite correct about Germany, Hitler had vowed never to surrender. His inflexibility in the face of certain defeat embittered the German High Command and cost tens of thousands of lives in battles between German and Allied troops, in bombing of cities with civilians, and in concentration camps.

In his next letter Lee is quick to point out that victory in Europe is not the end of the war: the shift of Army Air Force resources to the war in the Pacific had already begun.

Sunday evening
March 11, 1945

Dear Mother,

The news today is certainly full of good tidings. But it will take much more concentrated effort before final victory over the Axis. Plans are being shaped for transfer of the Air Forces European strength for the attack on Japan.

The weather over here now gives occasional [sic] hints of spring. The thatched English cottages have rainbow crocus blooming in their yards. (Send me all the 620 film you can get so that I can get some good pictures of Merry England in the spring. You might include some of your delicious cooking too (no eggs).

Movies seen lately: Song to Remember – life of Chopin with Paul Muni, Merle Oberon, Cornel Wilde; very good. Hanover Square – slow chiller. Keys of the Kingdom – Gregory Peck; very good.

I am glad that you have been able to correspond with the parents and wives of the crew of the Blue Hen Chick. I know that we are happy that our comradeship extends among our loved ones at home. Now that our combat tour is over and we go our several ways I hope that our friendships will continue.

Love,
Lee

Shirley fervently hoped that her older brother would be home for the May 27th graduation ceremony at Dickinson Junior College. In March she was busy with the drama club show, Campus Thunder, which featured ". . . a spectacular presentation of *The Wedding of the Painted Doll*. Shirley Minker, popular campus singer and star of this year's show, sings the tuneful old song accompanied by a chorus of beautiful dolls." (The *Campus Office*-R 1945) In between rehearsals, classes, and making the Dean's list, Shirley kept in touch with a number of servicemen. She regularly updated her brother on the location of high school friends in the Army, Marine Corps and Navy, several of whom were killed in action or taken prisoner of war.

Wednesday
March 14, 1945

Dear Lee

I guess it's alright if I write to you. I haven't heard anything to the contrary, so I'm hoping that this letter will reach you safely. I haven't written for a while 'cause since we had your cable we were holding all your mail. But, I had your letter last Saturday saying that you had decided to stay, so here I am!

Fred is in Luxembourg now, Lee. I just had a letter this morning; and he moved from France to Luxembourg just a few days ago. He hasn't seen any fighting, yet, but it sounds as though he'll be seeing some before too long. I had a letter from Allen and he's still safe and sound through all the fighting he has seen. Also, heard from Taylor Eder, Jeos Keper, and Francis McEvery. I also ran into Dick and Jimmy Rothnell at the station. He's in the Merchant Marine, you know, and he just came back from a trip over to France.

I imagine that by now you have returned from your rest leave. What will you do now? Go on more missions! I hope you can move the date of your arrival back in this country up about six weeks. We graduate on May 27, and I'd love to have you here. Well, I'm going to sign off now, and hope that you are able to decipher this scrawl. Say hello to all your crew members for me, and take care of yourself.

Lots of love,

Shirley

Three weeks of rest in the English countryside gave Lee the time to reflect on his experience in combat. The carefree college student of three years ago had been transformed in entirely unexpected ways. On March 19, 1945 with the war nearly over, Lee sent his dad a powerful picture of each hour of a "typical mission;" from the early morning briefing to suiting up for high altitudes in an unheated plane, to take off over the "cold, grey channel," to the relief and let down after bombs away.

Monday evening
March 19, 1945

Dear Dad,

Perhaps you would like to know about a typical mission day with the 8th United States Air Force.

After 1700 [hours] supper I stop at the base weather office to check up on tomorrow's weather, for bad weather is Germany's greatest ally in her vain attempt to stop the non-stop night and day, strategic and tactical air bombardment and espionage by the Air Forces of the United Nations. Then I check the availability list in the squadron orderly room to find if I am available for a mission and who will make up my crew. (experienced crews break in men from newly arrived crews.) I check the board – if it is red there is an alert for a mission, if green there is a stand-by (until 2230 etc.) if white we are released for training. (The board often changes several times a night.) I visit the gunners for an hour or so (chat, censor letters, sample a package from home, see that they are ready to fly) and then return to my barracks and bed about 2130.

At 0300 the squadron C.Q. snaps on a barracks light and wakes the men checked off for flying. He tells briefing time, bomb load and gas load. Speculation as to the target begins as we get up at 0400 (we allot about fifteen minutes to dress, fifteen to wash, fifteen to eat and fifteen to get to briefing) and check through the orderly room on the way to the mess hall. (half pre-mission breakfasts are of real, fresh, fried eggs.) Just before checking into briefing I make a quick check of my flying equipment and put on a set of suntans over G.I.O.D. long winter underwear so my electric heated suit will not be too close to my skin. Pilots, navigators and bombardiers attend a general briefing together at 0500 and then split up for more specific separate briefings. (gunners have a short briefing half an hour earlier before going to the planes to put in guns, check positions.) At [the] briefing information is given on formation, wing and division order, route and assembly, altitudes, temperature, weather, primary and secondary targets, enemy resistence [sic], friendly fighter escort, call signs, colors of the day, escape procedure and special instructions.

About 0545 I go to my locker to dress. I put on a two piece green General Electric wire lined A-3 electric heated flying suit and over that a light green coverall type summer flying suit. (for very cold days a heavy green wool lined jacket too.) Heavy wool socks, a light felt electric heated shoe and a heavy fleece lined rubber boot protect my feet; electric heated leather gloves over silk inner gloves protect my hands. I also wear a wool lined leather flying helmet with built in radio head phones, plastic sun goggles with electric heat filaments to prevent clouding up and a radio throat mike. Over all I wear a forty pound back-pack type parachute. And I carry a rubber oxygen mask, a steel flac helmet and a cord for my electric suit. A truck takes me to my plane – Kirkland "A" Able, 719, Blue Hen Chick, on hardstand 14 – about 0605. After a quick check with crew chief and engineer I assemble the crew in the waist for a last check of each man (position, equipment) a last briefing and a prayer with God. I start engines, wave to crew chief and taxi out to perimeter track and take off runway. At 0700, I pull out on the runway, make a quick check, note the green light from the control tower and give it the gun.

An actual mission is one continuous surge between tense eager expectancy and weary monotony – the thrill as power surges to lift the great silver bird in flight, the jockeying to form in squadron – group — wing — division and airforce formation by 1200 planes, England — a cloud covered hearsay – a gilt of sunlit fields and towns – A symphony in early morning shades of blue, the cold grey channel, Germany, cold, a stick of Wrigleys Spearmint Gum, oxygen, fascinating flac, escorting Mustang and Thunderbolt fighters, unidentified contrails, more flac – close and black – the plane staggers from the concussion, peaceful smoking target, prop wash rocking the formation, # 1 prop surging and running away, I'm tired, the channel and England again, low altitude, off oxygen at last, wolf down a Hershey bar.

I land about 1500, check with the crew chief about the plane (# 1 prop governor) and ride a truck back to the briefing room. I redress and down Red Cross cocoa and sandwiches while talking over the mission and calming down. (shots of scotch are provided too – supervised by a Flight Surgeon). I attend pilot's critique and then go to supper at about 1700.

Yours,
Lee

B-17 coming in for landing
Photo taken by Ralph Minker, March 1945
Courtesy Historical Society of Delaware

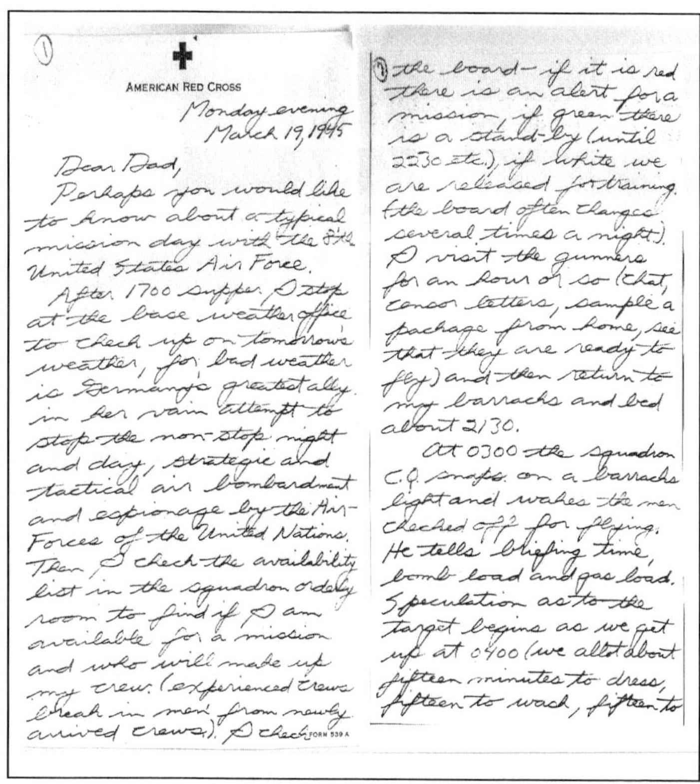

1

AMERICAN RED CROSS

Monday evening
March 19, 1945

Dear Dad,

Perhaps you would like to know about a typical mission day with the 8th United States Air Force.

After 1700 supper I stop at the base weather office to check up on tomorrow's weather, for bad weather is Germany's greatest ally in her vain attempt to stop the non-stop night and day, strategic and tactical air bombardment and espionage by the Air Forces of the United Nations. Then I check the availability list in the squadron orderly room to find if I am available for a mission and who will make up my crew. (experienced crews break in men from newly arrived crews). I check

FORM 539 A

2 the board – if it is red there is an alert for a mission, if green there is a stand-by (until 2230 etc.), if white we are released for training. (the board often changes several times a night). I visit the gunners for an hour or so (chat, censor letters, sample a package from home, see that they are ready to fly) and then return to my barracks and bed about 2130.

At 0300 the squadron C.Q. snaps on a barracks light and wakes the men checked off for flying. He tells briefing time, bomb load and gas load. Speculation as to the target begins as we get up at 0400 (we allot about fifteen minutes to dress, fifteen to wash, fifteen to

The first two pages of the March 19, 1945 letter describing a "typical mission". Courtesy Historical Society of Delaware

Lee had his first drink, a shot of scotch, on the order of the flight surgeon Captain Vernon 'Doc' Voltz, after a particularly difficult mission. His practice had been to give his post-mission ration to one of the crew. Upon return, the pilot's critique included a debriefing by an intelligence officer who filled out the requisite Interrogation Form for each crew after each mission. Lee succeeded in bringing the family into his world – one so different from springtime in Wilmington. Ralph Sr. readily shared his son's description of a typical mission with many friends, including Governor Walter Bacon.

The death of President Roosevelt in Warm Springs, Georgia

on April 12, 1945 – just a month before the end of the war — was more of a blow on the home front than it was for those in battle. FDR had been president for 12 years, during which time he led the American people through the two greatest crises of the twentieth century: the Great Depression and World War II. There are new concerns on the home front as the death of FDR leaves a relatively unknown leader, Harry Truman, to finish up the war. In November 1944, shortly after the election, Edna had written, "I tremble to think of Truman at the head of the nation." Her feeling was shared by many others in April 1945. The burst of spring growth in the gardens at the Ferris School is a sign of hope in Wilmington, along with news reports that Germany will soon be defeated. Yet the family grew increasingly uneasy; there are no letters from England for several weeks. Silence from a serviceman could be an ominous sign, producing tension that could only be relieved by a letter.

On April 1, 1945 First Lieutenant Ralph L. Minker was "...designated PFF Lead Crew having been chosen for this day through evaluation of their training, capabilities, knowledge, character, leadership and ability to accept responsibility."

April 9, 1945

Dearest Lee:

Another bright, spring morning. The asparagus crop is away ahead of schedule this year, and last Saturday I was able to cut enough of ours to have for dinner yesterday. We had some frost Friday night, which I fear has hurt the fruit buds. The campus is covered with violets and the dogwood trees in the wood are beginning to show white. Things are happening fast these days, both in Europe and in the Pacific; but they cannot happen too fast for those of us who have loved ones in the service.

Love
Mother

April 18, 1945

Dearest Lee:

I expect you received the news of the President's death almost as soon as we did, and I suppose you, like many of us, immediately asked "How will Truman ever carry on?" He certainly needs our good wishes and prayers. What a tragedy to lose both Roosevelt and Wilkie, who seemed to know as much about international affairs and some idea of what some of us are striving to attain.

Have you been unusually busy lately? We haven't had any word from you since March 19th.

With all my love.

Mother

April 19, 1945

Dear Lee:

The description of a typical mission of the Blue Hen Chick is a classic. How much I have enjoyed it, and dozens of others with whom I've shared it! It was written March 19 and got here in good time!

Here's hoping all is going well, It's pretty tough not to hear from you oftener. Even your signature would help. How about the picture of the Blue Hen Chick?

The best to you, kid.

As ever,
Dad

Too tired from 4:00 a.m. briefings and nine-hour missions to write letters, Lee used his leave to see the English countryside.

The lack of mail from overseas was felt keenly in the Minker household, Lee's sister, Bernice, asked that he find time to drop a line to ease his parents' worry about his safety. Even though the war in Europe was coming to a conclusion, men were still dying every day in land and air battles. The 8th continued to bomb airfields, submarine yards, and marshalling yards throughout March and April. By April 20, Hitler's 56th and final birthday, the Allied forces were closing in on the ruins of Berlin.

Saturday, April 20, 1945

Dear Lee,

We have been anxiously awaiting a letter from you for four weeks now. Please try to find time to drop a line of some sort so mom and pop won't worry too much. You know how they are.

Mother and Daddy are taking a trip to Raleigh, North Carolina this weekend to pick up a runaway. They left yesterday and expect to be home Sunday night. It's a 400 mile trip so it takes quite a while. Granny Minker is staying with Granny Jones and me 'til they arrive home.

The iris are beginning to bloom in the garden. We have two flowers, iris and pansies, which are really doing well.

It hardly seems possible that I have little over a month left in my high-school career. We graduate on the thirteenth of June in long white dresses and summer tux's. Shirley is out of college on the twenty-seventh of May. If you had remained in college we would have had three graduations in the Minker family in 1945.

I'm going to try to go up to Williamsport on the 11th of next month to see Shirley reign over the May Day. They're also holding the play that weekend so I'll have quite a time.

Pilot is becoming quite a dog, towering over his poor old mammy. They both are full of ticks and come in daily covered with mud from the creek. The pup is rapidly becoming better mannered than his mother ever thought to be.

Well, I'll try to write more often now that we're just marking time until finals and graduation.

Lots of love
Luck,
Bernice

As a second tour pilot, Lee now flew with "local crews" comprised of men finishing their tour or new replacements. On Monday, April 16 he flew A/C #44-8783, a B-17 with pathfinder equipment to German defense facilities in the harbor of Royan, France. The bombardier, Captain Stub Warfle, was the lead bombardier for the squadron. The success of each mission depended in large part on the lead aircraft whose job it was to navigate to the target, locate the specific aiming point, solve the bomb problem, and then lead the formation back home. The 447th B.G. suffered its last loss of a crewman and a plane on April 19, 1945, on the mission to Dresden. When the high squadron was attacked by two ME262s, the number one engine of *Dead Man's Hand* (A/C 42-31188), piloted by Lt. Robert F. Glazener caught fire, causing the plane to go down. The entire crew bailed out, Glazener and seven of the crew eventually made it back to the allied lines. The co-pilot, Second Lieutenant Harold Cramer, did not survive and is buried at the American Military Cemetery in Lorraine, France.

On Saturday April 21, First Lieutenant Ralph Minker at the controls of A/C#44-8786, led the Diamond Group of the 4B Wing to the airfield at Ingolstadt, north of Munich. The briefing started at 0400 hours, takeoff began at 0619. The target was cloud covered so they hit the secondary target – the marshalling yards in the town of Ingolstadt – before heading for home. Ingolstadt was the hub for six rail lines which branched out from southeast Germany. There were no losses in what turned out to be the 447th's final mission of the war. The four squadrons of the 447th Bomb Group had flown 258 missions in sixteen months, suffered over 1,100 causalities and men missing in action, and lost 130 aircraft. When a more thorough accounting of the losses could be done, the total number of their airmen lost in battle was over 400. Of that number, just over 200 lie in military cemeteries in Europe.

Wednesday evening
April 25, 1945

Dear Mother,

For the past month I have not written a letter because of a combination of flying fatigue and spring fever. But now I am refreshed and will write regularly again. I am okay so please don't worry.

What a lot has happened in just one month! Final victory of the United Nations in Europe is almost here; President Roosevelt has passed on and left us to carry on his plans and dreams for world peace and security; spring has come in full glory; the fury of war mounts in the Far East.

Our airbase is now transformed into a busy training center in anticipation of the day when hostilities finally cease in Europe.

Rumors are flying thick and fast of course but as yet there is nothing definite. Pilots are getting reviews of transition training flying techniques, instrument flying, night flying and engineering. Navigators and bombardiers are being checked on night and day navigation – dead reckoning, pilotage, celestial, radio and radar. Crews are being processed, planes are being overhauled and records are being put in order. Maybe our fourth of July date will have to be changed.

Your packages of film and food have arrived and are being put to good use. You had better not send any more though. Your letters have been coming through very well.

Love,
Lee

In the U.S., the news reports of the San Francisco Conference in late April of 1945 brought hope for a new way for nations to work together. Delegates from fifty nations gathered to determine how to keep the peace in the postwar world. This group grew out of the January 1, 1942 "Declaration by United Nations" that were allied against the Axis powers and united in the struggle for victory over Hitlerism. Now the same nations, and others who later signed the pact, came together to design a new organization, the two month conference eventually created the charter for the United Nations. Lee's service had made war all too real for the Minker family who recognized that a new world view was desperately needed.

V- E MAIL

[April 25, 1945]

Dearest Lee:

This is a day which I hope will go down in history as

the beginning of a new period – for it marks the opening of the San Francisco conference. We are all praying that something constructive to the peace of the world be done.

One almost hates to pick up the newspapers these days, for there are so many stories of German atrocities and cruelties to prisoners of war. How in the world we will ever re-educate this generation of German youth I can't imagine.

Love from all of us.

Mother

The war in Europe rapidly drew to a close. By April 20, the Russians had surrounded Berlin; by April 21, Patton's Third Army was at the Elbe River within striking distance of Berlin. With all lost, Adolph Hitler and his mistress Eva Braun, committed suicide in his bunker under the Reich Chancellery in Berlin on April 30, 1945. The German Reich collapsed; the formal peace in Europe was just days away.

The Eighth flew one last combat mission on April 25, the 447th B. G. "stood down" for that final mission to the Skoda Armament plant at Pilsen, Czechoslovakia. The German anti-aircraft guns were still deadly, six B-17s were lost, another 180 were damaged by flak. (Neillands 2001) Twenty-six crewmen died on this last mission.

V-E Day, May 8, 1945, brought an end to missions over Germany. After an unprecedented effort lasting more than three years, at a cost of the lives of 79,265 American airmen of the 8th AAF and over 50 percent of their heavy bombers, the Air War in Europe was over. "The achievements of Allied air power were attained only with difficulty and great cost in men, material, and effort. Its success depended on the courage, fortitude, and gallant action of the officers and men of the air crews and commands." (*Strategic Bombing Summary Report*, September 30, 1945.)

For the Minker family, the war would not be over until Lee came home. They waited eagerly for news of his furlough. They realized that the war was unfinished; Lee could be reassigned to the Pacific as the 8th AAF was preparing the transition to the war against Japan in the Pacific. To the combat crews still in England it was clear that the war – and their part in it – would not be finished until Japan was defeated. The May 1st memo from General "Hap" Arnold, Commander of the U.S. Army Air Forces, conveys the joy of victory, the necessity of the war yet to be won, and the immediate problem for the next few months – waiting for redeployment. Still, the letters from Wilmington have one theme: "When will you be home?"

THIS PAGE IS UNCLASSIFIED

RESTRICTED

HEADQUARTERS USAAF STATION 126
APO 559 US ARMY

1 May 1945

SUBJECT: Message from General H. H. Arnold.

TO: All Personnel.

1. The following message from the Commanding General, AAF, will be of interest to all personnel. This letter will be posted on all Bulletin Boards.

"I believe the following Memorandum, resulting from my visits with your personnel, will serve a fruitful purpose. It is directed to each member of the Army Air Forces and, at your discretion, should be widely publicized:

MEMORANDUM TO ALL OFFICERS AND MEN OF THE AAF IN THE ETO AND MTO:

1. The war against Germany is drawing to a victorious conclusion, and for the manner in which you have waged the air battle in that war I extend my heartiest congratulations to each and every one of you. Concurrently, I should like to dwell a bit on what lies ahead.

2. Before the peace of the world is secure, it is essential that the full weight of our armed forces be directed against Japan. This is necessary in order that a quick and decisive termination of the struggle in the Pacific may be assured. It will require many of you to augment the increasing strength of the AAF personnel now engaged against Japan. Constant thought and study are being given to the numerous phases of your redeployment, prior to demobilization, by all of us here in Washington. Completed plans are even now being implemented. You will be moved just as rapidly as available troop ships and air transports can ply the sea and the air from your ports to the USA and back again.

3. When the demobilization phase begins, those of you who have served longest in Europe and Africa, with minor exceptions, will return to your homes. However, we must first assure that all the Air Forces, together with their service elements, which will be required for an early decisive victory are brought to bear upon Japan. To do this, those of you having the least service overseas will be returned to the USA for leaves and furloughs at home after which you will be reassembled and given shakedown training before departing for the Pacific.

4. The problem of mastering new aircraft will confront many of you as you join the Japanese war. There are differences in the techniques required for the operation and maintenance of the B-29's and other new types. You will find that it takes time to learn them. For this reason your pretraining period in the USA may be extended.

5. After the violence of the war against Germany, considerable time may be required for the readjustment to peace. A force sufficient to assure this readjustment must, therefore, remain in Europe. Those of you, having served neither the longest nor the least, but who have gained experience sufficient to guarantee the success of such a mission, will make up the occupational Air Force. Your return to the USA will be possible through replacement and rotation...This will be accomplished at the earliest date practicable but probably not until the termination of the war in the Pacific.

6. The toughest part of the next several months will be the waiting period. Waiting for your unit to begin its movement--waiting for transportation. I realize this full well, but we, assisted by your commanders, will do everything within our power not only to keep you usefully employed but also to provide you with as wide a variety of recreation as it is possible to obtain.

7. In conclusion, I want you to understand clearly that I am as anxious to see you all go home again as you are to get there. However, we must not lose sight of the fact that there is another job for us to do - in the Pacific. Some of you, but not all, will be needed for its accomplishment. This job will not be easy but I am confident that the war against Japan will demonstrate once more the high morale and esprit which has been common to all the Army Air Force personnel throughout the world. ---SIGNED ARNOLD!"

BY ORDER OF LIEUTENANT COLONEL THORUP:

GLENN W. JOHNSTON
Captain, Air Corps
Assistant Adjutant

39

RESTRICTED

Memo from General "Hap" Arnold announcing V-E Day and the issues of redeployment. Official Unit Histories, 447th Bombardment Group. U.S. Air Force Historical Research Agency.

447th Bomb Group
Monthly Operations Reports

November 1945	Missions 222 - 243	Month	Total
	Missions	*22*	*243*
	Sorties	*821*	*7072*
	Aircraft Lost	*1*	*130*
	Crews Lost	*1*	*98*
	Personnel Killed	*1*	*62*
	Missing	*8*	*908*
	Wounded & injured	*1*	*120*

Final Totals for the 447th Bomb Group

The human tragedy reflected in the numbers below are only a partial indication of the great cost of lives and planes in the Air War over Europe. There were 48 bombardment groups stationed in England, each of which suffered similar or even more severe losses than the 447th. The final count, according to the official AAF report in 1946, was 79,265 airmen lost in the battle for Europe. The 447th Bomb Group lost over 400 men and half of its planes.

April 1945	Missions 244 - 258	Month	Total
	Missions	*15*	*258*
	Sorties	*543*	*7615*
	Aircraft Lost	*1*	*130*
	Crews Lost	*1*	*98*
	Personnel Killed	*1*	*62* *Over 400**
	Missing(MIA & POW)	*8*	*908*
	Wounded & injured	*1*	*120*

*The data is taken from the original Comparative Data Monthly Operations Report as recorded in Rattlesden 1943 - 1945 and on file at the National Archives. The actual number of personnel killed was over 400 when a more thorough accounting of the MIA and POW personnel could be done. In addition, some personnel reported as wounded later died of their injuries.

Chapter Twelve

Until You Walk in the Front Door

May 7, 1945 - September 2, 1945

Dates: May 7, 1945 to September 2, 1945	Location: Rattlesden Air Base, England & Wales

May 7 & 8, 1945	Germany surrendered, Victory in Europe is declared.
May 1 – 8, 1945	The 8th AAF dropped food to the Netherlands in Operation Chow Hound.
May 13, 1945	Lee received promotion to captain.
Late July, 1945	Rattlesden Air Base closed. Remaining troops are transported to Wales for embarkation orders.
Aug. 6, 1945	The first atomic bomb dropped on Hiroshima.
Aug. 9, 1945	The second atomic bomb dropped on Nagasaki.
Aug. 15, 1945	The Japanese government agreed to unconditional surrender.
Aug. 26, 1945	Lee sailed for home on the Queen Elizabeth. The ship is also carrying Lieutenant Colonel Jimmy Stewart and Governor Lehman of New York.
Aug. 31	The Queen Elizabeth docked in NY harbor; the 14,860 troops are welcomed by the big bands of Sammy Kaye and Cab Calloway in New York Harbor.
Sept. 2	President Truman declared Victory in Japan (V-J day).

Berlin, once a beautiful medieval city, endured relentless bombing by both the British RAF and the U.S. 8th AAF. The armies of the United States and Great Britain, with Russia on the Eastern front, closed in on the beleaguered city in early May. Street fighting and bombing destroyed 70% of Berlin, leaving rubble where majestic buildings had housed the Third Reich. On May 7, 1945, the faltering German government sent General Alfred Jodl to Rheims, France where he signed the document accepting the unconditional surrender. May 8, 1945 was designated Victory in Europe (V-E) Day. The strategic bombing campaign carried out by the Eighth Air Force and the RAF was decisive in winning the war against Nazi Germany.

When the peace was announced on May 7, 1945 Edna wrote immediately declaring, "There will be no wild celebrations." She underestimated the people of Wilmington, on May 8 people and streamers filled the downtown streets. The men and women of

Rattlesden celebrated in fine style with crepe paper, flags, four cakes and a dance.

Form 2247

RESTRICTED

AMERICAN RED CROSS

Month ending
May 31, 1945

Monthly Narrative Report
Carroll Emery, Staff Assistant
SAF-102-2-GB-30

This month ends up with us all deep in the throes of Victory. I still find myself listening to planes overhead at night and wonder if they're "our" of "theirs", and I can't yet feel comfortable in a room at night with all the blackout drapes wide open. But think before too long I'll get used to peace again and in the meantime, isn't it wonderful.

Victory Day was very considerate and landed right on our bi-monthly dance night. So that day found me going up and down ladders all day and decorating the club within an inch of its life with all the flags, crepe paper, etc. Headquarters so thoughtfully sent us. The results were really quite, if I do say so myself in all modesty. Consolidated Mess also helped out by making us four huge beautifully decorated cakes for the occasion. Came the dance and we all lived through it——but never will I forget V-E Day in the E.T.O. I'm afraid our beloved G.I.'s participated a wee bit too much in celebration and to call it a rat race would be mild. Howeve , the casualty list was low and everyone had the time of their lives——except my poor feet. So we really brought Victory in.

On V-1 and VO2 Days we served free food all day. Our doughnuts from headquarters really came in handy for the occasion.

Now for the other activities of the month. We had our other dance, which was nice but slightly more sub-dued than the V-E Day Dance. For this we had for an orchestra, the Century Bombers from Thorp-Abbott that really turn out some very sweet music.

My camera club is still thriving and weekly meetings are still well attended. As of these nice Sundays we've been bicycling out to local spots of interest and taking pictures like mad. I'm getting so I have that dark room technique down pretty well.

My dancing class is still very well attended. Have been having the girls out every week for them to work out on. The only trouble is with this is that they are so much more interested in the girls than they are in learning to dance.

A Miss Helton who has been our saviour since the base originated by bringing out and chaperoning a large group of girls for all our dances, provided and evening of fun. She brought about twenty-five girls out and we had about that many or a few more G.I.'s, and we spent the evening playing games under her supervision. I didnt quite know what to do when she switched them to playing post office and spin the bottle—but naturally the G.I.'s thought it was keen, and I was merely a guest. Was very pleased and complemented when the English girls presented me with three lovely handkerchiefs in appreciation of the fun they've had at our dances and dancing class.

RESTRICTED

21.

The VE Day celebrations at Rattlesden as reported by Carol Emory of the American Red Cross. Official Unit History, 447th Bombardment Group, U.S. Air Force Historical Research Agency

Celebration in downtown Wilmington, Delaware on V-E Day.
Delaware Public Archives

May 7, 1945

Dearest Lee:

We have just been through one of the greatest weeks in history, haven't we? And now daddy just called to say that Eisenhower has announced that this is V-E Day. We are still waiting for any announcement from the President or Churchill, but this surely must be it. Our hearts are full. I suppose at this hour every mother is thinking of her own son first and then trying to think of the whole picture. As we think of you our hearts swell with pride at the wonderful way you have carried on. I hate to think of what you have had to go through and see at a time when you should have been experiencing the joys of youth; but that cannot be undone now. I am glad that there have been and will be some weeks of rest and relaxation and peace. We know we still have responsibilities and that many hard years lie ahead.

Your beautiful Mother's Day card came this morning and I appreciate it more than you know. I will celebrate my 50th birthday on Thursday of this week. It frightens me sometimes to see the years come creeping on. There is so much still to be done. But I have three fine children to be thankful for. They will be able to do some of the things which I have not. This will be the third Mother's Day that you have been away from home. I feel sure we will be together when the next one comes around.

Mrs. Insho called me Friday night. I had written her at the time Leland was reported missing. They have not heard since around Easter time but of course are most hopeful now that so many German prisoners are being released. Of course she was asking all about you. Bob Durnham, the one who was in Bernice's class at A.I., has been reported killed in action in the Pacific.

Yesterday was Communion Sunday at Grace. The first table is always in memory of those of you who ordinarily would be there with us.

If this is really V-E day there will be no wild celebrations. The churches are to be open for prayer. The business houses are to close, I believe, but no schools. We all realize that while this is a time of thanksgiving and praise there is still much to be done before the war is over and we have to stick to our jobs.

Take care of yourself, dear, and let us hear from you as often as you feel you can write.

With all my love.

Mother

May 8, 1945

Dear Bernice,

It is V-E day at last!

You can probably imagine the joy, relief, and thanksgiving felt by us over here. But all realize that our war is only half finished; the peace is yet to be won.

I note that I am five letters behind in writing to you. So Solly (CBI slang). It hardly seems that you are in the last hectic days of your senior year of high school. Do you feel all grown up? What are your plans for the future—summer, fall? Are you going to sing with the Brandywiners? (Julia hopes to this summer – I hear.) How is Walt?

Here monotonous, stop gap training drags on. There is good weather again after a week of cold and rain.

Love,

Lee

Ferris School for Boys
BOX 230
Wilmington, Delaware

May 10, 1945

My dear Lee: -

The news of the last few days has been very welcome. It is difficult to imagine how the Nazi ideology could so completely grip people with the potentialities of the Germans. Yet we have seen it take place – and the "spanking" we have given them is just the beginning of the work necessary to a changed point of view.

I think you sense how I feel toward the news – I am counting the days until you are able to return and resume your preparation for your greater work of the future. You proved to yourself that you can take what comes – and I can see many satisfactions coming your way as you put your ability and spirit into some of the big tasks that lie before us. Opportunities for understanding and skillful leaders was never greater – and I am thrilled to think of the possibilities of your life.

You haven't replied to my suggestions about golf. Perhaps you thought I was rubbing it in a little after reading the scores you sent home of one of your attempts at the game. I think you'd get a kick out of it – and it's something we could have some fun out of together.

The best to you now! Remember we're with you every minute.

Sincerely,
Dad

By the spring of 1945 the Dutch people were near starvation. The five years of German occupation, together with unusually cold and snowy weather during the winter of 1944-45, resulted in severe food shortages. To make matters even worse, in September of 1944 the Germans barred food from coming into the harbors in retaliation for a Dutch railway worker strike. The British and Americans responded swiftly to the crisis in Holland. On May 1, 1945 nearly 400 B-17s, their bomb bays packed with food parcels, flew over the channel on *Operation Chowhound*: a new mission to bring food to the starving Dutch. There was no assurance that the Allied planes would not be fired on by the Nazis who still occupied Holland, as the surrender had not been signed. Over the next week, some 5,200 flying fortresses dropped 12,000 tons of food over Holland to people who waited near specially marked circles made with white sheets. (In later years, these flights were the most important of the war to Lee Minker.) One B-17 in *Operation Chowhound* went down over the North Sea, killing ten of the crew.

The ground crews got to see the results of the bombing on 'Victory Tours' when combat pilots flew them over Europe. "...the Station continued to conduct Victory Tours over the continent. These tours are very popular among the 'ground-pounders' who have not had the opportunity to view the actual areas of warfare. Cook's Tours, as they were more commonly called, were flown at 2,500 feet which ensured clear vision of bombed areas." (447th B.G. Administrative Report, 1 June 1945) The low-level flying gave Lee a close-up view of bombing results that combat pilots seldom see. His May 27 description of a bombed-out Germany is testimony to the utter futility of war. During May, the flying fortresses were also pressed into service to return refugees to their homeland or refugee centers. On May 13, a month before his 21st birthday, Lee was promoted to captain. Only fourteen months earlier he had received his commission as a second lieutenant at Pecos Field, Texas.

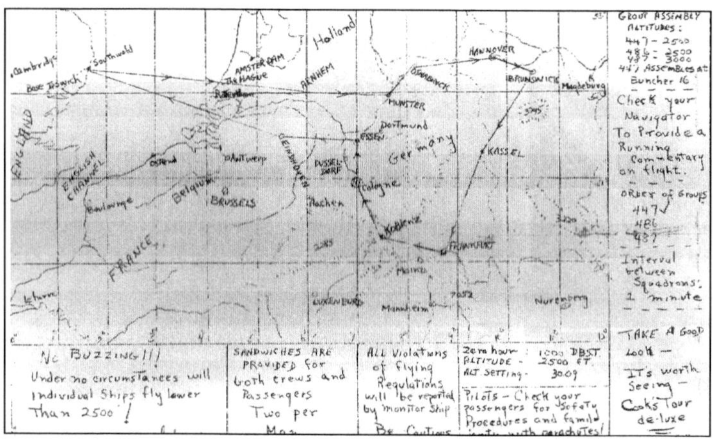

Map and orders for the "Liberty Tours" also known as "Cook's Tour."
May 1944
Note the direction to pilots about no buzzing
Courtesy Historical Society of Delaware

Wednesday evening
May 16, 1945

Dear Mother,

Today is a beautiful day – just like a May day back home.

Have you had a chance to work in the garden this spring? Have you been able to get a reliable boy to work in the garden? Has Ginger taught Pilot to detour around the flower beds? How was the iris this spring? Did they do okay along the road? What other spring flowers do you have? Did you prune and clean up dead growth and debris? What have you planted this spring?

As yet no redeployment news has been received here. The discharge point system will have no effect on pilot officer's however. Refresher training courses are in full swing until further notice.

With the end of the war in Europe censorship regulations have been relaxed in the U.K. Just don't mention anything which might help the Japs. I believe that I have told you most of what you might want to know already, but now I can tell you where I am located – East Anglia, Rattlesden, Suffolk, ten miles northwest of Stowemarket.

I am glad you had a chance to talk to Bob Cassel [friend from Dickinson] and Olaf Larsen [Radioman for the Blue Hen Chick.] They are fine fellows.

Love,
Lee

Announced just after V-E day, the Advanced Service Rating Score system required 85 points for discharge. Servicemen received one point for each month in the army, one point for each month in combat, five points for each campaign decoration, and two points for each child under 18 years. Those lacking in sufficient points would most likely be transferred to the Pacific for the attack on Japan. The system would have no impact on Lee; he had already signed on for a second tour of duty, plus the invasion would need seasoned pilots.

In the summer of 1945, the family at home was busier than was their flier in England. Shirley graduated from Dickinson Junior College on May 24; Bernice graduated from Tower Hill High School on June 13. Shirley and Bernice each set aside a graduation ticket for their brother, only to be disappointed when he did not return home. Nevertheless, as the war wound down, the Minker sisters had a wonderful time at parties, ceremonies, and other summer festivities. Shirley was continually on the go in May, with singing, the yearbook, and performing duties as the maid-of-honor during the May Day celebration. She barely found time to write to her brother. Her letters are a reminder of the cost of war – boys wounded, released from POW camps, or killed in action.

Shirley Minker, Maid of Honor to the May Queen, is the first girl to the right of the Queen's throne. Courtesy Lycoming College archives

---

Monday night
May 21, 1945

Dear Lee: --

Gee, I hope you don't really think I'm neglecting you lately but times have been so very busy around here that I don't realize where the days and weeks go. I know that you're even busier than I am, but for me it seems pretty bad. I finished my last exam today and now I have all the rest of the year to loaf around. Yes, this is our last week of school, Sunday I'm hoping to graduate from this famed institution and from there I'm on my own.

Since I last wrote to you so much has happened — the main one, of course, being the fall and unconditional surrender of Germany. I felt so wonderful when I heard the news, but was sobered by the realization that we have yet another victory to earn in the East before all is at peace again. I hope it isn't too much longer.

Fred is still over in Germany. I had a letter from him yesterday written the day after the German surrender. He didn't seem to know just what he was going to do. I don't think he's been over long enough to get a furlough and I don't even know whether or not he is going on to the Pacific. Of course, you know, we're hoping that you are coming home and you better keep that Fourth of July date with us! An awful lot of people here have had fellows from the Air Corps in Italy arrive home already! I'm singing at a wedding for one of the girls about the middle of June!

I had a wonderful letter from Taylor Edler and he's with the Marines on Okinawa. Allen Covender should be getting home some day soon, I think. He's been over two years this spring and I would think he'd have his 85 points if he wanted to be discharged.

The TWA line has just established a plane service between here and Pittsburgh. Timmie [chum from college] is very disappointed that they didn't do it sooner, so that she could have flown home once in a while. I don't believe it costs much more than the train, and it's so much shorter!

Mother has undoubtedly written you that Olaf Larsen [radio operator of the Blue Hen Chick] called her and is coming to see her. She was just thrilled to death, Lee. But now! I have to say something to you. Don't send the married men down to visit us. Bernice and I hate to waste our time and talents. See that you send some eligible bachelors the next time or we'll take care of you!

Take care of yourself now and do try and keep that date we all have together on the Fourth. Give my love to the "Blue Hen Chick" too.

Lots of love,
Shirley

Censorship was relaxed in May, so information could now be shared with the families at home. Lee was finally able to tell his parents the location in England of the base and report on missions. He looked back at the war only briefly, rather talked about a career and most welcome of all – fresh milk, a baseball game, and a date with his girl. All the alternatives for the immediate future included further military service. The plans for an all-out attack on Japan had been made, the first amphibious assault was to take place on November 1, 1945 on Kyushu with a second landing scheduled for March 1, 1946 on Honshu. Truman was advised that an invasion of Japan would cost between 250,000 and one million Allied casualties, plus an equal number of Japanese.

By the second week of May, Rattlesden became a training unit. "With the cessation of hostilities and the possibility of a rapid move, great emphasis was placed on combat crew training in lines that would be prepare the Group for an overseas movement. Intense priority was placed on an intensive fourteen-day program designed to produce a high rate of navigational and pilot efficiency." (*Air Exec's Summary Report*, May 1945, 447th B.G.) Experienced pilots, who could be retrained to fly the long range B-29, were needed for combat in the Pacific. The only new topic of conversation at the base was rumors about redeployment.

Thursday evening
May 24, 1945

Dear Dad,

A cool spell has come over England this week with intermittent rain showers: At present it seems as if it will be sometime after mid-June when I can come home from this changeable climate – 4th of July maybe.

I have been promoted to Captain recently by the way.

During my eight months and thirty seven combat missions with the 8th Air Force I have taken part in the battles of the Rhineland, Ardennes and Central Germany. I have had one special mission not included in a regular battle. I have been awarded the Air Medal and five oak leaf clusters.

When I return to the States I will probably get a thirty day furlough home and then report to Atlantic City for assignment. During furlough I want to get a good rest and eat good food. (What does milk taste like?) It would be great if we could have a family reunion dinner, a visit to Dickinson and the seashore. I can take time out to learn something of golf and tennis and get the garden in shape. We will have to see the power laden Blue Rocks and renew old acquaintances. I must pay my respects to Miss Julia B. Taylor too. [his high school girl friend]

There will be several choices for reassignment: 1. Instructing – can't see it.

2. A.T.C. (Air Transport Command) – could see a C-54 (maybe you could inquire as to the chances).

3. Retraining for more combat maybe, would like to be an operations officer.

It would be a good idea to check my summer uniforms. Please don't send any packages but keep sending letters.

See you all soon.

Lee

Sunday evening
May 27, 1945

Dear Mother,

This is a beautiful May Sunday evening. I can't help but wonder how it is back home. Rumors are flying thick and fast but still nothing has been announced.

Enclosed you will find film negatives which should be of interest when developed. London, crew, buddies, etc. More will follow seperately [sic]. I am sending a receipt for another government money order, play program and briefing sheet for a Victory Tour of Germany.

Recently I flew on a Victory Tour of Germany (one of a series) planned to give air and ground personnel of the 8th Air Force a low altitude close-up view of the results of their bombing missions, a view of Europe and a sample of flying. The damage to the German cities is indescribable, especially in railway yards and business centers. I wish every American could see the utter ruin so as to see, and realize the real slaughter of total war. Rotterdam is more than half weed covered lots where buildings once stood before the German blitz of 1940. Every German city is only a shell of half-walls and rubble, hopeless and bare; the sun gleams mockingly on millions of glass particles in the ruins. The country is a beautiful spring green in field and forest with neat, honest orange roofed farmhouses, but not a permanent bridge is standing, and all roads, railways, canals and rivers are blocked at least once every half mile. Germany is beaten and paralyzed totally and horribly.

Received your letter of May nineteenth today which seems okay. How is my mail coming through now?

Say hello to everybody for me.

Yours,
Lee

May 28, 1945

Dearest Lee:-

Mrs. Inscho called yesterday to tell me that Leland had been liberated from a German prison, and she was looking for him to come home. This morning we received a note from Olaf, saying he was disappointed in not being able to visit us. Evidently they are very strict with passes for he says it will be impossible for him to get away. He said some mighty nice things about you.

Yesterday's paper announced the Eighth Air Force is being sent to Japan, but did not say anything about stop offs in the U.S.A. From all accounts there must be little left of the city of Tokio [sic] by now. Of course there are all kinds of rumors going around Japan getting ready to make peace, but one cannot count on any of them being true.

I want to get you a small box off this week, Lee, but unless I hear from you within the next few days it will not contain anything of real worth. A mother and daddy like to do something real special for their boy when he is 21, but it seems we will have to wait until you return. Please if there is anything you need or want don't hesitate to tell us.

Love to you, Lee, and let us hear as much of your plans as you know and are permitted to tell.

Mother

Shirley hoped until graduation day that her brother would be back from England to share in the celebration. After all, the war was over! Lee's ticket went unused as redeployment plans remained uncertain. Family celebrations once taken for granted often had empty places during the war. For the fortunate families like the Minkers, the absence was not permanent. For 292,000 U.S. families however, a Gold Star banner in the window was a sad reminder of the permanent loss they had suffered. Since WW I a banner with a blue star placed in the window symbolized someone in the service. If the person was killed, a gold star took the place of the blue.

Man-In-Service Flag Catalog: #1979.0445.42
Armed Forces History of technology, National Museum of American History

---

Wednesday afternoon
May 30, 1945

Dearest Lee: --

How's my big brother today? It's a rather windy and chilly Memorial Day here in Wilmington, but the sun is shining very brightly. Bernice has school all day today and dad is out playing golf with Uncle Marion, so I decided to sit down and write some letters. Here I am all through school, Lee, if you can believe it!

I kept hoping all the time that you might be able to make it somehow or other, Lee, but I guess it just wasn't supposed to happen. We did miss you a lot, you know. That's both of my commencements that you have missed now. I don't think that's very nice of you! Bernice graduates the 13th of June, so try and make it! I'm just kidding you, I guess you know.

This morning I tried out for a lead in the Brandywiners. They are giving Iolanthe and I have the title-role. It isn't such a very big part, but big enough for me to start with! Bernice also got a part and we both think we're pretty hot stuff. Rehearsals start next Tuesday night and go through almost all the rest of the summer! Bernice and I are going to get our driver's licence [sic] so that we can get where we want to this summer!

Write now when you can and have a good time. I'm going to try and catch up on my reading 'cause you are miles ahead of me. Bye for now and hope to see you soon.

Lots of love –
Shirley

May 31, 1945

Dearest Lee:-

[N.B. The first line of Edna's May 31, 1945 letter is not readable.]

. . . letter written only a week ago and received this afternoon, - that you are now Captain Lee Minker and that you expect to get home for 30 days sometime next month. We'll certainly try to see that you get all the rest you want and some good food, including plenty of Grade A milk. Grandmother Minker will be on hand with her rolls and pies and I'll try to put in my share. I did send off your birthday box, but there's nothing valuable in it and if it does not reach you we shall not worry about that.

Love to you, Captain.

Mother

Throughout June and July, Lee flew training flights that he considered "monotonous" but in fact, were preparation for probable transfer to the Pacific. Bored and impatient, he flooded family members with questions, sent his sisters lists of movies he had seen and the books he had read. In an effort to keep the troops occupied, the recreation unit showed 26 movies on base in May. In June everyone at Rattlesden was busy inventorying equipment, readying it for return to the U.S. and redeployment to Japan. Weekly, the family made plans that included Lee, only to be frustrated at yet another delay for the anticipated furlough. Now it was Bernice's turn to press her brother to be home for her graduation, on June 13th from Tower Hill High School. Lee's promotion to captain was met with delight by his proud parents, sisters, and a grandmother who is rendered speechless by the news.

June 1, 1945

Dear Captain,

Today we recieved [sic] your letter with the news of your promotion and of your approximate arrival at home. I wish, now that you're in charge of the army, that you could rush your furlough a little so that you can be home for my graduation, June thirteenth.

Big news reached me last weekend when Dad came up to Williamsport to cart Shirley home from school. I was accepted at Centinary Jr. College in Hackettstown, N. J. That was quite a relief as all the colleges are filled, practically and rejections are the rule, not the exception. So many more girls have the money to go to school now than ever before it's worth your life to get in.

We sure had a swell time in Williamsport, even though it rained practically the whole time we were there. Mother seemed to enjoy herself and it did her good to get away.

This evening one of the boys at the school took Shirley out to teach her to drive. I'd had previous lessons from Walter so felt pretty superior, knowing all the gears and stuff. You have to take a test when you get your permit in Delaware now, so we're practicing for that.

Well, it's time for me to turn in.

Bernice

V – MAIL

June 6, 1945

My dear Lee:

Well, you made the headlines again! Congratulations on that captaincy. I am certainly proud of you and happy for you. A few people may write you but several dozen have spoken to me about their joy over your advancement. Grandmother Minker was so thrilled she couldn't even talk over the phone to Aunt Eunice after she had called Aunt Eunice to give her the news. She had to hang up and call her an hour later.

What a job I have keeping up with my family: All of you are doing so splendidly on the front page or the back page regularly so that it is rare to think of three days passing without the local papers carrying some news article about a member of the family. I can hardly say how I feel about it -- the way we are able to get into the constructive efforts of the community and nation.

A great week end at Dickinson! Everybody asked for you. I spoke to several of your original class, i.e. the girls.

It's good to think you may be home soon. I'll order the milk you drink it.

The best to you.

As always,

DAD

Thursday
June 7, 1945

Dearest "Cap" –

Gee whiz, you really are doing quite well for a beginner and considering that you had the misfortune to have the same name as Bernice and I do. I guess we'll really have to have a royal welcome for you when you get back in these parts. It really is wonderful though, Lee, and we are all awfully proud of our big brother. So many people have told me that they think it's wonderful, and then I just give them a long speech about you.

We had our first Brandywiner's rehearsal on Tuesday night and got along quite well. I knew a few more people than I did last year. I do hope that you can get home in time to see it, Lee, cause, in addition to Bernice and I having parts, I believe that a Miss Taylor [Julia Taylor, Lee's girlfriend] is also gracing us with her presence! She only has a speaking part, as I understand it, but she won't be home for about three weeks yet.

Bernice and I went over to "A.I" [A.I. duPont High School] last Sunday to the Baccalaureate service. I felt almost like an alien 'cause I didn't know many people there. It's been very cold here lately so that I think they are actually going to have some cool weather for graduation. I can remember that yours was a scorcher, and so was mine. That all seems so long ago to me, and, I guess that it seems even longer to you. Bernice's [graduation from Tower Hill High School] is next Wednesday and luckily, we don't have rehearsal then.

Well, Lee, it's about time for lunch now so I'm going to say good-bye again. Be good, now and do come home soon. Don't forget to bring your crew, though! Write when you can, cause your letters have been coming through pretty fast lately!

Lots of love,
Shirley

BERNICE MINKER

Junior Varsity Hockey, '44; Varsity Basketball, '45; Tennis; Chorus; Assembly Committee; Operetta Cast; College, Centenary.

Bernice Minker's photo, Tower Hill Yearbook of 1945
Tower Hill School archives.

As superintendent of the Ferris Industrial School, Ralph Minker Sr. had to continually search for staff during the war. With so many men away or involved in war work, Bernice's friend Walter was recruited to help out in one of the cottages. By spring of 1945 in Delaware, German POW's were the principal source of emergency workers. The labor shortage was soon to end as the servicemen and women came home by the tens of thousands, changing the landscape for the entire labor market.

Monday nite
June 9, 1945

Dear Lee,

At last summer seems to have arrived in Wilmington. After a cold spell lasting several weeks, the weather finally changed today into warm, summer weather. Thank goodness it's held off this long, though, as it seem horrible to be sitting in school during summery days.

High school ends for me next Wednesday night. I sure hope you can get home for the commencement program and am holding a reserved seat for you. A fellow in the class is giving a dinner at the country club before the fatal hour and another is throwing open house afterwards. Some fun!

Last Tuesday night rehearsals for Iolanthe got under way. Shirley and Walt and I, benevolent 1 yr. members that we are, smiled sympathetically at the newcomers, giving the impression that we were old hands at the game. The Brandywiners really are a swell bunch of folks though, and no one feels lost in their midst for long.

Since the shortage of help Walt has been working here on Sundays, driving, etc. He is now with the assistance of Mr. Arthur, trying to amuse fifty Ball Cottage boys.

Don't forget our date Wednesday night.

---Lots of Love Luck,
Bernice

Tower Hill High School Graduating Class of 1945. Bernice Minker is in the second row, the last girl on the right. Courtesy Tower Hill School archives.

June 10, 1945 marked the second anniversary of the 447th Bomb Group at Rattlesden. The airmen celebrated the occasion with impressive style.

The big deal of the month was our huge 250 Mission, Two Year Anniversary Party June 10. It was an all out affair...there was a softball game at noon, USO band concerts, a beer and cocktail hour, dinner for all the G.I.'s and two enlisted and two officers dances at night...We decorated the club for the occasion and gave all the girls corsages plus the lovely programs the base had printed. Really a big affair. – (report by Carol Emory, Red Cross staff assistant, June 1945, Offical Unit History 447th B. G.)

June 16, 1945 marked Lee's twenty-first birthday. A seasoned combat pilot at age 21 was not the future that Rev. and Mrs. Minker, Sr. had envisioned for their son. The spirit of the sacrifice of the American people during WW II is conveyed in Edna's 21st birthday letter. Millions of families, like the Minkers, sent clean-cut kids to crush the evil of Nazi Germany, in the strong belief that the work had to be done, and each son or daughter was needed – no matter what the cost.

V – MAIL

June 14, 1945

Dearest Lee:-

Today is just about as hot as that day 21 years ago when you arrived at the Homeopathic Hospital, Wilmington. It was a happy occasion and little did daddy and I dream that you would be celebrating your 21st birthday away from home,- certainly not on foreign soil and in the Army. From that day to this we have been proud of you and we thank God that, although you are not with us today, you have been spared and we are looking forward to seeing you before many weeks roll by. I guess I will wait until you arrive before baking the birthday cake which has always been a part of the celebration each year for you three children.

We are ordering tickets for Brandywiners (one for you, too) for the last week in July, feeling pretty sure that you will be with us then.

I do hope it is possible for you to be having some kind of a let-up and celebration on this, one of your most important, birthday. Of course you know we are all thinking of you and wishing for you the very best.

With all my love.
Mother

Saturday evening
June 16, 1945

Dear Mother,

Today I am twenty one years old. I do not feel any different today than I did yesterday but I know that I have grown, especially during the last twenty eight months in the Air Forces. I only hope that I am growing as you and Dad would want me to.

Plans have been changed again since my recent cablegram to you. At present it is very probable that I will be here another month. This afternoon I received your letter of June eighth; continue writing until I get home, to help relieve the great monotony of just sitting around.

Yesterday a troupe of sports stars serving the E.T.O.

[European Theatre of Operations] visited the base to talk about and demonstrate their sport. Captain Horton Smith of the Army Service Forces represented golf, George Lott and Tommy Faulkenburg represented tennis and Sol Sniff represented ping pong. In the evening movies of the 1944 World Series and football season were shown.

Love to you all.

Lee

Lee did not get home for Bernice's high school graduation, but did find time to send her a book of poetry as a gift. He did get orders to ship home at the end of June and excitedly sent a telegram to his parents. But the delays in demobilization continued into July, his seat for the Brandywiner's production of Gilbert and Sullivan's *Iolanthe*, featuring the Minker sisters, was empty.

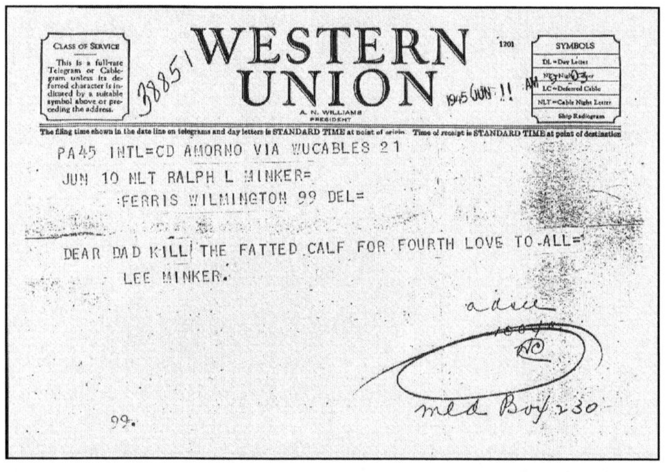

WESTERN UNION

A. N. WILLIAMS, PRESIDENT

1945 JUN 11

PA45 INTL=CD AMORNO VIA WUCABLES 21

JUN 10 NLT RALPH L MINKER=

:FERRIS WILMINGTON 99 DEL=

DEAR DAD KILL THE FATTED CALF FOR FOURTH LOVE TO ALL=

LEE MINKER.

Telegram announcing Lee's homecoming in early July 1945. Courtesy Historical Society of Delaware

Tuesday evening
July 3, 1945

Dear Mother,

I am still sweating out shipment home. The flying echelon of the 447th Bomb Group (Heavy) has left for the U.S.A. and the ground echelon has been alerted for an August first boat ride. I had hoped to fly home but that now seems out of the question. I now hope to be able to return to the States with the group ground echelon. At any rate I will not be home till August as things now stand.

Enclosed is a receipt for $ 230 which the Finance Department is sending home for me. It might be well to keep some of it on hand for use during my furlough although I will receive a partial or maybe even another full payment before then. We must file a corrected income tax return covering my promotion to Captain too. Are you investing my money equally in war bonds, building and loan stock and a savings fund?

I am leaving for a pass to London in the morning.

Love,
Lee

July 2, 1945

Dear Lee,

Today I received your letter with the Wordsworth collection enclosed. Certainly that is one of the most outstanding graduation presents I collected. Thank you.

Since we expected you home for the 4th Shirley and I

have curtailed our writing but will start again. Try and hurry for we were all very disappointed to hear of the delay.

Last week mother spent in Ocean Grove, attending the W.C.S. [Women's Christian Society] conference there. She studied hard but appears to be rested up.

Walt enlisted in the Navy the other day and went to New York to spend today and tomorrow taking his physical. It takes them two days to get around to him.

While Mother was away Granny Minker came out and stayed. She baked rolls and rusks and two lemon pies plus a batch of cinnamon buns. Were they delish!! Sat. night Uncle Marian and his family ate dinner here, since they brought Mom back from the shore.

Lots of Love Luck,
Bernice

With the war in Europe over, the Army Air Force wasted no time in closing the bases in England in preparation for redeployment. Men and material would now be concentrated on winning the war in the Pacific Theater. On April 1, 1945 the Americans launched the amphibious invasion of the heavily fortified island of Okinawa. Strategically situated south of Japan, Okinawa became the last battle of World War II. By the time the Battle of Okinawa ended on July 2, 1945 the final toll of American casualties was the highest experienced in any campaign against the Japanese. Total American battle casualties were 49,151, of which 12,520 were killed or missing and 36,631 wounded. The toll for the Japanese who were dug into the caves of the rocky island was even higher; more than 107,000 Japanese and Okinawan conscripts were killed. More than 100,000 Okinawan civilians died, many of whom committed suicide when faced with capture. The Battle of Okinawa harshly demonstrated to military planners the high price that each side would pay for the invasion of Japan.

In July 1945 Truman, Churchill and Stalin met at Potsdam, Germany and called on the Japanese to accept "unconditional surrender" to the Allies. Japan was warned that unless they agreed to end the war, Japan would face "prompt and utter destruction." During the Potsdam Conference, Truman learned of the successful explosion of the atomic bomb in the desert of New Mexico. Truman informed Stalin of this event, but surprisingly Stalin appeared disinterested. The Russians knew of the American and British efforts to develop the atomic bomb and were secretly working on an atomic bomb project of their own.

Friday evening
July 6, 1945

Dear Shirley,

How are you this fine summer evening? I have just returned from a three day pass to London but still there is no news of shipping home.

While in London I saw Churchill booed and hissed in a last minute tour of the Socialist Labor Center of South London. The people are extremely bitter about the vested interests and titles in the Conservative National Party and vote Socialist because the only alternative is Liberal, and the Liberals do not even have enough candidates to control Parliament.

I attended a very fine British movie, The Way to The Stars, the story of an airfield under the RAF and the AAF. It was a very well done and true picture. British pictures, when good have a freshness and sincerity not often achieved by American but much of their production would not interest us.

But it is a problem to keep busy and happy over here now. Recently I saw a USO Campshow (fair entertainment as usual). And Music for Millions (good). I have read the July Reader's Digest (good as usual) and am now attempting the Republic of Plato.

There has been no letter from home since I last wrote. I hope that my mail is still being forwarded.

How are you doing in your driving lessons? How is Iolanthe shaping up? Have you a job yet? Has your nose peeled yet this summer? Where is Fred now and what are his prospects? What is the gossip back there? What are you doing in your time off? Have you weeded in the garden? How are Ginger and Pilot? Have you got any 620 film stored up? Etc?

Love,
Lee

July 9, 1945

Dear Lee,

Well, I've just a few minutes before practice so I thought I'd drop you a few lines. The show is progressing very slowly at this point.

This morning Shirley and I both got up early to go in town about jobs – she to the Delaware Hospital, I to Bird-Speaksman's. She landed her job – as a cardiograph worker, starting tomorrow but mine fell through. Seems like no one wants a person just for the summer and jobs are really tough to get.

Shirley and I have spent today and ourselves rushing

in and out of town. Part of the time was spent getting Julia's present. We finally decided on a leather, velvet lined jewelry case with a pair of gold horses head earrings to stick in. O-K? We're going to present it to her tonight at Brandywiners.

Well, have to be buzzin' along 'cause practice is at 8:00 but those [were] swell shots of your plane today. Or are they yours? Well, so long.

Lots of love, luck
Bernice

Most of the air echelon left Rattlesden Air Base June 29 and 30th 1945; the ground echelon sailed on *USAT Joseph T. Robinson* and *USAT Benjamin R. Milam* from Liverpool on August 1 and 3, 1945. Rattlesden Air Base closed in late July 1945, leaving behind Quonset huts, the three runways and 55 ghostly hard stands that had been home to the Flying Fortresses of the 447th Bomb Group. Captain Minker moved with the remaining troops to Wales to await embarkation orders. After so many months of plans that changed, the interminable wait for return to the U.S. was almost over.

Friday evening
July 20, 1945

Dear Mother,

Greetings and salutations for the last time from Rattlesden. Sunday fifty four pilots, co-pilots and bombardiers are shipping from this air base to the 70th Redeployment Depot at Chorley [Middlesex, England].

(seven navigators are leaving Saturday). After a day of processing we will sweat for at least ten days probably, until we board a boat for the U.S.A. Then –

I had a big last pass in England early this week. I hope that someday the rest of the family can see England—London, Liverpool, Cambridge, Oxford, Brighton, Edinburgh, Scotland, Wales. This is a great little country.

Plays seen while on pass: The Cure for Love (very good); Robert Donat is great as lead and director of this past Lancashire comedy); the Skin of Our Teeth (good; very modern Thorton Wilder comic history of the world; (Vivian Leigh is great); Dear Ruth (very good army production of current Broadway hit.)

The last letter received from you was written July fourteenth. I suppose it will be the last I receive for a while but maybe I will be home before too long.

Love,
Lee

Japan rejected the demand for unconditional surrender on July 28, 1945. The possibility of assignment to the Pacific became more likely for the troops in the European Theater. Then on August 6, 1945, the U.S. dropped the first atomic bomb on Hiroshima, Japan; the second atomic bomb was dropped on Nagasaki on August 9. Japan finally accepted the Allied terms of surrender on August 14, 1945. The letters from Wilmington described wild celebrations downtown as the city emptied onto the streets in complete jubilation. Their great relief that the war was over was diminished by the horror of this new destructive weapon. After nearly four years of war, each member of the Minker family shared their joy over the end of the violence and longing for a future in a world at peace in their last letters written in August 1945.

The Japanese envoys, Foreign Minister Mamoru Shigemitsu and General Yoshijiro Umezu, signed the Instrument of Surrender on the deck of the battleship Missouri on September 2, 1945. General Douglas MacArthur, Commander in the Southwest Pacific and Supreme Commander for the Allied Powers, signed for the United States. World War II was over.

V – MAIL

Dear Mother, *8-7-45*

Well I am still sitting and waiting. Maybe I will see you in September.

Probably some mail will be forwarded from my old address soon. Save them please. You can write me at the above temporary address now. (V-Mail).

Today the announcement of the new atomic bomb came out, a horrible warning and a great promise for the future.

Yesterday I saw the movie Winged Victory; a good show, pretty accurate but melodramatic.

Recently I went to Blackpool, a very American amusement resort.

Love to all,
Lee

Thursday, August 16, 1945

Dearest Lee:-

Your letter of the 7th came this morning, but we are hoping that the sentence "maybe I will see you in

September" is not true. Of course we realize that the waiting is a hundred times harder on you than on us at home. We have not written because you told us not to. In this morning's Inquirer [Wilmington morning paper] is the news that yesterday the troopship Benjamin R. Milan arrived at Boston carrying, among others, members of the 709th Bomber Group; so we were all pepped up thinking you might be in Wilmington before the end of the week. I have always thought that you would get word thru by telephone as soon as you landed in the U.S.A., but the girls seem to think that you won't call until you know just when you will get in Wilmington.

When the news came on Tuesday night [of the surrender of Japan] of course our first thought was of you. We wondered whether you would hear it if you were in the middle of the ocean. We all went into church, for daddy had it open for prayer. Of course there was wild jubilation downtown, but we came home about 10 o'clock. Last night we all went to the communion service held especially for the occasion. Our first table, as usual, was for those of you who are still away from home. I do hope I can have you by my side in church before too many weeks roll by.

It is wonderful feeling to look out on a beautiful morning such as this and realize that once more the world is at peace. At the same time it brings an awful responsibility for the months and days ahead. You may know that already gas and fuel oil rationing has been lifted. There are so many things which we do not know about yet, but we will still have to be patient. I think the end came before anyone was prepared for it. The atomic bomb is truly an awful thing when used in warfare, and I am glad the Japanese had sense enough to realize that.

I still think the sentence saying you would see us in September was written when you were rather "down" and tired of the waiting; and that we will see you sometime this month. I have always said you would be home on the Queen Mary or Queen Elizabeth. I notice that the Queen Mary is scheduled to arrive next Wednesday. Your mail here is piling up.

Now keep your chin up. With these late developments maybe it won't be too long before you are discharged from the army and able to get back into college. We have so very much to be thankful for, don't we?

With all our love,

Mother

[August 16, 1945]
Thursday

Dear Lee,

Well, what a disappointment we all had this morning when your letter came. We had hoped you'd be home sometime this week, since we saw in the paper that the 709th landed in Boston yesterday.

Lots has certainly happened since we've last written. The war is over!! Tuesday we had just started out for the movie when sirens and horns began blowing all over the place. People ran out on the streets, some laughing, others crying husterically. We got to 4th and Market, then abandoned the bus to walk. What a fight to walk up the pavement crowded with people! We finally made it, in about half an hour, to 9th and decided to go to church. There we met mother and Shirley who had driven in. May, Shirley, Walt and I got out as soon as we could and tore back to the center of the city, which was really rockin'. By this time all motor traffic up Market had ceased and people surged up and down, throwing paper, waving flags, screaming and singing. We met Dar and Ruth, then ran into two fellows from Brandywiners with their girls. The ten of us formed a long line with the boys on the ends and went rocketing up and down, seeing people we knew, shouting and laughing. About 10:30 we discovered how hungry we were and set out to find a place to eat. Settled at the Kozy Korner we planned what to do next – we all went out to Dars, as things were getting a little rough down town.

Yesterday practically no one worked and we drove around a dead town viewing the remains of the celebration. At 1:15 the church held communion and it was most impressive.

I've been busying myself getting ready for college, making clothes and stuff. It starts on the 16th and I got the orientation week schedule today. I'm really all excited and can scarcely wait to be off.

Well, I'd better be off now, or lunch won't be ready when mom gets home.

Lots of Love Luck
Bernice

August 16

BERNICE MINKER
BRINDLEY ROAD
WILMINGTON, 99, DEL.

Thursday

Dear Lee,

Well, what a disappointment we all had this morning when your letter came. We had hoped you'd be home sometime this week, since we saw in the paper that the 709th landed in Boston yesterday.

Lots has certainly happened since we've last written. The war is over!! Tuesday night Walt ~~and~~ I had just started out for the movie when sirens and horns began blowing all over the place. People ran out on the street, some laughing, others crying hysterically. We got to 4th and Market, then abandoned the bus to walk. What a fight to walk up the pavements crowded with people! We finally made it, in about half an hour, to 9th and decided to go to church. There we met mother and Shirley, who had driven in. May, Shirley, Walt and I got out as

Opening page of Bernice Minker's letter describing the V-J Day celebration in Wilmington.
Courtsey Historical Society of Delaware

Capt. R. L. Minker
127th Redeployment, Bl # 18
A.P.O. # 652, C/O P.M.
New York City

8-17-45

Dear Mother,

Peace has come at last – Thank God! You can probably picture the joy and thanks deep in the hearts of us in the service.

Good news today: I was alerted for return to the U.S.A. Probably sometime within a week I will move to an embarkation point for shipment, probably by boat, to a U.S. port and Camp Dix, New Jersey. Probably I will then get a thirty day leave; maybe after that I will be released and be able to return to "civilian" life. While home I want to fly at N.C.A.A.B.[New Castle Army Air Base], (must have four hours to get August flying pay), relax and play. Don't write any more for I'll see you soon.

Love,
Lee

Monday, August 20, 1945

Dearest Lee:-

I have finished scanning the paper for a list of ships and men arriving this week, but have found nothing which would indicate that you are to be among them. Every Sunday when we sit down to dinner together we say, "Well, by another Sunday I guess Lee will be home".

Love to you and write whenever you can.

Mother

Tuesday night
August 21, 1945

My dear Lee: --

How's it going over there now or would you just rather not say! I know how disgusted you must feel because I'm quite disgusted. I'm just not going to believe you're here until I see you walk in the front door. Anyhow, that's the way it goes!

Have you been doing any celebrating lately? I mean since the war is over! We have been having a wonderful couple of days last week and I have never seen Wilmington go so completely crazy. I felt so happy that I didn't know whether to laugh or cry first. But, it's made an awful lot of difference here already. There is no gas rationing which is really the most wonderful thing. It seems so funny not to have to worry about everything like gas stamps, Lee, 'cause it seems that has been going on for years.

We're really going to celebrate when you come home. See you soon.

Love as always,
Shirley

From:

To: REV. & MRS. R.L. MINKER
P.O. BOX 230
WILMINGTON, 99,
DELAWARE

0-77072
CAPT. R. L. MINKER, JR
127th Repl. Bn, Bl. #18
A.P.O. #652, % P.M.
New York City
(Sender's complete address above)

(CENSOR'S STAMP)

See Instruction No. 2

8-25-45

Dear Mother and Dad,

I am coming home!!! When H.M.S. Queen Elizabeth next docks in New York I will be cheering from her deck. At last — it will be great to be home again.

Remember that it may take a couple days to travel from New York to Camp Dix to Wilmington. I will get in touch with you as soon as I know how things will proceed. Does Wilmington play a Labor Day doubleheader home?

See you soon.

Love to all, Lee

Have received three letters.

HAVE YOU FILLED IN COMPLETE ADDRESS AT TOP?

REPLY BY V---MAIL

HAVE YOU FILLED IN COMPLETE ADDRESS AT TOP?

Lee's last correspondence from overseas, a hurried V-Mail informing the family that AT LAST he is coming home! Courtesy Historical Society of Delaware

0-77-72
Capt. R. L. Minker, Jr.
127th Repl.Bn, BL # 18
A.P.O. # 653, C/O P.M.
New York city

8-25-45

Dear Mother and Dad,

I am coming home!!! When H.M.S. Queen Elizabeth docks in New York I will be cheering from her deck. At last --------------- it will be great to be home again.

Remember that it may take a couple days to travel from New York to Camp Dix to Wilmington. I will get in touch with you as soon as I know how things will proceed. Does Wilmington play a Labor Day doubleheader home?

See you soon.

Love to all,
Lee

Have received three letters.

Lee walked the decks of the *Queen Elizabeth* with Governor Lehman of New York during the five-day crossing aboard the crowded ship. Colonel Jimmy Stewart proved to be a good companion during the poker games that helped to pass the time. He took several photos from the deck, enjoyed the music and welcoming crowds, and marveled that he really was back home.

Lee Minker took this picture of the New York skyline from the deck of the Queen Elizabeth on September 1, 1945.
Courtesy Historical Society of Delaware

September 1, 1945

"With name bands playing hot jive on the open pier and her deep-throated horns bellowing signals to the Lilliputian tugs, the giant Queen Elizabeth docked at W. Fiftieth Street early yesterday afternoon amid the noisiest welcome since V-E Day."

(The New York Times, pp. 1 and 26.)

He disembarked from the *Queen Elizabeth* on September 1, a very different young man than the boy who left for training on February 23, 1943. He took the bus to Trenton, New Jersey and from there rode the ferry across to Wilmington. Mother, Dad, Shirley and Bernice were waiting at the ferry dock.

The celebration at the ferry landing was emotional for the family when Captain Minker arrived in Wilmington just after Labor Day, 1945. The love, support, and remarkable correspondence of his mother and dad and two sisters sustained him through 18 months of training and seven months of combat.

On Sunday, September 8, Lee sat down to a family dinner with fresh milk, grandmother's pocketbook rolls and lemon pie. He had served 30 months in the Armed Forces, brought his Flying Fortress and crew back safely from the German skies — despite flak, bad weather, engine failure, run-away propellers, and *Luftwaffe* fighters – thirty seven times. Now he was home, a whole lifetime ahead of him.

An ordinary and an extraordinary story
of an American family.

A EULOGY OF AFFIRMATION

46th Anniversary Reunion of the
447th Bomb Group of the 8th Army Air Force
1991

Gordon Dodge, my co-pilot, has sent me a birthday gift – the planting of a tree in my name in Israel. First, as a gesture of peace in a land and a world hurting for lack of peace. Second, as a way to fight polluted air which can kill and cripple human life.

My friends, that gift is a type of eulogy, an affirmation of me, an affirmation of Gordon Dodge, and an affirmation of our veteran's group. We have fought in war for the freedom of life to flourish on planet earth. That fight is not over: that fight has many fronts and facets. The gift of a tree is a living eulogy: action, not just words: while we are still alive.

I remember the way we were! We were a group of strangers then. We were civilians being converted into uniformed military men. We were land-based creatures, learning to use the air to define a land-based way of life. Again, I repeat, we were a group of strangers. A world war had enveloped the United States. As we came together our lives were at risk.

Our President, Franklin Roosevelt, told us that we were fighting for four great freedoms: first, freedom of expression; second of belief and worship; third, freedom from economic want; fourth, freedom from fear and rumor of war. Each of these freedoms is interconnected and each is worldwide in scope.

My friends, we were in England in both the hell and hope of wartime. We helped to make a great victory happen and to open hard locked doors to a better future. Some of us died in that struggle. Some of us have died since that time. We who are here today shall follow after them. In the meantime, however, we still have a solemn responsibility to give witness to who we are and have been, to say to each other and those who passed away: still standing for peace with justice, still faithful to a common cause.

Ralph L. Minker
Retired Pastor, United Methodist Church

Ralph Minker at 447th B.G. Memorial May, 1985
Rattlesden, England
Photo by Sandra O'Connell

Ralph Minker at WWII Memorial Jan. 2005
Washington, D.C.
Photo by Carol Schreiner

Blue Hen Chick

In early September, 1944, B-17G -95-BO 43-38719 rolled off the production line in the Boeing Seattle plant. It was delivered to the Air Force at Great Falls Montana, arriving at Lincoln, Nebraska on September 9, and finally Dow Field, Maine, before being ferried to England on September 27. The aircraft was immediately assigned to the 709th Bomb Squadron, 447th Bomb Group, reaching Rattlesden the first week of October. The first combat mission for A/C #43-38719 came on October 7, 1944 when the group went to Merceberg. Assigned to the Minker crew in early November, the pilot, Ralph "Lee" Minker, named her the *Blue Hen Chick* for the famous fighting hens of the revolutionary war of the state of Delaware.

Blue Hen Chick flew 67 combat missions, and in spite of being hit by flak on numerous occasions and sustaining damage from two accidents, returned to the reclamation center in Kingman, Arizona where it was sold for scrap. (Details and photos courtesy Mr. Rob Kirkwood)

Blue Hen Chick, May 12, 1945 Flyover.
Photo by Mark Brown, 3rd Air Division photographer

MISSIONS FLOWN BY Ralph L. Minker
Oct 1944 - April 1945
447TH BOMB GROUP 709TH SQUADRON

No.	Date	Target	AirCraft #	Name
1	Thursday 26 Oct 1944	Oil plant at Hannover	43-38605	*Big Ass Bird*
2	Thursday, 2 Nov 1944	Synthetic oil plant at Merceburg	43-37795	*Dixie Marie*
3	Thursday, 9 Nov 1944	Transportation targets at Saarbrucken	42-107215	*Li'l Eight ball**
4	Thursday, 16 Nov 1944	Ground troop support Duren	43-38719	***Blue Hen Chick***
5	Saturday, 25 Nov 1944	Synthetic oil plant at Merceburg	43-38230	*Wolf Wagon**
6	Sunday, 26 Nov 1944	Marshalling yard at Hamm	43-37667	*Barbara Jane*
7	Monday, 27 Nov 1944	Marshalling yard at Bingen	42-97296	*Royal Flush**
8	Monday, 4 Dec 1944	Marshalling Yards at Mainz	43-38719	***Blue Hen Chick***
9	Wednesday, 5 Dec 1944	Merseburg	43-38719	***Blue Hen Chick***
10	Monday, 11 Dec 1944	Marshalling Yards at Giessen	43-38719	***Blue Hen Chick***
11	Tuesday, 12 Dec 1944	Marshalling Yards at Darmstadt	43-38719	***Blue Hen Chick***
12	Sunday, 24 Dec 1944	Babenhausen Airfield	43-38719	***Blue Hen Chick***
13	Thursday, 28 Dec 1944	Marshalling Yards at Koblenz	43-38719	***Blue Hen Chick***
14	Saturday, 30 Dec 1944	Marshalling Yards at Mannheim	43-38719	***Blue Hen Chick***
15	Monday, 1 Jan 1945	Oil plant at Dollbergen	42-107215	Li'l Eight ball
16	Wednesday, 3 Jan 1945	Marshalling Yards at Koblenz	43-38524	*Blonde Bomber II*
17	Friday, 5 Jan 1945	Communications Ctr. at Waxweiler	44-6016	*TNT Jeanie*

18	Saturday, 6 Jan 1945	Marshalling Yards at Worms	43-38719	***Blue Hen Chick***
19	Sunday, 7 Jan 1945	Marshalling Yards at Paderborn	43-38719	***Blue Hen Chick***
20	Monday, 8 Jan 1945	Marshalling Yards at Frankfurt	43-38719	***Blue Hen Chick***
21	Wednesday, 10 Jan 1945	Marshalling Yards at Karlsruhe	43-38719	***Blue Hen Chick***
22	Sunday, 14 Jan 1945	Oil Refinery at Magdeburg	43-38719	***Blue Hen Chick***
23	Monday, 15 Jan 1945	Aircraft Plant Augsburg	43-38719	***Blue Hen Chick***
24	Tuesday, 16 Jan 1945	Oil Plant at Dessau	42-32080	
25	Saturday, 20 Jan 1945	Marshalling Yards at Heilbronn	43-38719	***Blue Hen Chick***
26	Sunday, 21 Jan 1945	Mannheim	43-38719	***Blue Hen Chick***
27	Monday, 29 Jan 1945	Marshalling Yards at Kassel	43-38719	***Blue Hen Chick***
28	Thursday, 1 Feb 1945	Rail Bridge Wesel	43-38719	***Blue Hen Chick***
29	Tuesday, 7 Feb 1945	Oil Refinery at Bohlen	43-38719	***Blue Hen Chick***
30	Wednesday, 14 Feb 1945	Highway Bridge Wesel	43-38719	***Blue Hen Chick***
31	Friday, 16 Feb 1945	Rail Bridge Wesel	43-38719	***Blue Hen Chick***
32	Monday, 20 Feb 1945	Marshalling Yards at Nurnberg	43-38719	***Blue Hen Chick***
33	Sunday, Feb 25 1945	Rail line Neuberg	43-38719	***Blue Hen Chick***
34	Monday 26 Feb 1945	Railway Station Berlin	43-38719	***Blue Hen Chick***
35	Tuesday, Feb 27 1945	Communication Center at Leipzig	43-38719	***Blue Hen Chick***
36	Monday 16 April 1945	Harbour facilities Royan, France	A/C # 783	*Path Finder*
37	Saturday 21 April 1945	Airfield at Inglostadt	A/C # 786	*Path Finder*

* Planes that flew 100 or more missions without mechanical failure.

Week of May 1 - 6 — *Operation ChowHound*

Victory Tours

History 447th Bomb Group, by Doyle Shields,

National Archives — RG 18 Boxes 1559 - 1649

Blue Hen Chick Mission summary, Rob Kirkwood, 1999

HISTORY OF THE *Blue Hen Chick* "43-38719 A"
AIRCRAFT TYPE: B-17G-BO

Mission No.	Date			Pilot	Target
	September	28,	1944		Assigned to 447th Bomb Group, 709th Squadron
1	October	7,	1944	Otto	Merseburg
2	October	15,	1944	Westrope	Cologne
3	October	17,	1944	Cohen	Cologne
4	October	19,	1944	Johnson	Mannheim
5	October	22,	1944	Johnson	Marshalling yards at Munster
6	October	25,	1944	Gilbert	Oil plant at Hamburg
7	October	26,	1944	Horton	Industrial plant at Hannover
8	November	11,	1944	Horton	Marshalling yards at Oberlahnstein
9	November	16,	1944	Minker	Duren area
10	December	4,	1944	Minker	Marshalling yards at Mainz
11	December	6,	1944	Minker	Merseburg
12	December	11,	1944	Minker	Marshalling yards at Giessen
13	December	12,	1944	Minker	Marshalling yards at Darmstadt
14	December	18,	1944	Beighley	Marshalling yards at Mainz
15	December	24,	1944	Minker	Airfields at Babenhausen
16	December	28,	1944	Minker	Marshalling yards at Koblenz
17	December	30,	1944	Minker	Marshalling yards at Mannheim
18	January	6,	1945	Minker	Marshalling yards at Worms
19	January	7,	1945	Minker	Miscellaneous targets in Western Germany
20	January	8,	1945	Minker	Marshalling yards at Frankfurt
21	January	10,	1945	Minker	Marshalling yards at Karlsruhe
22	January	13,	1945	Minker	Rail bridge at Mainz
23	January	14,	1945	Minker	Oil refinery at Madgeburg
24	January	15,	1945	Minker	Messerschmitt aircraft plant at Augsburg
25	January	20,	1945	Minker	Marshalling yards at Heilbronn
26	January	21,	1945	Minker	Mannheim
27	January	29,	1945	Minker	Henschel aircraft plant at Kassel
28	February	1,	1945	Minker	Rail bridge at Wesel
29	February	6,	1945	Minker	Oil refinery at Bohlen
30	February	9,	1945	Summers	Munitions plant at Weimar
31	February	14,	1945	Minker	Highway bridge across the Rhine river at Wesel
32	February	16,	1945	Minker	Railroad bridge at Wesel
33	February	19,	1945	Schwab	Railroad bridge at Wesel
34	February	20,	1945	Minker	Marshalling yards at Nurnbereg

No.	Date			Pilot	Target
35	February	23,	1945	Coleman	Marshalling yards at Crailsheim
36	February	25,	1945	Minker	Rail line at Neuberg
37	February	26,	1945	Minker	Berlin/Alexanderplatz railway station
38	February	27,	1945	Minker	Communication center in Liepzip
39	March	1,	1945	Mustaleski	Marshalling yards at Ulm
40	March	2,	1945	Mustaleski	Oil refinery at Dresden
41	March	7,	1945	Mustaleski	Oil plants at Datteln-Emscher Lippe
42	March	8,	1945	Mustaleski	Marshalling yards at Frankfurt
43	March	10,	1945	Mustaleski	Marshalling yards at Dortman (2)
44	March	14,	1945	Bricker	Munitions plant at Hannover
45	March	15,	1945	Mustaleski	Marshalling yards at Oranienburg
46	March	17,	1945	Dewey	Oil target at Ruhland
47	March	18,	1945	Summers	Berlin
48	March	19,	1945	Summers	Motor transport Industries at Zwickau
49	March	20,	1945	Summers	U-Boat yards at Hamburg
50	March	21,	1945	Bates	Wittmundhafen Air field
51	March	24,	1945	Mustaleski	Airfield at Varrelbusch
52	March	28,	1945	Mustaleski	Hanomag Armored fighting vehicle plant at Hannover
53	March	30,	1945	Mustaleski	Communications target at Hamburg
54	March	31,	1945	Mustaleski	Airfield at Brandenburg
55	April	3,	1945	Dreyer	Submarine yards at Keil
56	April	7,	1945	Lehner	Marshalling yards at Schwerin
57	April	8,	1945	Mustaleski	Marshalling yards at Plauen
58	April	9,	1945	Dreyer	Airfield at Neuberg
59	April	10,	1945	Vantetten	Airfield at Brandenburg/Briest
60	April	11,	1945	Broughton	Airfield at Ingolstadt
61	April	14,	1945	Mustaleski	Bordeaux/Royan area-destroying coastal defenses
62	April	15,	1945	Mustaleski	Bordeaux/Royan area-destroying coastal defenses
63	April	16,	1945	Mustaleski	Bordeaux/Royan area-destroying coastal defenses
64	April	19,	1945	Mustaleski	Rail target in the Dresden area
65	April	20,	1945	Coleman	Marshalling yards at Neuruppin
66*	April	21,	1945	Golden	Airfield at Ingolstadt

July 9, 1945 **Returned to the United States-Bradley Field, Boston, Mass.**
December 17, 1945 **Sent to Reclamation Finance Center-Kingsman Arizona. Sold for scrap.**

* = Shields book, page 319 lists # 719 as having flown 67 missions.

Prepared by Rob Kirkwood, son of John Kirkwood, navigator of the 2nd crew of The Blue Hen.

RESOURCES

Primary Resources

Civilian Home Front, Wilmington V-E Day celebration, May 8, 1945. Box #14, Photograph 2619, Delaware Public Archives.

Ferris Wheel, April, 1943, Ferris Industrial School, Historical Society of Delaware, Wilmington, Delaware.

Grant, Denis. Personal Interview, March 26, 2005.

Kirkwood, John and Rob, private collection of photographs.

Ralph L. Minker papers and scrapbook, 1943 - 1945. Historical Society of Delaware, Wilmington, Delaware.

Official Unit Histories, 447th Bombardment Group. Digital images converted by David Warren, 447bg.com, from microfilm on file at Maxwell Air Force Base, U.S. Air Force Historical Research Agency.

Operations records of the 447th Bombardment Group. Record Group No. 18, Stack Area 190, Row 58, Compartment 31, Shelves 5 – 7, Box #'s 1553 - 1570 and Box #'s 1635 – 1649. National Archives and Records Administration, College Park, Maryland.

Sellars, Robin. Interview with Ralph Minker, March 1999. Reichelt Oral History Program, Florida State University, Tallahassee, Florida. Transcript, copy of Ralph L. Minker.

Stevenson, Patrick. Interview with Ralph Minker, January 2000. Dickinson College, Carlisle, Pennsylvania. Video tape and transcript.

Warfle, Elywyn (Stub). Personal Interview, October, 2004.

World War II Collection. Historical Society of Delaware, Wilmington, Delaware.

Books and Papers

Bernstein, Mark and Alex Lubertozzi, *World War II on the Air. Edward R. Murrow and the broadcasts that riveted a nation*. Text and recordings. Sourcebooks, 2003.

Cameron, Rebecca Hancock. *Training to Fly: Military Flight Training 1907 – 1945*. Air Force History and Museums Program, Government Printing Office,1999.

Kaplan, Philip. *Bombers: The Air Crew Experience*. New York: Barnes and Noble, 2000.

Keegan, John. *The Second World War*. New York: Penguin Books, 1989

Lawrence, Samuel. *Pledging Allegiance: American Identity and the Bond Drive of World War II*. Washington D.C.: Smithsonian Institution Press, 1997.

Lingeman, Richard. *Don't You Know There's a War On? The American Home Front 1941 - 1945*. New York:Thunder's Mouth Press/Nations Books. 1970, 2003.

Neillands, Robin. *The Bomber War: The Allied Air Offensive Against Nazi Germany*. New York: Overlook Press, 2001.

McLaughlin, Brigadier General J. Kemp. *The Mighty Eighth in World War II, A Memoir*. Lexington:The University Press of Kentucky, 2000.

Shields, Doyle and the Men of the 447th. *History 447th Bomb Group*. 1996.

Smith, J. Douglas and Richard Jensen. *World War II on the Web*. Wilmington, Delaware: Scholarly Resources Books, 2003.

Stevenson, Patrick. "The Good Soldier for the Good War" Dickinson College, May 4, 2000.

Warfle, Colonel Elwyn J. (Stub). *One Lucky Bastard*. Mount Vernon, Virginia: Mount Vernon Publishing, 2002.

Newspapers

[The] *Campus Office-R*, March 1945, Williamsport Junior College. Lycoming College Archives.

New York Times, September, 1945. microfilm

[Wilmington] *Journal Every Evening*. 1943 -1945. microfilm

Wilmington Morning News. 1943 – 1945. microfilm

Web sites

447th Bomb Group e-Museum
www.447bg.com

Air Force Historical Research Agency
www.au.af.mil/au/afhra/

Air Force Link
www.af.mil/history/

Collings Foundation
www.collingsfoundation.org

Dirks, Tim. Film History of the 1940s.
www.filmsite.org

Eighth Air Force Historical Society
www.8thafhs.org

Gila River Camp map
www.cr.nps.gov/history/online_books/

Mighty Eighth Air Force Museum
www.mightyeighth.org

National Museum of the United States Air Force
www.wpafb.af.mil/museum/

Operation Chowhound
http: //usersinterestroom.nl~heijink

State of Delaware
www.state.de.us

Stevenson, "The Good Soldier for the Good War."
www.dickinson.edu/~history/rlm/

A Note about the Editorial Team

Ralph Lee Minker wrote over 300 letters to his family as a young man coming of age in World War II. He exchanged letters with his parents and two sisters during pilot training, and while flying 37 combat missions. He came back a captain, the youngest member of the 447th B.G.'s *Lucky Bastards' Club*. Ralph received his discharge in the fall of 1945, returned to Dickinson College in Carlisle, Pennsylvania, graduating in 1947. He then followed his father's footsteps at Boston University School of Theology. Ordained a Methodist Minister in 1950, Reverend Minker served eight churches in the Delaware and Maryland Conference of the United Methodist Church before retiring in 1990. Captain Ralph Minker's service was recognized in 2003 by the 709th U.S. Air Force Reserve squadron stationed in Dover, Delaware when they named a C-5 transport plane, *Spirit of the Blue Hen*. In 2005 Ralph L. Minker was inducted into the Delaware Aviation Hall of Fame.

Sandra O'Connell and Ralph Minker were married in March 1980. She discovered the power of the Minker family correspondence when they read each letter on its 50th anniversary in 1993-1995. These first readings and a meeting in 2000 with WWII historian, Harry Butowsky, led inevitably (after five years of work) to *An American Family in World War II*. Sandra was the lead researcher and writer on Ralph's missions and the home front issues. Prior writing experience includes nine years as technology editor for *HR magazine*, where she contributed over 80 articles on the application of technology to human resources. This is her first venture into the field of history.

Dr. Harry A. Butowsky serves as historian and web manager with the National Service History Program in Washington, DC. He is the author of *World War II in the Pacific*, a National Historic Landmark Study, six other Landmark Studies as well as sixty articles on military, labor, science and constitutional history. Since 1980 Dr. Butowsky has served on the faculty of George

Mason University in Fairfax, Virginia where he teaches the History of World War I and World War II. Ralph Minker has participated in his World War II classes to talk about the *Blue Hen Chick* and the Eighth Air Force in 1944 and 1945. Dr. Butowsky has presented dozens of papers at numerous professional organizations and is a frequent speaker for community organizations. Harry served as military historian for *An American Family in World War II.*

WA